Information Hiding Techniques for Steganography and Digital Watermarking

For quite a long time, computer security was a rather narrow field of study that was populated mainly by theoretical computer scientists, electrical engineers, and applied mathematicians. With the proliferation of open systems in general, and the Internet and the World Wide Web (WWW) in particular, this situation has changed fundamentally. Today, computer and network practitioners are equally interested in computer security, since they require technologies and solutions that can be used to secure applications related to electronic commerce (e-commerce). Against this background, the field of computer security has become very broad and includes many topics of interest. The aim of this series is to publish state-of-the-art, high-standard technical books on topics related to computer security. Further information about the series can be found on the WWW by following the URL:

http://www.ifi.unizh.ch/~oppliger/serieseditor.html.

Also, if you would like to contribute to the series and write a book about a topic related to computer security, feel free to contact either the Commissioning Editor/Acquisitions Editor or the Series Editor at Artech House.

Recent Titles in the Artech House Computer Security Series

Rolf Oppliger, *Series Editor*

Information Hiding Techniques for Steganography and Digital Watermarking, Stefan Katzenbeisser and Fabien A. P. Petitcolas,

Security Technologies for the World Wide Web, Rolf Oppliger

For a complete listing of the *Artech House Computing Library*,
turn to the back of this book.

Information Hiding Techniques for Steganography and Digital Watermarking

Stefan Katzenbeisser
Fabien A. P. Petitcolas
editors

Artech House
Boston • London

Library of Congress Cataloging-in-Publication Data
Information hiding techniques for steganography and digital watermarking / Stefan Katzenbeisser, Fabien A.P. Petitcolas, editors.
        p. cm. — (Artech House computing library)
    Includes bibliographical references and index.
    ISBN 1-58053-035-4 (alk. paper)
        1. Computer security. 2. Data protection. 3. Watermarks. I. Katzenbeisser, Stefan. II. Petitcolas, Fabien A.P.

QA76.9.A25 I54144   2000   99-052317
005.8—dc21   CIP

British Library Cataloguing in Publication Data
Information hiding techniques for steganography and digital
        watermarking. — (Artech House computing library)
        1.Cryptography 2. Data encryption (Computer science)
        3. Copyright
        I. Katzenbeisser, Stefan II. Petitcolas, Fabien A.P.
        005.8'2

        ISBN 1-58053-035-4

Cover design by Igor Valdman

© 2000 ARTECH HOUSE, INC.
685 Canton Street
Norwood, MA 02062

International Standard Book Number: 1-58053-035-4
Library of Congress Catalog Card Number: 99-052317

10 9 8 7 6 5 4 3 2 1

Contents

List of figures

Foreword

Ross J. Anderson

Every few years, computer security has to re-invent itself. New technologies and new applications bring new threats, and force us to invent new protection mechanisms. Cryptography became important when businesses started to build networked computer systems; virus epidemics started once large numbers of PC users were swapping programs; and when the Internet took off, the firewall industry was one of the first to benefit.

One of the newest hot spots in security research is information hiding. It is driven by two of the biggest policy issues of the information age—copyright protection and state surveillance.

The ease with which perfect copies can be made of digital music and video has made the entertainment industry nervous that their content might be pirated much more than currently happens with analogue home taping. The growing popularity of MP3 encoded music has sharpened these fears. Part of the solution may come from a change in the way music and video are sold; after all, the software industry has largely abandoned copy-control mechanisms in favor of a business model that combines frequent upgrades, online registration for technical support, prosecution of large-scale pirates, and the networking of everything from business applications to games. But in the case of music and video, it is hoped that technical protection mechanisms will also provide part of the solution. One of these mechanisms is copyright marking—hiding copyright notices and serial numbers in the audio or video in such a way that they are difficult for pirates to remove.

The growth of the Internet has also made government intelligence and police agencies nervous. They say that widely available encryption software could make wiretapping more difficult; their common reaction is to try to restrict the strength of encryption algorithms or require that spare copies of the keys are available somewhere for them to sieze. Civil liberties advocates are outraged at this and denounce it as an intolerable assault on privacy. Both of these views are somewhat simplistic. Most police communications intelligence is not about wiretapping, so much as tracing networks of contacts; and the typical criminal communications tool is the prepaid mobile phone. The issue in both cases is not the secrecy of communications, but their traceability. Communications can also be hidden using the kind of techniques developed for copyright marking, and these can help criminals evade any laws against using "unapproved" cryptography.

As well as being important for copyright protection and to any long-term resolution of the crypto versus law enforcement debate, information hiding is also important for privacy. Large amounts of personal information, from census returns to medical records, are de-identified for processing by researchers; sometimes this is done well, while other times it is possible to re-identify the data subjects without too much effort.

With these forces driving it, research in information hiding has grown explosively. The progress made in the last five years is comparable to that in cryptology during 1945-1990. A large number of systems have been proposed; many of them have been broken; we now have a fair idea of what works, what doesn't, and where the interesting research directions are.

I am therefore delighted that we see here the first serious technical book on information hiding, which I expect will be the standard reference on the subject for many years to come.

Preface

This book provides an overview of steganography and digital watermarking, two areas of research which are generally referred to as "information hiding." Steganography studies ways to make communication invisible by hiding secrets in innocuous messages, whereas watermarking originated from the need for copyright protection of digital media.

Until recently, information hiding techniques received much less attention from the research community and from industry than cryptography. This situation is, however, changing rapidly and the first academic conference on this topic was organized in 1996. The main driving force is concern over protecting copyright; as audio, video, and other works become available in digital form, the ease with which perfect copies can be made may lead to large-scale unauthorized copying, and this is of great concern to the music, film, book, and software publishing industries.

Information hiding brings together researchers with very different backgrounds: electrical engineering, signal and image processing, computer science, and cryptography to name but a few. So far a comprehensive and unified treatment of this relatively new area of research has been missing. The available information was spread over countless papers and conference proceedings. According to a major bibliographic information system, 103 papers dealing with watermarking appeared in 1998, whereas two appeared in 1992, which again provides evidence for the growing importance of steganography and watermarking. The aim of this book is to provide both a tutorial and a comprehensive reference volume.

Chapter 1 introduces the field of information hiding, thereby drawing a panorama of possible applications. Part I of this book deals with steganography. Fundamental principles are discussed and steganographic applications are presented in Chapters 2 and 3. Breaking steganographic communication is the main topic of Chapter 4.

In Part II, watermarking systems are described. Goals and requirements of watermarking systems are discussed in Chapter 5. Chapter 6 provides a survey of methods used in the field. The crucial issue of "robustness" is the theme of Chapter 7. Fingerprinting is discussed in Chapter 8. Finally, the legal implications of copyright on the Internet in combination with watermarking techniques are discussed in the last chapter.

Acknowledgements

It is our great pleasure to thank the contributors to this volume. Despite the many calls on their time, they managed to provide chapters dealing with their main topic of research. It has required considerable effort on their part, and their cooperation and assistance are greatly appreciated. For us, it has been a distinct pleasure to edit this volume and work with them.

We also want to thank Viki Williams, Susanna Taggart, Michael Webb, and Hilary Sardella from Artech House for helping us master all the difficulties which arose during the production process of this book. Furthermore, we want to thank Philipp Tomsich for setting up a shared computer account and Raimund Kirner for preparing illustrations. Finally, we want to mention all anonymous referees who provided useful feedback which greatly helped us in the development of this work.

Stefan C. Katzenbeisser
Fabien A. P. Petitcolas

Vienna and Cambridge
June, 1999

Chapter 1

Introduction to information hiding

Fabien A. P. Petitcolas

As audio, video, and other works become available in digital form, the ease with which perfect copies can be made, may lead to large-scale unauthorized copying which might undermine the music, film, book, and software publishing industries. These concerns over protecting copyright have triggered significant research to find ways to hide copyright messages and serial numbers into digital media; the idea is that the latter can help to identify copyright violators, and the former to prosecute them.

At the same time, moves by various governments to restrict the availability of encryption services have motivated people to study methods by which private messages can be embedded in seemingly innocuous cover messages.

There are a number of other applications driving interest in the subject of information hiding and we will describe some of them in this chapter to show how broad this topic is. But before doing this, we will introduce the main subdisciplines of information hiding related to computer systems and give a brief history of this fascinating area of research.

1.1 MAIN SUBDISCIPLINES OF INFORMATION HIDING

Covert channels have been defined by Lampson [1], in the context of multilevel secure systems (e.g., military computer systems), as communication paths that were neither designed nor intended to transfer information at all. These channels are typically used by untrustworthy programs to leak information to their owner while performing a service for another program. These communication channels have been studied at length in the past to find ways to confine such programs [2]. We will not extend much more on this topic except as an example of covert communication on Ethernet networks (see Section 2.7.2) and in the context of image downgrading (see Section 3.2.3).

Anonymity is finding ways to hide the metacontent of messages, that is, the sender and the recipients of a message. Early examples include anonymous remailers as described by Chaum [3] and onion routing, proposed by Goldschlag, Reed, and Syverson [4]. The idea is that one can obscure the trail of a message by using a set of remailers or routers as long as the intermediaries do not collude; so trust remains the cornerstone of these tools. Note that there are different variants depending on who is "anonymized"; sender, receiver, or both. Web applications have focused on receiver anonymity while email users are concerned with sender anonymity.

An important subdiscipline of information hiding is *steganography*. While cryptography is about protecting the content of messages, steganography is about concealing their very existence. This modern adaptation of *steganographia* (Trithemius, 1462–1516), assumed from Greek στεγανό-ς, γραφ-ειν literally means "covered writing" [5], and is usually interpreted to mean hiding information in other information (Figure 1.2 shows the cover page of Trithemius' book). Examples include sending a message to a spy by marking certain letters in a newspaper using invisible ink, and adding subperceptible echo at certain places in an audio recording. The general model of hiding data in other data will be illustrated in Chapter 2 and the main steganographic techniques will be reviewed in Chapter 3.

Watermarking, as opposed to steganography, has the additional requirement of robustness against possible attacks. In this context, the term "robustness" is still not very clear; it mainly depends on the application, but a successful attack will simply try to make the mark undetectable. We will show ways to achieve this in Chapter 7. Robustness has strong implications in the overall design of a watermarking system and this is one of the reasons why we will treat steganography and digital watermarking separately in this book.

Watermarks do not always need to be hidden, as some systems use *visible digital watermarks* [6], but most of the literature has focussed on *imperceptible* (invisible, transparent, or inaudible, depending on the context) digital watermarks which have wider applications. Visible digital watermarks are strongly linked to the original paper watermarks which appeared at the end of the 13th century (see Section 5.2.1). Modern visible watermarks may be visual patterns (e.g., a company logo or copyright sign) overlaid on digital images and are widely used by many photographers who do not trust invisible watermarking techniques (see [7]).

From this brief overview the reader may have already noticed another fundamental difference between steganography and watermarking. The information hidden by a watermarking system is always associated to the digital object to be protected or to its owner while steganographic systems just hide any information. The "robustness" criteria are also different, since steganography is mainly concerned with detection of the hidden message while watermarking concerns potential removal by a pirate. Finally, steganographic communications are usually point-to-point (between sender and receiver) while watermarking techniques are usually one-to-many.

Precise terminology for these two subdisciplines of information hiding will be given in Chapters 2 and 5.

1.2   A BRIEF HISTORY OF INFORMATION HIDING

In this section we do not intend to cover the whole history of information hiding, rather just give the important landmarks. For more details the reader is referred to Kahn [8] and [9, 10].

1.2.1   Technical steganography

The most famous examples of steganography go back to antiquity. In his *Histories* [11], Herodotus (c. 486–425 B.C.) tells how around 440 B.C. Histiæus shaved the head of his most trusted slave and tattooed it with a message which disappeared after the hair had regrown. The purpose was to instigate a revolt against the Persians. Astonishingly, the method was still used by some German spies at the beginning of the 20th century [12]. Herodotus also tells how Demeratus, a Greek at the Persian court, warned Sparta of an imminent invasion by Xerxes, King of Persia: he removed the wax from a writing tablet, wrote his message on the wood underneath and then covered the message with wax. The tablet looked exactly like a blank one (it almost fooled the recipient as well as the customs men). A large number of techniques were invented or reported by Æneas the Tactician [13], including letters hidden in messengers' soles or women's earrings, text written on wood tablets and then whitewashed, and notes carried by pigeons. He also proposed hiding text by changing the heights of letterstrokes or by making very small holes above or below letters in a cover-text. This latter technique was still in use during the 17th century, but was improved by Wilkins (1614–1672) who used invisible ink to print very small dots instead of making holes [14] and was reused again by German spies during both World Wars [8, p. 83]. A modern adaptation of this technique is still in use for document security [15] and prints blocks of tiny pixels across a page to encode information such as date, printer identifier, and user identifier.

In 1857, Brewster already suggested hiding secret messages "in spaces not larger than a full stop or small dot of ink" [16] and by 1860 the basic problems of making tiny images had been solved by Dragon, a French photographer: during the Franco-Prussian War of 1870–1871, while Paris was besieged, messages on microfilm were sent out by pigeon post [17, 18]. During the Russo-Japanese war of 1905, microscopic images were hidden in ears, nostrils, and under fingernails [19]. Finally, Brewster's idea became real by World War I when messages to and from spies were reduced to *microdots* by several stages of photographic reduction and then stuck on top of printed periods or commas in innocuous cover material such as magazines [12, 20].

Invisible inks have been used extensively. They were originally made of available organic substances (such as milk or urine) or "salt armoniack dissolved in water" [14, V, pp. 37–47] and developed with heat; progress in chemistry helped to create more sophisticated combinations of ink and developer by the first World War, but the technology fell into disuse with the invention of "universal developers" which could determine which parts of a piece of paper had been wetted from the effects on the surfaces of the fibers [8, pp. 523–525]. This leads to the more familiar application-specific information hiding and marking technologies found in the world of secure printing [21, 22]. Watermarks in paper are a very old anticounterfeiting technique; more recent innovations include special ultraviolet fluorescent inks used in printing traveler's checks. As the lamps used in photocopiers have a high ultra-violet content, it can be arranged that photocopies come out overprinted with "void" in large letters. The reader is referred to van Renesse [21, 22] for a survey of recent developments.

Another example comes from architecture: since its early days, artists have understood that works of sculpture or painting appear different from certain angles, and established rules for perspective and anamorphosis [23]. Through the 16th and 17th centuries anamorphic images supplied an ideal means of camouflaging dangerous political statements and heretical ideas [24]. A masterpiece of hidden anamorphic imagery—the *Vexierbild*—was created in the 1530s by Shö, a Nürnberg engraver, pupil of Dürer (1471–1528); when one looks at it straight on, one sees a strange landscape, but looking from the side reveals portraits of famous kings.

1.2.2   Linguistic steganography

A widely used method of linguistic steganography is the acrostic. The most famous example is probably Giovanni Boccaccio's (1313–1375) *Amorosa visione* which is said to be the "world's hugest acrostic" [25, pp. 105–106]. Boccaccio first wrote three sonnets—containing about 1,500 letters all together—and then wrote other poems such that the initial of the successive tercets correspond exactly to the letters of the sonnets. Another famous example of acrostic comes from the *Hypnerotomachia Poliphili* [26],[1] published in 1499. This puzzling and enigmatic book, written anonymously, reveals the guilty love between a monk and a woman: the first letter of the thirty eight chapters spelled out "Poliam frater Franciscus Columna peramavit."[2]

Expanding on the simple idea of the acrostic, monks and other literate people found ways to better conceal messages mainly into text. By the 16th and 17th centuries, there had arisen a large amount of literature on steganography and many of the methods depended on novel means of encoding information. In his 400 page book *Schola Steganographica* [27], Gaspar Schott (1608–1666) expands the "Ave Maria" code proposed by Trithemius in *Polygraphiæ*, together with *Steganographia* (see Figure 1.2) two of the first known books in the field of cryptography and steganography. The expanded code uses 40 tables, each of which contains 24 entries (one for each letter of the alphabet of that time) in four languages: Latin, German, Italian, and French. Each letter of the plain-text is replaced by the word or phrase that appears in the corresponding table entry and the stego-text ends up looking like a prayer, a simple correspondence letter, or a magic spell. Schott also explains how to hide messages in music scores; each note corresponds to a letter (Figure 1.1). Another method, based on the number of occurrences of notes used by J. S. Bach, is mentioned by Bauer [28]. John Wilkins, showed how "two Musicians may discourse with one another by playing upon their instruments of musick as well as by talking with their instruments of speech" [14, XVIII, pp. 143–150]. He also explains how one can hide secretly a message into a geometric drawing using points, lines, or triangles: "the point, the ends of the lines and the angles of the figures do each of them by their different situation express a several letter" [14, XI, pp. 88–96].

An improvement is made when the message is hidden at random locations in the cover-text. This idea is the core of many current steganographic systems. In a security protocol developed in ancient China, the sender and the receiver had copies of a paper mask with a number of holes cut at random locations. The sender would place his mask over a sheet of paper, write the secret message into the holes, remove the mask, and then compose a cover message incorporating the code ideograms. The receiver could read the secret message at once by placing his mask over the resulting letter. In the early 16th century Cardan (1501–1576), an Italian mathematician, reinvented this method which is now known as the Cardan grille.

The presence of errors or stylistic features at predetermined points in the cover material is another way to select the location of the embedded information. An

---

1 The English version of 1592 was published under title "The Strife of Love in a Dreame" in London.

2 Translated as: "Brother Francesco Colonna passionately loves Polia." Colonna was a monk, still alive when the book was published.

Figure 1.1   Hiding information in music scores: Gaspar Schott simply maps the letters of the alphabet to the notes. Clearly, one should not try to play the music [27, p. 322]. Courtesy of the Whipple Science Museum, Cambridge, England.

early example was a technique used by Francis Bacon (1561–1626) in his *biliterarie* alphabet [29, pp. 266], which seems to be linked to the controversy of whether he wrote the works attributed to Shakespeare [30]. In this method each letter is encoded in a five-bit binary code and embedded in the cover-text by printing the letters in either normal or italic fonts. The variability of 16th century typography acted as camouflage. Similar techniques have been used in an electronic publishing pilot project: copyright messages and serial numbers have been hidden in the line spacing and other format features of documents (e.g., Brassil et al. [31]). It was found that shifting text lines up or down by one-three-hundredth of an inch to encode zeros and ones was robust against multigeneration photocopying and could not be noticed by most people.

Further examples come from the world of mathematical tables. Publishers of logarithm tables and astronomical ephemerides in the 17th and 18th century used to introduce errors deliberately in the least significant digits (e.g., [32]). To this day, database and mailing list vendors insert bogus entries in order to identify customers who try to resell their products.

Figure 1.2   Title page of Trithemius' *Steganographia* (printed 1606 in Frankfurt, Germany). Many of Trithemius' works—including the *Steganographia*—are obscured by his strong belief in occult powers (i.e., he wrote on alchemy and the power of angels, classified witches into four categories, fixed the creation of the world at 5206 B.C., and explained how to transmit messages through telepathy with the help of planetary angels and religious incantations). Courtesy of H. Frodl, Austrian National Library, Vienna, Austria.

1.2.3   Copyright enforcement

A last example of an old solution that is being reused against forgery and for copy protection is the catalog of signed images of Claude Gellée of Lorraine (1600–1682), also known as Claude Lorrain. Lorrain's reputation as a landscape painter was such that he was attracting imitations. So, he introduced a method for protecting his intellectual property nearly 100 years before any relevant law was introduced.[3] From some time around 1635 until the end of his life in 1682, Lorrain kept a book that he called the *Liber Veritatis*. The *Liber Veritatis* was a collection of drawings in the form of a sketchbook. The book was specially made for him, with a scheme of alternating pages, four blue pages followed by four white, which repeated in this manner and contained around 195 drawings.

Baldinucci (1624?–1696), the second biographer of Lorrain, reported that the purpose in creating the Liber Veritatis was to protect Lorrain against forgery.[4] In fact, any comparison between drawings and paintings goes to show that the former were designed to serve as a "check" on the latter and from the Liber any very careful observer could tell whether a given painting was a forgery or not.

Similar techniques are being used today. ImageLock [35], for instance, keeps a central database of image digests and periodically searches the Web for images having the same digest. Tracking systems based on private watermarks (e.g., [36]) also require central databases. Unfortunately, apart from the extent of the problem (which is now global) nothing much has changed, since such services still do not provide any proof of infringement. Chapters 5 and 7 will investigate these problems further.

1.2.4   Wisdom from cryptography

Although steganography is different from cryptography, we can borrow many of the techniques and much practical wisdom from the latter, a more thoroughly researched discipline. In 1883, Auguste Kerckhoffs enunciated the first principles of cryptographic engineering, in which he advises that we assume the method used to encipher data is known to the opponent, so security must lie only in the choice of key [37][5]. The history of cryptology since then has repeatedly shown the folly of "security-by-obscurity"—the assumption that the enemy will remain ignorant of the system in use, one of the latest examples being mobile phones [38].

---

3 According to Samuelson [33, p. 16], the first "copyright" law was the "Statute of Anne" introduced by the English Parliament in 1710.

4 An English translation of the biography is in [34].

5 "Il faut qu'il n'exige pas le secret, et qu'il puisse sans inconvénient tomber entre les mains de l'ennemi." [37, p. 12]

Applying this wisdom, we obtain a tentative definition of a secure stego-system: one where an opponent who understands the system, but does not know the key, can obtain no evidence (or even grounds for suspicion) that a communication has taken place. It will remain a central principle that steganographic processes intended for wide use should be published, just like commercial cryptographic algorithms and protocols. This teaching of Kerckhoffs holds with particular force for watermarking techniques intended for use in evidence, which "must be designed and certified on the assumption that they will be examined in detail by a hostile expert," Anderson [39, Prin. 1].

So one might expect that designers of copyright marking systems would publish the mechanisms they use, and rely on the secrecy of the keys employed. Sadly, this is not the case; many purveyors of such systems keep their mechanisms subject to nondisclosure agreements, sometimes offering the rationale that a patent is pending.

That any of these security-by-obscurity systems ever worked was a matter of luck. Yet many steganographic systems available today just embed the "hidden" data in the least significant bits (see Section 3.2) of an audio or video file—which is trivial for a capable opponent to detect and remove.

1.3   SOME APPLICATIONS OF INFORMATION HIDING

Unobtrusive communications are required by military and intelligence agencies: even if the content is encrypted, the detection of a signal on a modern battlefield may lead rapidly to an attack on the signaler. For this reason, military communications use techniques such as spread spectrum modulation or meteor scatter transmission to make signals hard for the enemy to detect or jam. Basics of spread spectrum modulation are reviewed in Section 6.4.1 and meteor-burst communications are studied by Schilling et al. [40]. Criminals also place great value on unobtrusive communications and their preferred technologies include prepaid mobile phones and hacked corporate switchboards through which calls can be rerouted (e.g., [41]). As a side effect, law enforcement and counterintelligence agencies are interested in understanding these technologies and their weaknesses, so as to detect and trace hidden messages.

Information hiding techniques also underlie many attacks on "multilevel secure" systems used by military organizations. A virus or other malicious code propagates itself from "low security" to "high security" levels and then signals data downwards using a covert channel in the operating system or by hiding information directly in data that may be declassified [42] (see also Section 2.7.2).

Information hiding techniques can also be used in situations where plausible deniability[6] is required. "The obvious motivation for plausible deniability is when the two communicating parties are engaged in an activity which is somehow illicit, and they wish to avoid being caught" [43] but more legitimate motives include fair voting, personal privacy, or limitation of liability. One possible mechanism providing such property is the steganographic file system, presented by Anderson, Needham, and Shamir: if a user knows a file's name, he can retrieve it; but if he does not, he cannot even obtain evidence that the file exists [44].

Anonymous communications, including anonymous remailers and Web prox-ies [3], are required by legitimate users to vote privately in online elections, make political claims, consume sexual material, preserve online free speech, or to use digital cash. But the same techniques can be abused for defamation, blackmail, or unsolicited commercial mailing. The ethical positions of the players in the in-formation hiding game are not very clear so the design of techniques providing such facilities requires careful thought about the possible abuses, which might be nonobvious.

The healthcare industry and especially medical imaging systems may benefit from information hiding techniques. They use standards such as DICOM (digital imaging and communications in medicine) which separates image data from the caption, such as the name of the patient, the date, and the physician. Sometimes the link between image and patient is lost, thus, embedding the name of the patient in the image could be a useful safety measure [45, 46]. It is still an open question whether such marking would have any effect on the accuracy of the diagnosis but recent studies by Cosman et al. [47] revealing that lossy compression has little effect, let us believe that this might be feasible. Another emerging technique related to the healthcare industry is hiding messages in DNA sequences [48]. This could be used to protect intellectual property in medicine, molecular biology or genetics.

A number of other applications of information hiding have been proposed in the context of multimedia applications. In many cases they can use techniques already developed for copyright marking directly; in others, they can use adapted schemes or shed interesting light on technical issues. They include the following:

- **Automatic monitoring of copyrighted material on the Web**: A robot searches the Web for marked material and hence identifies potential illegal usage. An alternative technique downloads images from the Internet, com-putes a digest of them, and compares this digest with digests registered in its database [35, 49]. We will revisit these tools later in Section 7.3.2, and show that the actual benefits are not as good as the advertised ones.

---

6 The term "plausible deniability" was introduced by Roe [43] and refers to the converse prob-lem of nonrepudiation, that is, the property such that a sender should not be able to falsely deny that he sent a message.

- **Automatic audit of radio transmissions**: A computer can listen to a radio station and look for marks, which indicate that a particular piece of music, or advertisement, has been broadcast [50, 51].
- **Data augmentation**: Information is added for the benefit of the public. This can be details about the work, annotations, other channels [52], or purchasing information (nearest shop, price, producer, etc.) so that someone listening to the radio in a car could simply press a button to order the compact disc. This can also be hidden information used to index pictures or music tracks in order to provide more efficient retrieval from databases (e.g., [45, 53]).
- **Tamper proofing**: The information hidden in a digital object may be a signed "summary" of it, which can be used to prevent or to detect unauthorized modifications (e.g., [54, 55]).

Some of these applications and techniques will be detailed in the next chapters. We tried to keep chapters simple enough such that any computer science graduate student can understand them without much problem. Note however that steganography and digital watermarking require some background in various disciplines including cryptography, image processing, information theory, and statistics. It is outside the scope of this book to detail all the basic techniques on which information hiding techniques are built. If more background is required, we refer the reader to Menezes [56] for cryptography, Jain [57] for image processing, and Cover [58] for information theory.

REFERENCES

[1] Lampson, B. W., "A Note on the Confinement Problem," *Communications of the ACM*, vol. 16, no. 10, Oct. 1973, pp. 613–615.

[2] Gligor, V., "A Guide to Understanding Covert Channel Analysis of Trusted Systems," Technical Report NCSC-TG-030, National Computer Security Center, Ft. George G. Meade, Maryland, USA, Nov. 1993.

[3] Chaum, D., "Untraceable Electronic Mail, Return Addresses and Digital Pseudonyms," *Communications of the ACM*, vol. 24, no. 2, Feb. 1981, pp. 84–88.

[4] Goldschlag, D. M., M. G. Reed, and P. F. Syverson, "Hiding routing information," in *Information Hiding: First International Workshop, Proceedings*, vol. 1174 of *Lecture Notes in Computer Science*, Springer, 1996, pp. 137–150.

[5] Murray, A. H., and R. W. Burchfiled (eds.), *The Oxford English dictionary: being a corrected re-issue*, Oxford, England: Clarendon Press, 1933.

[6] Braudaway, G. W., K. A. Magerlein, and F. Mintzer, "Protecting publicly-available images with a visible image watermark," in *Proceedings of the SPIE 2659, Optical Security and Counterfeit Deterrence Techniques*, 1996, pp. 126–133.

[7] "The Stockphoto mailing list," <http://stockphoto.joelday.com/>, 1998. Discussions on photography in general and new technologies in particular.

[8] Kahn, D., *The Codebreakers—The Story of Secret Writing*, New York, New York, USA: Scribner, 1996.

[9] Petitcolas, F. A. P., R. J. Anderson, and M. G. Kuhn, "Information Hiding—A Survey," *Proceedings of the IEEE*, vol. 87, no. 7, Jul. 1999, pp. 1062–1078.

[10] Kobayashi, M., "Digital Watermarking: Historical Roots," Technical Report RT0199, IBM Research, Tokyo Research Laboratories, Japan, Apr. 1997.

[11] Herodotus, *The Histories*, London, England: J. M. Dent & Sons, Ltd, 1992.

[12] Newman, B., *Secrets of German Espionage*, London: Robert Hale Ltd, 1940.

[13] Tacticus, A., *How to Survive Under Siege / Aineias the Tactician*, Oxford, England: Clarendon Press, pp. 84–90 and 183–193, Clarendon ancient history series, 1990.

[14] Wilkins, J., *Mercury: or the Secret and Swift Messenger: Shewing, How a Man May With Privacy and Speed Communicate His Thoughts to a Friend at Any Distance*, London: printed for Rich Baldwin, near the Oxford-Arms in Warnick-lane, 2nd ed., 1694.

[15] "Aliroo home page," <http://www.aliroo.com/>, 1997. WitnesSoft and ScarLet security software.

[16] Brewster, D., "Microscope," in *Encyclopædia Britannica or the Dictionary of Arts, Sciences, and General Literature*, vol. XIV, Edinburgh, IX—Application of photography to the microscope, pp. 801–802, 8th ed., 1857.

[17] Hayhurst, J., "The Pigeon Post into Paris 1870–1871," 1970. <http://www.windowlink.com/jdhayhurst/pigeon/pigeon.html>.

[18] Tissandier, G., *Les merveilles de la photographie*, Boulevard Saint Germain, Paris, France: Librairie Hachette & Cie, VI—Les dépêches microscopiques du siège de Paris, pp. 233–248, Bibliothèque des merveilles, 1874.

[19] Stevens, G. W. W., *Microphotography—Photography and Photofabrication at Extreme Resolutions*, London: Chapman & Hall, 1968.

[20] Hoover, J. E., "The Enemy's Masterpiece of Espionage," *The Reader's Digest*, vol. 48, May 1946, pp. 49–53. London edition.

[21] van Renesse, R. L. (ed.), *Proceedings of the SPIE 2659, Optical Security and Counterfeit Deterrence Techniques*, 1996.

[22] van Renesse, R. L. (ed.), *Proceedings of the SPIE 3314, Optical Security and Counterfeit Deterrence Techniques II*, 1998.

[23] Baltrušaitis, J., *Anamorphoses ou thaumaturgus opticus*, Paris, France: Flammarion, pp. 5 and 15–19, Les perspectives dépravées, 1984.

[24] Seckel, A., "Your Mind's Eye: Illusions & Paradoxes of the Visual System," Lecture for the National Science Week, University of Cambridge, England, 1998.

[25] Wilkins, E. H., *A History of Italian Literature*, London: Geoffrey Cumberlege, Oxford University Press, 1954.

[26] Anonymous, *Hypnerotomachia Poliphili: the Dream Battles of Polia's Lover*, 1st ed., 1499.

[27] Schott, G., *Schola steganographica*, Jobus Hertz, printer, 1680.

[28] Bauer, F. L., *Decrypted Secrets—Methods and Maxims of Cryptology*, Berlin, Heidelberg, Germany: Springer-Verlag, 1997.

[29] Bacon, F., *Of the Advancement and Proficiencie of Learning or the Partitions of Sciences*, Leon Lichfield, Oxford, for R. Young and E. Forest, vol. VI, pp. 257–271, 1640.

[30] Leary, P., *The Second Cryptographic Shakespeare: a Monograph Wherein the Poems and Plays Attributed to William Shakespeare are Proven to Contain the Enciphered Name of the Concealed Author, Francis Bacon*, Omaha, Nebraska, USA: Westchester House, 2nd

ed., 1990.

[31] Brassil, J., et al., "Electronic Marking and Identification Techniques to Discourage Document Copying," in *Proceedings of INFOCOM'94*, 1994, pp. 1278–1287.

[32] Wagner, N. R., "Fingerprinting," in *Symposium on Security and Privacy*, Technical Commitee on Security & Privacy, IEEE Computer Society, Oakland, California, USA, 25–27 Apr. 1983, pp. 18–22.

[33] Samuelson, P., "Copyright and Digital Libraries," *Communications of the ACM*, vol. 38, no. 4, Apr. 1995, pp. 15–21 and 110.

[34] Röthlisberger, M., *Claude Lorrain: The Paintings*, New York, New York, USA: Hacker Art Books, vol. I: Critical Catalogue, Sources—F. Baldinucci. Translation from Italian of "Notizie de' Proffessori del Disegno," Filippo Baldinucci (1624?–1696), vol. IV, Florence 1728., pp. 53–63, 1979.

[35] "ImageLock home page," <http://www.imagelock.com/>, 1999.

[36] Cox, I. J., et al., "A Secure, Robust Watermark for Multimedia," in *Information Hiding: First International Workshop, Proceedings*, vol. 1174 of *Lecture Notes in Computer Science*, Springer, 1996, pp. 183–206.

[37] Kerckhoffs, A., "La Cryptographie Militaire," *Journal des Sciences Militaires*, vol. 9, Jan. 1883, pp. 5–38.

[38] Piper, F., and M. Walker, "Cryptographic Solutions for Voice Technology and GSM," *Network Security*, Dec. 1998, pp. 14–19.

[39] Anderson, R. J., "Liability and Computer Security: Nine Principles," in *Computer Security—Third European Symposium on Research in Computer Security*, vol. 875 of *Lecture Notes in Computer Science*, Springer, 1994, pp. 231–245.

[40] Schilling, D. L. (ed.), *Meteor Burst Communications: Theory and Practice*, Wiley series in telecommunications, New York: J. Wiley and Sons, 1993.

[41] Mulhall, T., "Where Have All The Hackers Gone? A Study in Motivation, Deterrence and Crime Displacement," *Computers and Security*, vol. 16, no. 4, 1997, pp. 277–315.

[42] Kurak, C., and J. McHugh, "A Cautionary Note on Image Downgrading," in *Computer Security Applications Conference*, San Antonio, Texas, USA, Dec. 1992, pp. 153–159.

[43] Roe, M., *Cryptography and Evidence*, Ph.D. thesis, University of Cambridge, Clare College, 18 Nov. 1997.

[44] Anderson, R. J., R. M. Needham, and A. Shamir, "The Steganographic File System," in *Proceedings of the Second International Workshop on Information Hiding*, vol. 1525 of *Lecture Notes in Computer Science*, Springer, 1998, pp. 73–82.

[45] Anderson, R. J., and F. A. P. Petitcolas, "On The Limits of Steganography," *IEEE Journal of Selected Areas in Communications*, vol. 16, no. 4, May 1998, pp. 474–481.

[46] Hilton, D., "Matching Digital Watermarking Methods to Real Data," Computer Laboratory Seminars, University of Cambridge, 1999.

[47] Cosman, P. C., et al., "Thoracic CT Images: Effect of Lossy Image Compression on Diagnostic Accuracy," *Radiology*, vol. 190, no. 2, Feb. 1994, pp. 517–524.

[48] Taylor Clelland, C., V. Risca, and C. Bancroft, "Hiding Messages in DNA Microdots," *Nature*, vol. 399, 10 Jun. 1999, pp. 533–534.

[49] "Digimarc home page," <http://www.digimarc.com/>, 1997.

[50] Blagden, D., and N. Johnson, "Broadcast Monitoring: a Practical Application of Audio Watermarking," Announced for publication in *Proceedings of the SPIE 3657, Security and Watermarking of Multimedia Contents* but withdrawn. Presented at the conference.

[51] Willard, R., "ICE (Identification Coding, Embedded)," Preprint 3516 (D2-3) of the

Audio Engineering Society, 1993. Presented at the 74th Convention of the AES, Berlin, 16–19 March, 1993.

[52] Gerzon, M. A., and P. G. Graven, "A High-Rate Buried-Data Channel for Audio CD," *Journal of the Audio Engineering Society*, vol. 43, no. 1/2, Jan.–Feb. 1995, pp. 3–22.

[53] Johnson, N. F., "In Search of the Right Image: Recognition and Tracking of Images in Image Databases, Collections, and The Internet," Technical report, George Mason University, Center for Secure Information Systems, Jun. 1999.

[54] Friedman, G. L., "The Trustworthy Digital Camera: Restoring Credibility to the Photographic Image," *IEEE Transactions on Consumer Electronics*, vol. 39, no. 4, Nov. 1993, pp. 905–910.

[55] Lin, C.-Y., and S.-F. Chang, "Issues for Authenticating MPEG Video," in *Proceedings of the SPIE 3657, Security and Watermarking of Multimedia Contents*, 1999, pp. 54–65.

[56] Menezes, A. J., P. C. van Oorschot, and S. A. Vanstone, *Handbook of Applied Cryptography*, Boca Raton, Florida: CRC Press, 1997.

[57] Jain, A. K., *Fundamentals of Digital Image Processing*, Englewood Cliffs: Prentice-Hall, 1989.

[58] Cover, T. M., and J. A. Thomas, *Elements of Information Theory*, New York, Chichester: John Wiley & Sons, 1991.

Part I

Secret writing and steganography

Chapter 2

Principles of steganography

Stefan C. Katzenbeisser

The "classic" model for invisible communication was first proposed by Simmons [1] as the "prisoners' problem." Alice[1] and Bob are arrested for some crime and are thrown in two different cells. They want to develop an escape plan, but unfortunately all communications between each other are arbitrated by a warden named Wendy. She will not let them communicate through encryption and if she notices any suspicious communication, she will place them in solitary confinement and thus suppress the exchange of all messages. So both parties must communicate invisibly in order not to arouse Wendy's suspicion; they have to set up a *subliminal channel*. A practical way to do so is to hide meaningful information in some harmless message: Bob could, for instance, create a picture of a blue cow lying on a green meadow and send this piece of modern art to Alice. Wendy has no idea that the colors of the objects in the picture transmit information.

Throughout this book we will make the (for an actual prison perhaps unrealistic) assumption that Alice and Bob have access to computer systems in their cells and are able to exchange messages in many different formats (e.g., text, digital images, digital sound, etc.).

---

1 In the field of cryptography, communication protocols usually involve two fictional characters named Alice and Bob. The standard convention is to name the participants in the protocol alphabetically (Carol and Dave often succeed Alice and Bob in a multiperson protocol), or with a name whose first character matches the first letter of their role (e.g., Wendy the warden). We will follow this convention here.

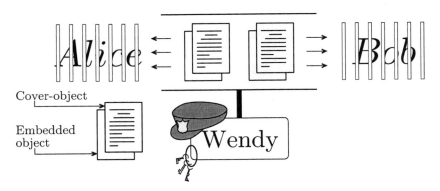

Figure 2.1   The prisoners' problem, illustrated. Courtesy of Scott Craver, reprinted from [2].

Unfortunately there are other problems which may hinder the escape of Alice and Bob. Wendy may alter the message Bob has sent to Alice. For example, she could change the color of Bob's cow to red, and so destroy the information; she then acts as an *active warden*. Even worse, if she acts in a *malicious* way, she could forge messages and send a message to one of the prisoners through the subliminal channel while pretending to be the other.

The above model is generally applicable to many situations in which invisible communication—*steganography*—takes place. Alice and Bob represent two communication parties, wanting to exchange secret information invisibly. The warden Wendy represents an eavesdropper who is able to read and probably alter messages sent between the communication partners (see Figure 2.1).

Whereas cryptographic techniques try to conceal the contents of a message, steganography goes yet a bit further: it tries to hide the fact that a communication even exists. Two people can communicate covertly by exchanging unclassified messages containing confidential information. Both parties have to take the presence of a *passive*, *active* or even *malicious* attacker into account.

2.1   FRAMEWORKS FOR SECRET COMMUNICATION

Most applications of steganography follow one general principle, illustrated in Figure 2.2. Alice, who wants to share a secret message m with Bob, randomly chooses (using the private random source r) a harmless message c, called *cover-object*, which can be transmitted to Bob without raising suspicion, and embeds the secret message into c, probably by using a key k, called *stego-key*. Alice therefore changes the cover c to a *stego-object* s. This must be done in a very careful way, so that a third

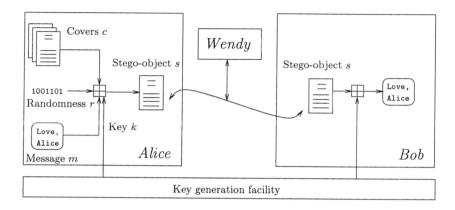

Figure 2.2   Schematic description of steganography: Alice randomly chooses a cover c using her private random source r and embeds the message m in c using a key k, creating the stego-object s which she passes on to Bob. Bob reconstructs m with the key k he shares with Alice.

party, knowing only the apparently harmless message s, cannot detect the existence of the secret. In a "perfect" system, a normal cover should not be distinguishable from a stego-object, neither by a human nor by a computer looking for statistical pattern. Theoretically, covers could be any computer-readable data such as image files, digital sound, or written text.

Alice then transmits s over an insecure channel to Bob and hopes that Wendy will not notice the embedded message. Bob can reconstruct m since he knows the embedding method used by Alice and has access to the key k used in the embedding process. This extraction process should be possible *without* the original cover c.

A third person watching the communication should not be able to decide whether the sender is *active* in the sense that he sends covers containing secret messages rather than covers without additional information. More formally, if an observer has access to a set $\{c_1, \ldots, c_n\}$ of cover-objects transmitted between both communication parties, he should be unable to decide which cover-objects c_i contain secret information. Thus, the security of invisible communication lies mainly in the inability to distinguish cover-objects from stego-objects.

In practice however, not all data can be used as cover for secret communication, since the modifications employed in the embedding process should not be visible to anyone not involved in the communication process. This fact requires the cover to contain sufficient redundant data, which can be replaced by secret information. As an example, due to measuring errors, any data which are the result of some physical scanning process will contain a stochastic component called *noise*. Such random artifacts can be used for the submission of secret information, as we will see in the next few chapters. In fact, it turns out that noisy data has more advantageous properties in most steganographic applications.

Obviously a cover should never be used twice, since an attacker who has access to two "versions" of one cover can easily detect and possibly reconstruct the message. To avoid accidental reuse, both sender and receiver should destroy all covers they have already used for information transfer.

In the literature there are basically three types of steganographic protocols: *pure steganography*, *secret key steganography*, and *public key steganography*; the latter is based on principles of public key cryptography. In the following subsections, all three types will be discussed.

2.1.1   Pure steganography

We call a steganographic system which does not require the prior exchange of some secret information (like a stego-key) *pure steganography*. Formally, the embedding process can be described as a mapping $E : C \times M \to C$, where C is the set of possible covers and M the set of possible messages.[2] The extraction process consists of a mapping $D : C \to M$, extracting the secret message out of a cover. Clearly, it is necessary that $|C| \geq |M|$. Both sender and receiver must have access to the embedding and extraction algorithm, but the algorithms should not be public.

Definition 2.1 (Pure steganography) *The quadruple $\mathfrak{S} = \langle C, M, D, E \rangle$, where C is the set of possible covers, M the set of secret messages with $|C| \geq |M|$, $E : C \times M \to C$ the embedding function and $D : C \to M$, the extraction function, with the property that $D(E(c, m)) = m$ for all $m \in M$ and $c \in C$ is called a pure steganographic system.*

In most practical steganographic systems the set C is chosen to consist of meaning-ful, and apparently harmless messages (like the set of all meaningful digital images, or like texts produced using Trithemius' tables discussed in Chapter 1), two com-munication partners would be able to exchange without raising suspicion. The embedding process is defined in a way that a cover and the corresponding stego-object are perceptually similar. Formally, perceptual similarity can be defined via a *similarity function*:

---

2 More generally, the embedding process can be seen as a relation on the sets $C \times M$ and C (i.e., $E \subset C \times M \times C$), provided that for every two elements (c_1, m_1) and $(c_2, m_2) \in C \times M$, $m_1 \neq m_2$, $E(c_1, m_1) \cap E(c_2, m_2) = \emptyset$. However, for simplicity of notation we will assume a functional relationship throughout this chapter.

Definition 2.2 (Similarity function) *Let C be a nonempty set. A function sim :*
$C^2 \rightarrow (-\infty, 1]$ *is called similarity function on C, if for $x, y \in C$*

$$sim(x, y) = 1 \quad \Leftrightarrow \quad x = y$$

For $x \neq y$, $sim(x, y) < 1$

In the case of digital images or digital sound the correlation between two signals can
be used as a similarity function. Therefore, most practical steganographic systems
try to fulfill the condition $sim(c, E(c, m)) \approx 1$ for all $m \in M$ and $c \in C$.

Covers which have not been used before should be private to the sender (i.e., an
attacker should not have access to the covers used for secret communication). For
instance, the sender could create covers through the use of recording or scanning
techniques. For every communication process, a cover is randomly chosen. Rather
than selecting one cover at random the sender could also look through the database
of usable covers and select one that the embedding process will change the least.
Such a selection process can be done via the similarity function *sim*. In the encoding
phase, the sender chooses a cover c with the property

$$c = \max_{x \in C} \; sim(x, E(x, m)) \tag{2.1}$$

If the cover is the result of some scanning process, the original can be digitized again
and again. Due to the noise in the hardware, every process will produce a slightly
different cover. The sender could select one, best suitable for communication. Such
a technique, called *selection method of invisibility*, is detailed in [3].

Some researchers propose public cover databases. Since an attacker who has
access to the original version of a cover can easily detect the secret, the sender
chooses one element c out of the database and performs some modifications to get
a cover c'. He then uses this new cover for secret communication. This method,
however, is not free of dangers. If an attacker has knowledge of the modification
techniques used, he can create the "plain" cover (i.e., the cover without the secret
information) himself and break the communication. Even if he does not know the
techniques which have been applied, he could create a similar cover by comparing
c to the stego-object.

Some steganographic methods combine traditional cryptography with steganography: the sender encrypts the secret message prior to the embedding process.
Clearly, such a combination increases the security of the overall communication
process, as it is more difficult for an attacker to detect embedded ciphertext (which
itself has a rather random appearance) in a cover. Strong steganographic systems,
however, do not need prior enciphering.

2.1.2   Secret key steganography

With pure steganography, no information (apart from the functions E and D) is required to start the communication process; the security of the system thus depends entirely on its secrecy. This is not very secure in practice because this violates Kerckhoffs' principle (see Section 1.2.4). So we must assume that Wendy knows the algorithm Alice and Bob use for information transfer. In theory, she is able to extract information out of every cover sent between Alice and Bob. The security of a steganographic system should thus rely on some secret information traded by Alice and Bob, the *stego-key*. Without knowledge of this key, nobody should be able to extract secret information out of the cover.

A secret key steganography system is similar to a symmetric cipher: the sender chooses a cover c and embeds the secret message into c using a secret key k. If the key used in the embedding process is known to the receiver, he can reverse the process and extract the secret message. Anyone who does not know the secret key should not be able to obtain evidence of the encoded information. Again, the cover c and the stego-object can be perceptually similar.

Definition 2.3 (Secret key steganography) *The quintuple* $\mathfrak{S} = \langle C, M, K, D_K, E_K \rangle$, *where C is the set of possible covers, M the set of secret messages with $|C| \geq |M|$, K the set of secret keys, $E_K : C \times M \times K \to C$ and $D_K : C \times K \to M$ with the property that $D_K(E_K(c, m, k), k) = m$ for all $m \in M$, $c \in C$ and $k \in K$, is called a secret key steganographic system.*

Secret key steganography requires the exchange of some key, although the transmission of additional secret information subverts the original intention of invisible communication. So as in cryptography, we assume that all communication parties are able to trade secret keys through a secure channel. Alice and Bob could agree on a stego-key before imprisonment. However, by using some characteristic features of the cover and a secure hash function H it is possible to calculate a key used for secret communication directly out of the cover: $k = H(feature)$. If the embedding process does not change the "feature," the receiver is able to recalculate the key. Obviously such a feature has to be highly "cover dependent" to reach an adequate level of security (however, the security depends on the secrecy of H, thus violating Kerckhoffs' principle again). If the cover is a digital image, one could take all most significant bits of the cover's color values as a "feature." This method could be also used to calculate a secret session key out of a general key k' valid for a longer period of time, if the hash function depends on k'.

Some algorithms additionally require the knowledge of the original cover (or some other information not derivable from the stego-object) in the decoding phase. Such systems are of limited interest, because their use requires the transmission of the original cover, a problem strongly related to key-exchange in traditional cryptography. These algorithms can be seen as a special case of secret key steganographic systems in which $K = C$ or $K = C \times K'$ where K' denotes an additional set of secret keys.

2.1.3 Public key steganography

As in public key cryptography, public key steganography does not rely on the exchange of a secret key. Public key steganography systems require the use of two keys, one private and one public key; the public key is stored in a public database. Whereas the public key is used in the embedding process, the secret key is used to reconstruct the secret message.

One way to build a public key steganography system is the use of a public key cryptosystem. We will assume that Alice and Bob can exchange public keys of some public key cryptography algorithm before imprisonment (this is, however, a more reasonable assumption). Public key steganography utilizes the fact that the decoding function D in a steganography system can be applied to any cover c, whether or not it already contains a secret message (recall that D is a function on the entire set C). In the latter case, a random element of M will be the result, we will call it "natural randomness" of the cover. If one assumes that this natural randomness is statistically indistinguishable from ciphertext produced by some public key cryptosystem, a secure steganography system can be built by embedding ciphertext rather than unencrypted secret messages.

A protocol which allows public key steganography has been proposed by Anderson in [4, 5]; it relies on the fact that encrypted information is random enough to "hide in plain sight": Alice encrypts the information with Bob's public key to obtain a random-looking message and embeds it in a channel known to Bob (and hence also to Wendy), thereby replacing some of the "natural randomness" with which every communication process is accompanied. We will assume that both the cryptographic algorithms and the embedding functions are publicly known. Bob, who cannot decide a priori if secret information is transmitted in a specific cover, will suspect the arrival of a message and will simply try to extract and decrypt it using his private key. If the cover actually contained information, the decrypted information is Alice's message.

Since we assumed that Wendy knows the embedding method used, she can try to extract the secret message sent from Alice to Bob. However, if the encryption method produces random-looking ciphertext, Wendy will have no evidence that the extracted information is more than some random bits. She thus cannot decide if the extracted information is meaningful or just part of the natural randomness, unless she is able to break the cryptosystem.

A more crucial point is that Bob must suspect the use of a steganographic technique and try to decode every cover he receives from Alice (he may not even know Alice personally). If the stego-message is not targeted towards a specific person, but for example is posted in an Internet newsgroup, the problem worsens. Although the protocol also works in this case (only the intended receiver can decrypt the secret message, since only he has the correct private key) all possible receivers have to try to decode every posted object.

Craver [2] extended this protocol to simulate pure steganography using both public and private key steganography. In most applications, pure steganography is preferred, since no stego-key must be shared between the communication partners, although a pure steganography protocol does not provide any security if an attacker knows the embedding method. By implementing a key-exchange protocol using public key steganography, Alice and Bob can exchange a secret key k which they can later use in a secret key steganography system. Since no stego-key (besides their public encryption key) must be known a priori, we can refer to the communication process as pure steganography, although it does not conform to Definition 2.1.

In this protocol, Alice first generates a random public/private key pair for use with any public-key cryptosystem. Then she embeds the public key in a channel known to and viewable by Bob (and hence also Wendy). Neither Wendy nor Bob can determine whether the channel contains more than random bits. However, Bob suspects that the stego-object sent by Alice contains Alice's public key and tries to extract it. He uses the received public key to embed a randomly chosen key k along with a short message of acknowledgement, both encrypted with Alice's public key, in a cover and sends it to Alice. Again, Wendy can try to extract the secret information sent by Bob, but will likely notice only random-looking ciphertext. Alice suspects the arrival of a message from Bob, extracts the secret information and decrypts it with her private key. Now Alice and Bob share a stego-key k. This protocol is illustrated in Figure 2.3.

However, the protocol is (at the first step) susceptible to a man-in-the-middle attack. If Wendy is active, she can catch the first stego-object sent from Alice to Bob and replace Alice's public key with her own. Bob will encrypt the random secret key k using Wendy's public key instead of Alice's. Now Wendy knows the key k chosen by Bob and can forward it to Alice: she encrypts it with Alice's public key, embeds it in a cover and sends the result to Alice. Although Alice correctly receives k, she is not aware of the fact that Wendy also has access to k.

It is conjectured that neither public key steganography nor pure steganography is possible in the presence of a malicious warden. Wendy could fool Bob by starting a public key steganography protocol or the extended protocol given above in the name of Alice. Since Bob has no way to verify the validity of the public key sent

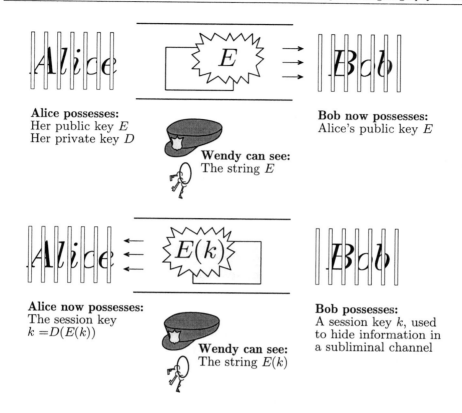

Alice possesses:
Her public key E
Her private key D

Wendy can see:
The string E

Bob now possesses:
Alice's public key E

Alice now possesses:
The session key
$k = D(E(k))$

Wendy can see:
The string $E(k)$

Bob possesses:
A session key k, used
to hide information in
a subliminal channel

Figure 2.3   Illustration of a steganographic key-exchange protocol. Courtesy of Scott Craver, reprinted from [2].

in the first step of the protocol, he cannot identify the key he received with Alice. This situation is very similar to public key cryptography, where a certification of the public key is required. In the case of pure steganography, Bob is not able to distinguish a message sent by Alice from a message by Wendy.

2.2   SECURITY OF STEGANOGRAPHY SYSTEMS

Although breaking a steganography system normally consists of three parts: detecting, extracting, and disabling embedded information (see Chapter 4), a system is already insecure if an attacker is able to prove the existence of a secret message. In developing a formal security model for steganography we must assume that an attacker has unlimited computation power and is able and willing to perform a variety of attacks. If he cannot confirm his hypothesis that a secret message is embedded in a cover, then a system is theoretically secure.

2.2.1   Perfect security

Cachin [6] gave a formal information-theoretic definition of the security of steganographic systems. The main idea is to refer to the selection of a cover as a random variable C with probability distribution P_C. The embedding of a secret message can be seen as a function defined in C; let P_S be the probability distribution of $E_K(c, m, k)$, that is the set of all stego-objects produced by the steganographic system. If a cover c is never used as a stego-object, then $P_S(c) = 0$. In order to calculate P_S, probability distributions on K and M must be imposed. Using the definition of the relative entropy $D(P_1 \| P_2)$ between two distributions P_1 and P_2 defined on the set Q,

$$D(P_1 \| P_2) = \sum_{q \in Q} P_1(q) \log_2 \frac{P_1(q)}{P_2(q)} \tag{2.2}$$

—which measures the inefficiency of assuming that the distribution is P_2 where the true distribution is P_1—the impact of the embedding process on the distribution P_C can be measured. Specifically, we define the security of a steganography system in terms of $D(P_C \| P_S)$:

Definition 2.4 (Perfect security) *Let $\mathfrak{S}$ be a steganography system, P_S the probability distribution of the stego-covers sent via the channel, and P_C the probability distribution of C. $\mathfrak{S}$ is called ε-secure against passive attackers, if*

$$D(P_C \| P_S) \leq \varepsilon$$

and perfectly secure if $\varepsilon = 0$

Since $D(P_C \| P_S)$ is zero if and only if both probability distributions are equal, we can conclude that a steganography system is (theoretically) perfectly secure, if the process of embedding a secret message in a cover does not alter the probability distribution of C. A perfectly secure system can be constructed out of a one-time pad:

Theorem 2.1 *There exists perfectly secure steganography systems.*

Proof: We give a constructive proof: let C be the set of all bitstrings of length n, P_C the uniform distribution on C, and e the secret message ($e \in C$). The sender selects one $c \in C$ at random and computes $s = c \oplus e$, where $\oplus$ is the bit-wise XOR operation. The resulting stego-covers s are uniformly distributed on C, so $P_C=P_S$ and $D(P_C\|P_S) = 0$. In the extraction process, the secret message e can be recovered by computing $s \oplus c$.

The above system is very simple but not useful, since no warden will let Alice and Bob exchange random strings.

2.2.2 Detecting secret messages

A passive attacker (Wendy) has to decide whether a cover c sent from Bob to Alice contains secret information or not. This task can be formalized as a statistical hypothesis-testing problem. Therefore, Wendy defines a test function $f : C \rightarrow \{0, 1\}$:

$$f(c) = \begin{cases} 1 & c \text{ contains a secret message} \\ 0 & \text{otherwise} \end{cases} \qquad (2.3)$$

which Wendy uses to classify covers as they are passed on via the insecure channel. In some cases Wendy will correctly classify the cover, in other cases she will not detect a hidden message, making a type-II error. It is also possible that Wendy falsely detects a hidden message in a cover which does not contain information; she then makes a type-I error. Practical steganography systems try to maximize the probability β that a passive attacker makes a type-II error. An ideal system would have $\beta = 1$. In the following paragraphs we will show that perfectly secure steganography systems (provided that an attacker makes a type-I error with probability zero) possess this property.

For ε-secure steganography systems the probabilities α and β that a passive attacker makes a type-I and type-II error are linked through the following theorem:

Theorem 2.2 (Cachin, 1998) *Let $\mathfrak{S}$ be a steganography system which is ε-secure against passive attackers, the probability β that the attacker does not detect a hidden message and the probability α that the attacker falsely detects a hidden message satisfy*

$$d(\alpha, \beta) \leq \varepsilon,$$

where $d(\alpha, \beta)$ is the binary relative entropy defined by

$$d(\alpha, \beta) = \alpha \log_2 \frac{\alpha}{1 - \beta} + (1 - \alpha) \log_2 \frac{1 - \alpha}{\beta}$$

In particular, if $\alpha = 0$, then $\beta \geq 2^{-\varepsilon}$

In order to prove Theorem 2.2, we need a special property of the relative entropy function: deterministic processing cannot increase the relative entropy between two distributions: let Q_0 and Q_1 be two random variables defined on the set Q with probability distributions P_{Q_0} and P_{Q_1} and f be a function $Q \rightarrow T$. Then, $D(P_{T_0} \| P_{T_1}) \leq D(P_{Q_0} \| P_{Q_1})$, where P_{T_0} and P_{T_1} denote the probability distributions of $f(Q_0)$ and $f(Q_1)$, see [6].

Proof: (of Theorem 2.2) In the case that the cover does not contain a secret message, the covers are distributed according to P_C. We consider the random variable $f(C)$ and calculate its distribution π_C. In the case $f(c) = 1$, the attacker makes a type-II error; thus $\pi_C(1) = \alpha$ and $\pi_C(0) = 1 - \alpha$. If the cover does not contain a secret message, the covers are distributed according to P_S. Again, we calculate the distribution π_S of $f(S)$. In the case that $f(s) = 0$, the attacker makes a type-I error since he does not detect a hidden message; thus $\pi_S(0) = \beta$ and $\pi_S(1) = 1 - \beta$. The relative entropy $D(\pi_C \| \pi_S)$ can be expressed as

$$
\begin{aligned}
D(\pi_C \| \pi_S) &= \sum_{q \in \{0,1\}} \pi_C(q) \log_2 \frac{\pi_C(q)}{\pi_S(q)} \\
&= (1 - \alpha) \log_2 \frac{1 - \alpha}{\beta} + \alpha \log_2 \frac{\alpha}{1 - \beta} \\
&= d(\alpha, \beta)
\end{aligned}
$$

Using the remark above, $d(\alpha, \beta) = D(\pi_C \| \pi_S) \leq D(P_C \| P_S) \leq \varepsilon$. Since $\lim_{\alpha \to 0} \alpha \log_2 \frac{\alpha}{1-\beta} = 0$ using De Hospital's rule, $d(0, \beta) = \log_2 \frac{1}{\beta}$. Thus, $\beta \geq 2^{-\varepsilon}$, if $\alpha = 0$.

Therefore, for ε-secure steganography systems with $\alpha = 0$ we can conclude that if $\varepsilon \to 0$, the probability $\beta \to 1$. If ε is small, an attacker will fail to detect embedded messages with very high probability.

2.3   INFORMATION HIDING IN NOISY DATA

As we have noted in Section 2.1, steganography utilizes the existence of redundant information in a communication process. Images or digital sound naturally contain such redundancies in the form of a noise component. In this section, we will assume without loss of generality that the cover c can be represented by a sequence of binary digits. In the case of a digital sound this sequence is just the sequence of samples over time; in the case of a digital image, a sequence can be obtained by vectorizing the image (i.e., by lining up the grayscale or color values in a left-to-right and top-to-bottom order). Let $\ell(c)$ be the number of elements in the sequence, m the secret message, and $\ell(m)$ its length in bits.

The general principle underlying most steganographic methods is to place the secret message in the noise component of a signal. If it is possible to code the information in such a way that it is indistinguishable from true random noise, an attacker has no chance in detecting the secret communication.

The simplest way of hiding information in a sequence of binary numbers is replacing the least significant bit (LSB) of every element with one bit of the secret message m. In floating point arithmetic, the least significant bit of the mantissa can be used instead. Since normally the size of the hidden message is much less than the number of bits available to hide the information ($\ell(m) \ll \ell(c)$) the rest of the LSB can be left unchanged. Since flipping the LSB of a byte (or a word) only means the addition or subtraction of a small quantity, the sender assumes that the difference will lie within the noise range and that it will therefore not be generally noticed. Obviously this technique does not provide a high level of security. An attacker can simply try to "decode" the cover, just as if he were the receiver. In addition, the algorithm changes the statistical properties of the cover significantly, even if the message consists of truly random bits.

This technique can be improved. Instead of using every cover-element for information transfer, it is possible to select only some elements in a rather random manner according to a secret key and leave the others unchanged. This selection can be done using a pseudorandom number generator; [7] report a system in which the output of the random number generator is used to spread the sequence of message bits over the cover by determining the number of cover-elements which are left unchanged between two elements used for information transfer. We will investigate these methods in detail in Chapter 3.

The last method is applicable to *stream covers* as well. A stream cover is a cover where the sender has no access to the entire sequence of numbers in the embedding process; think of an application which stores secret information in digital audio files while they are being recorded. On the other hand a cover is called a *random access cover* if the sender has access to the entire sequence of elements in the embedding process.

Aura [3] has introduced a flexible scheme applicable to random access covers, especially to digital images. He developed a secret key steganography system based on pseudorandom permutations. Due to the construction of the scheme, the secret information is distributed over the whole cover in a rather random manner; for details refer to Section 3.2.2.

2.4   ADAPTIVE VERSUS NONADAPTIVE ALGORITHMS

All methods presented in the last section have one general principle in common: they substitute insignificant parts (e.g., the noise component) of the cover with the secret message. Although these parts have specific statistical properties, the embedding process does not pay attention to them and changes the statistical profile of the cover significantly. A passive attacker could exploit this fact and break the system; see Chapter 4 for details. As definition 2.4 indicates, preserving the cover-distribution is essential in providing security.

2.4.1   Laplace filtering

The public domain program PGMStealth hides secret information in grayscale images by simply storing one bit of information in the LSB of every cover-pixel. By using the discrete Laplace operator it is possible to detect secret PGMStealth messages in grayscale images (an image p is represented by a (X,Y)-matrix):

$$\nabla^2 p(x,y) = p(x+1,y) + p(x-1,y) + p(x,y+1) + \\ p(x,y-1) - 4p(x,y) \tag{2.4}$$

Evaluating (2.4) at every point (x,y) gives the "Laplace filtered" image. Since we can expect neighboring pixels to have a similar color, the histogram of $\nabla^2 p(x,y)$ is tightly clustered around zero. Figure 2.4(a) shows eight histograms of Laplace filtered grayscale images printed in one coordinate system. Figure 2.4(b) shows the histograms of the same images after PGMStealth has done its work. Since the embedding process adds noise to the picture, which is statistically quite different from true random noise, the new histogram differs extremely. Laplace filtering does not prove the existence of a secret, but it will provide strong evidence that the picture was subject to modifications.

2.4.2   Using cover-models

To avoid such an attack, some researchers proposed to *model* the cover-characteristics and thus create *adaptive* steganography algorithms, a goal which is not easily achieved. It could be possible to code the secret information in such a way that it is statistically indistinguishable from true random noise. The secret information could then be placed in highly noisy image regions. Generally, such an approach requires the knowledge of an exact model of covers used for secret information transfer. However, setting up such a model is not easy and the whole strategy has the inherent danger that an attacker, who has greater resources and is

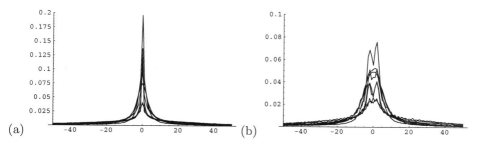

Figure 2.4 (a) Histograms of eight Laplace filtered images; (b) Histograms of eight Laplace filtered PGMStealth output images.

willing to spend more time on the problem, is able to deduce a better model, which he can use to detect patterns encoded in the cover by the nonsophisticated model the sender used.

A noise-model-dependent embedding process which uses digital images as cover-objects is presented in [8]. We shall summarize it here. Let f be the probability density function of the noise component (symmetric around zero), and η_i a sequence of independent random variables with the probability distribution defined by f. The sender first generates a "zero noise" image by averaging several versions of one cover and then selects $\ell(m)$ random pixels for information transfer, one for each message bit. The information is encoded by adding $|\eta_i|$ or $-|\eta_i|$ to these pixels, depending on the message bit to encode; the remainder of the pixels will be modified by η_i. These modifications should be consistent with the statistical noise model f.

By applying such a method, the embedding process becomes parametric; in most cases the decoding process is therefore also parametric and requires the knowledge of the original cover.

2.5   ACTIVE AND MALICIOUS ATTACKERS

During the design of a steganographic system special attention has to be paid to the presence of active and malicious attackers. Active attackers are able to change a cover during the communication process; Wendy could capture one stego-object sent from Alice to Bob, modify it and forward the result to Bob. It is a general assumption that an active attacker is not able to change the cover and its semantics entirely, but only make minor changes so that the original and the modified cover-object stay perceptually or semantically similar. An attacker is malicious if he forges messages or starts steganography protocols under the name of one communication partner. For attacks on steganographic systems see Chapters 4 and 7.

2.5.1   Active attackers: robust steganography

Steganographic systems are extremely sensitive to cover modifications, such as image processing techniques (like smoothing, filtering, and image transformations) in the case of digital images and filtering in the case of digital sound. But even a *lossy compression* can result in total information loss. Lossy compression techniques try to reduce the amount of information by removing imperceptible signal components and so often remove the secret information which has previously been added.

An active attacker, who is not able to extract or prove the existence of a secret message, thus can simply add random noise to the transmitted cover and so try to destroy the information. In the case of digital images, an attacker could also apply image processing techniques or convert the image to another file format. All of these techniques can be harmful to the secret communication. Another practical requirement for a steganography system therefore is *robustness*. A system is called robust if the embedded information cannot be altered without making drastic changes to the stego-object.

Definition 2.5 (Robustness) *Let* $\mathfrak{S}$ *be a steganography system and* $\wp$ *be a class of mappings* $C \to C$. $\mathfrak{S}$ *is* $\wp$-robust, *if for all* $p \in \wp$

$$D_K(p(E_K(c, m, k)), k) = D_K(E_K(c, m, k), k) = m \tag{2.5}$$

in the case of a secret key steganography system and

$$D(p(E(c, m))) = D(E(c, m)) = m \tag{2.6}$$

in the case of a pure steganography system, regardless of the choice of $m \in M$, $c \in C$, *and* $k \in K$.

It should be clear that there is a trade-off between *security* and *robustness*. The more robust a system will be against modifications of the cover, the less secure it can be, since robustness can only be achieved by redundant information encoding which will degrade the cover heavily and possibly alter the probability distribution P_S.

Many steganography systems are designed to be robust against a specific class of mappings (e.g., JPEG compression/decompression [9, 10], filtering, addition of white noise, etc.). An ideal system would be robust to all "α-similarity-preserving" mappings, (i.e., mappings $p : C \to C$ with the property $sim(c, p(c)) \geq \alpha$ and $\alpha \approx 1$). However, such systems are difficult to engineer and would have a low bandwidth due to the robustness of the encoding. On the other hand, a system is called α-weak, if for every cover a α-similarity-preserving mapping exists so that the encoded information is not recoverable in the sense of (2.5) and (2.6).

Generally, there are two approaches in making steganography robust. First, by foreseeing possible cover modifications [11, 12] the embedding process itself can be made robust so that modifications will not entirely destroy secret information. A second approach tries to reverse the modifications that have been applied by the attacker to the cover, so that the original stego-object can be restored. Bender et al. [13] proposed "affine coding," a counterstrategy against affine image transformations in order to recover secret messages embedded in stego-objects. They try to estimate the parameters of the transform by measuring the change in shape, size, and orientation of some encoded reference patterns. Since the transform is linear, the inverse transform can be applied to reconstruct the stego-cover.

Cox et al. [14] point out that robust algorithms have to place the information in the perceptually most significant parts of the signal, since information encoded in the noise component can be removed without great effort. For example, it is known that embedding rules operating in some transform domain of the cover-signal can be much more robust to modifications than embedding algorithms operating in the time domain. We will exploit these properties and construct robust steganographic systems which store information in the discrete cosine transform (DCT) coefficients of an image in Section 3.3.1. Empirical studies showed that these methods are robust to JPEG compression down to a quality level of about 60%. Other methods, mainly used in watermarking, survive JPEG compression down to a quality level of about 5%.

2.5.2   Supraliminal channels

If we assume that an active attacker can only make minor changes to a stego-object, then every cover contains some sort of perceptually significant information which cannot be removed without entirely changing the semantics of the cover. By encoding a secret message in a way that it forms such a perceptually significant part, information can be transmitted between two communication partners with high integrity. Craver [2] calls such a channel a *supraliminal channel*: "information is hidden in plain sight, so obviously, in fact, that it is impossible to modify without gross modifications to the transmitted objects."

The covers used for secret communication can be described by a *cover-plot*, a formal description of the perceptually significant parts of the cover. Let $\mathbb{S}$ be the set of all cover-plots and f be a function $f : \mathbb{S} \rightarrow \{0, 1\}^N$, called *cover-plot function*. To embed a bitstring $x \in \{0, 1\}^N$ in a supraliminal channel, Alice chooses one element $s \in f^{-1}(x)$ and sends a cover conforming to the cover-plot s over the insecure channel. Wendy probably suspects the use of a subliminal channel and changes the cover slightly in an attempt to remove secret messages encoded in the noise component, but is not able to change the cover-plot. Bob reconstructs the

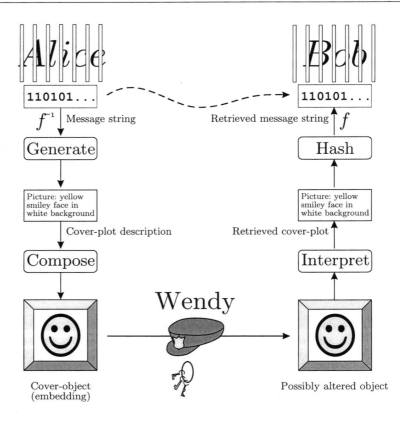

Figure 2.5   Schematic description of a supraliminal channel. Courtesy of Scott Craver, reprinted from [2].

cover-plot s out of the the cover he received and applies the function f in order to recover x; see Figure 2.5.

To be of practical interest, it must be possible to create a cover out of any cover-plot in a way that, if an active warden applies minor changes to the cover, the embedded bitstring does not change; (i.e., Wendy should not be able to convert the cover-plot s of the transmitted cover to s' so that $f(s) \neq f(s')$). Furthermore, it must be possible to exactly deduce a cover-plot out of every cover usable for secret communication. The function f should be publicly accessible and both f and f^{-1} feasible to compute. A cover which does not contain a secret message should map to a random string. Thus, the only difference between a stego-object and an innocent cover is that the string $f(s)$ possesses a meaning.

In order to communicate covertly using a supraliminal channel, Alice cannot explicitly hide a bitstring with an obvious meaning (like "Here is the plan to break out of jail. Love, Alice") since Wendy can simply recover the embedded information using the public function f. In such a case Alice and Bob would immediately face solitary confinement. If the encoded message, however, is a random secret key or apparently random-looking ciphertext, Wendy will have no evidence that the transmitted information is anything more than a random bitstring (unless she is able to break the cryptosystem) and will not raise suspicion.

A supraliminal channel can be used to implement a covert key exchange protocol. Alice generates a public key E and private key D, selects a cover-plot $s \in f^{-1}(E)$ and sends a cover conforming to s to Bob. Bob recovers E by computing the cover-plot and applying f. He chooses a random key k, encrypts it using E, chooses a cover conforming to a cover-plot $s' \in f^{-1}(E(k))$ and sends it back to Alice, who can recover $E(k)$ in an analogous way. She then decrypts $E(k)$ using her private key D. At no point does Wendy have evidence that the message encoded in the supraliminal channel is meaningful and that a key-exchange protocol is going on. Although the protocol is susceptible to a man-in-the-middle attack (like the one presented in Section 2.1.3), a nonmalicious warden cannot deduce k out of the information sent between Alice and Bob.

The main drawback of the system is, besides a low bandwidth due to the robustness of the encoding, its feasibility. It is not yet known whether a cover-plot function f can be implemented efficiently. Craver [2] suggested using the "unambiguously understandable" words in an audio-video clip as cover-plots and to define f via a hash function.

2.5.3 Malicious attackers: secure steganography

In the presence of a malicious attacker, robustness is not enough. If the embedding method is not dependent on some secret information shared by sender and receiver, (i.e., in the case of pure steganography or public key steganography) an attacker can forge messages, since the recipient is not able to verify the correctness of the sender's identity. Thus, to avoid such an attack, the algorithm must be robust and secure. We can define a *secure steganographic algorithm* in terms of four requirements:

- Messages are hidden using a public algorithm and a secret key; the secret key must identify the sender uniquely;
- Only a holder of the correct key can detect, extract, and prove the existence of the hidden message. Nobody else should be able to find any statistical evidence of a message's existence;

- Even if the enemy knows (or is able to select) the contents of one hidden message, he should have no chance of detecting others;
- It is computationally infeasible to detect hidden messages.

2.6   INFORMATION HIDING IN WRITTEN TEXT

Unlike noisy data, written text contains less redundant information which could be used for secret communication. Steganographic methods can try to encode the information directly in the text (and so exploit the natural redundancy of languages) or in the text format (e.g., by adjusting the interword or interline space).

Many ways have been proposed to store information directly in messages. Infrequent typing or spelling errors could be introduced, commas omitted, and words replaced by synonyms. Most of them are not serious options, as they degrade the text heavily. Additionally the embedding task requires the interaction of the user, it therefore cannot be automated.

On the other hand it is possible to create a text message for the sole purpose of being a cover for a secret communication. Wayner [15, 16] describes one of the most promising techniques, an automated version of Trithemius' tables. He uses context-free grammars (CFG) to create cover-texts and chooses the productions according to the secret message to be transmitted; refer to Section 3.7 for details. Thus, the secret information is not embedded in the cover, the cover itself (actually the way it has been produced by a CFG) *is* the secret message. If the grammar is unambiguous the receiver can extract the information by applying standard parsing techniques, methods which have been extensively studied in the construction of compilers. Every word which can be produced out of the grammar should form a meaningful message, otherwise an attacker will immediately raise suspicion.

If the cover-text is transmitted in a formatted form (like HTML, LaTeX or a Postscript file) information can be embedded in the format rather than in the message itself. Secret information can be stored in the size of interline or interword spaces [17–19]. If the space between two lines is smaller than some threshold, a "0" is encoded, otherwise a "1." A similar method can be used to transmit information in ASCII text: infrequent additional white space characters are introduced to form the secret message.

Many other (and more subtle) methods could be possible, for instance encoding information in the way a word processing system chooses line breakpoints. TeX, for example, uses a very sophisticated algorithm for computing line- and pagebreaks [20]; actually it classifies possible breakpoints by three values called *badness, penalty,* and *demerits.* Roughly speaking, the badness of a line is a measure for how much white space TeX would have to insert to achieve a "grouped style." Additionally, a penalty is assigned to every possible breakpoint, representing the "aesthetic cost" of breaking at a specific place. The demerits parameter of a line is then computed out of badness and penalty. TEX tries to choose a sequence of breakpoints such that the sum of all demerits in a paragraph is minimal. By adjusting several internal parameters it is possible to choose suboptimal breakpoints and so store additional information.

It is an open question whether secure and robust steganography is possible with text messages. An attacker can simply try to reformat the text and so destroy all information encoded in the text format. Additionally, text messages can be stored in different formats (like HTML, TEX's DVI, Postscript, PDF, or RTF); the conversion from one format to another might also be harmful to the embedded message.

2.7 EXAMPLES OF INVISIBLE COMMUNICATION

We want to conclude this chapter with a description of some applications and successful implementations of steganographic principles appearing in the scientific literature.

2.7.1 Subliminal channels in digital signature schemes

Simmons [21] showed that two people can communicate invisibly by exploiting weaknesses of digital signature schemes. Subliminal channels can be added to the ElGamal signature scheme, DSA, ESIGN, and some others. As an example, we want to show here how to construct a subliminal channel using the ElGamal [22] signature scheme. To generate ElGamal keys the user chooses a prime p, a generator g of $\mathbb{Z}_p^*$, and a random number $x < p$. The user calculates $y = g^x \bmod p$; the public key is the triple $\langle y, g, p \rangle$ and the private key is x. To sign a message M, the user first chooses a random number k such that k is relatively prime to $p - 1$, computes $a = g^k \bmod p$ and solves $M \equiv xa + kb \bmod (p - 1)$ for b. The signature is then the pair a and b. To verify a signature, confirm that $y^a a^b \equiv g^M \bmod p$.

To store an additional secret message in the digital signature, the receiver must have access to the sender's private key x. To send a secret message M' together with some harmless message M, M' plays the role of the random number k in the basic ElGamal scheme (i.e., the sender calculates $a = g^{M'} \bmod p$ and solves $M \equiv xa + M'b \bmod (p - 1)$ for b). The signature is again the pair a and b and can be verified as above. If the receiver has access to x, he can—subject to further conditions—reconstruct M' using the extended Euclidean algorithm. (In fact, there are also other weaknesses, see [23].) The detection of such subliminal channels in digital signature schemes stresses the need for *subliminal free digital signatures* [24], schemes which are proved to be free of subliminal channels.

2.7.2   Covert channels in operating systems

If both communication partners have access to one computer system (or if the communication partners are actually two processes running on one host), there are many other subtle methods of invisible communication. For decades the designers of operating systems have worried about the possibility of security leaks in high-security operating systems. The concern is that malicious programs could exploit *covert channels* to pass on sensitive information from a highly protected to a less protected system area. According to Lampson [25] a communication channel is covert if it was neither designed nor intended to transfer information at all; it uses entities not normally viewed as data objects to transfer information from one subject to another [26].

Covert channels can arise when one part of the system (i.e., a shared resource) operating at a specified security level is able to supply a service to another system part with a possibly different security level. Consider the following example: in an operating system, a process A acting at a high security level is able to write data onto a disk; another process B, operating at a lower security level, can access the file table (i.e., the names and sizes of all files created by the other process), although it has no access to the data itself. Such a situation can lead to a covert channel: A can send information to B by choosing appropriate file names and sizes. See [27] for details and a classification of covert channels.

Handel et al. [28] examined the Open System Interconnect (OSI) network model for possible covert channels usable to transmit secret information. They found many possible weaknesses (e.g., unused portions of data frames in the data link layer). There are even more subtle ways for sharing data; the timestamp of an IP packet can be used to transmit one bit of data (packets sent by even time increments represent logical zero, packets sent at odd time increments represent a logical one), the collision detection system in the Ethernet physical layer can be modified, and the Internet control message utilized; see also Sections 3.2.8 and 4.4.

2.7.3   Video communication systems

Steganography can be used to embed secret messages into a video stream recorded by video conferencing systems. Westfeld et al. [29] report a system that stores messages into a lossy DCT-based video compression scheme. They state that in an Integrated Services Digital Network (ISDN) video conferencing system a Global System for Mobile Communications (GSM) telephone conversation (up to 8 Kbps) could be embedded without severely degrading the video signal and thus making the secret communication apparent. This rate, however, depends on the nature of the video image used as cover.

2.7.4   Data hiding in executable files

Executable files contain lots of redundancies in the way independent subsequent instructions are scheduled or an instruction subset is chosen to solve a specific problem. Code obfuscation techniques, primarily developed to protect re-engineering of software products, can be used to store additional information in executable files. Such techniques try to transform a program P into a functionally equivalent program P' which is more difficult to reverse-engineer; in steganographic applications the secret information lies in the sequence of transformations applied.

Collberg et al. [30] point out that the only requirement is to keep the "observable" behavior intact (i.e., the behavior as experienced by the user). More precisely, if $P \rightarrow P'$ is a transformation of a source program P into a target program P', two conditions should hold: if P fails to terminate or terminates with an error message, P' may or may not terminate; otherwise, P' terminates and produces the same output as P. Collberg et al. [30, 31] list numerous techniques usable to obfuscate Java code. Among them are the "branch insertion" and "loop condition insertion" transforms. The first introduces an additional branch by writing two functionally equivalent code blocks, which are chosen according to a branch condition; the second transform extends a loop condition in a way that the total number of times the loop will execute is not affected.

2.8   CONCLUSION

On December 16, 1997, the London Daily Telegraph [32] quoted an unofficial European Union report on the existence of a system called ECHELON used to check European telecommunication: "Within Europe all email, telephone, and fax communications are routinely intercepted by the United States National Security Agency transferring all target information from the European mainland via the strategic hub of London then by satellite to Fort Meade in Maryland via the crucial hub at Menwith Hill in the North York moors in the UK." This and other incidents show that the use of cryptography or any other method which can be used to ensure privacy is essential for protecting civil liberties rights. Since more and more countries restrict the use of strong cryptography, alternative methods become increasingly important.

This chapter showed that invisible communication is possible in the computer age. Nearly any message possesses the potential of being a cover for secret communication; the noise component of digital images or digital sound can be modified, formatted wordprocessor output can contain secrets, messages can be created by CFG, the weakness of digital signature algorithms can be exploited, and even the communication of two processes in an operating system can be used to exchange classified information. Many of these techniques (and ways to defeat them) will be discussed in depth in the next chapters.

REFERENCES

[1] Simmons, G. J., "The Prisoners' Problem and the Subliminal Channel," in *Advances in Cryptology, Proceedings of CRYPTO '83*, Plenum Press, 1984, pp. 51–67.

[2] Craver, S., "On Public-Key Steganography in the Presence of an Active Warden," Technical Report RC 20931, IBM, 1997.

[3] Aura, T., "Practical Invisibility in Digital Communication," in *Information Hiding: First International Workshop, Proceedings*, vol. 1174 of *Lecture Notes in Computer Science*, Springer, 1996, pp. 265–278.

[4] Anderson, R. J., "Stretching the Limits of Steganography," in *Information Hiding: First International Workshop, Proceedings*, vol. 1174 of *Lecture Notes in Computer Science*, Springer, 1996, pp. 39–48.

[5] Anderson, R. J., and F. A. P. Petitcolas, "On The Limits of Steganography," *IEEE Journal of Selected Areas in Communications*, vol. 16, no. 4, 1998, pp. 474–481.

[6] Cachin, C., "An Information-Theoretic Model for Steganography," in *Proceedings of the Second International Workshop on Information Hiding*, vol. 1525 of *Lecture Notes in Computer Science*, Springer, 1998, pp. 306–318.

[7] Möller, S., A. Pfitzmann, and I. Stirand, "Computer Based Steganography: How It Works and Why Therefore Any Restrictions on Cryptography Are Nonsense, At Best," in *Information Hiding: First International Workshop, Proceedings*, vol. 1174 of *Lecture Notes in Computer Science*, Springer, 1996, pp. 7–21.

[8] Fridrich, J., "Innovative C4I Technologies (Secure Image Encryption and Hiding)," Technical report, final report for SBIR project No. AF97-043 (Phase I), AFRL, Rome, New York, 1998.

[9] Pennebaker, W. B., and J. L. Mitchell, *JPEG Still Image Compression Standard*, New York: Van Nostrand Reinhold, 1993.

[10] Wallace, G. K., "The JPEG Still Picture Compression Standard," *Communications of the ACM*, vol. 34, no. 4, 1991, pp. 30–44.

[11] Johnson, N. F., Z. Duric, and S. Jajodia, "A Role for Digital Watermarking in Electronic Commerce," to appear in *ACM Computing Surveys*.

[12] Johnson, N. F., "An Introduction to Watermark Recovery from Images," in *SANS Intrusion Detection and Response Conference, Proceedings*, 1999.

[13] Bender, W., D. Gruhl, and N. Morimoto, "Techniques for Data Hiding," *IBM Systems Journal*, vol. 35, no. 3/4, 1996, pp. 313–336.

[14] Cox, I. J., et al., "Secure Spread Spectrum Watermarking for Multimedia," Technical report, NEC Institute, 1995.

[15] Wayner, P., "Mimic Functions," *Cryptologia*, vol. XVI/3, 1992, pp. 193–214.

[16] Wayner, P., "Strong Theoretical Steganography," *Cryptologia*, vol. XIX/3, 1995, pp. 285–299.

[17] Brassil, J., N. F. Maxemchuk, and L. O'Gorman, "Electronic Marking and Identification Techniques to Discourage Document Copying," in *Proceedings of INFOCOM'94*, 1994, pp. 1278–1287.

[18] Low, S. H., N. F. Maxemchuk, and A. M. Lapone, "Document Identification for Copyright Protection Using Centroid Detection," *IEEE Transactions on Communications*, vol. 46, no. 3, 1998, pp. 372–383.

[19] Maxemchuk, N. F., "Electronic Document Distribution," *AT&T Technical Journal*, September/October 1994, pp. 73–80.

[20] Knuth, D. E., *The TEXbook*, Reading, MA: Addison Wesley, 1984.

[21] Simmons, G. J., "The Subliminal Channel and Digital Signatures," in *Advances in Cryptology, Proceedings of EUROCRYPT '84*, vol. 209 of *Lecture Notes in Computer Science*, Springer, 1985, pp. 364–378.

[22] ElGamal, T., "A Public-Key Cryptosystem and a Signature Scheme Based on Discrete Logarithms," in *Advances in Cryptology, Proceedings of CRYPTO '84*, vol. 196 of *Lecture Notes in Computer Science*, Springer, 1985, pp. 10–18.

[23] Anderson, R. J., et al., "The Newton Channel," in *Information Hiding: First International Workshop, Proceedings*, vol. 1174 of *Lecture Notes in Computer Science*, Springer, 1996, pp. 151–156.

[24] Desmedt, Y., "Subliminal-Free Authentication and Signature," in *Advances in Cryptology, Proceedings of EUROCRYPT '88*, vol. 330 of *Lecture Notes in Computer Science*, Berlin, New York: Springer, 1988, pp. 22–33.

[25] Lampson, B. W., "A Note on the Confinement Problem," *Communications of the ACM*, vol. 16, no. 10, 1973, pp. 613–615.

[26] Kemmerer, R. A., "Shared Resource Matrix Methodology: An Approach to Identifying Storage and Timing Channels," *ACM Transactions on Computer Systems*, vol. 1, no. 3, 1983, pp. 256–277.

[27] Meadows, C., and I. Moskowitz, "Covert Channels—A Context-Based Review," in *Information Hiding: First International Workshop, Proceedings*, vol. 1174 of *Lecture Notes in Computer Science*, Springer, 1996, pp. 73–93.

[28] Handel, T. G., and M. T. Sandford, "Data Hiding in the OSI Network Model," in *Information Hiding: First International Workshop, Proceedings*, vol. 1174 of *Lecture Notes in Computer Science*, Springer, 1996, pp. 23–38.

[29] Westfeld, A., and G. Wolf, "Steganography in a Video Conferencing System," in *Proceedings of the Second International Workshop on Information Hiding*, vol. 1525 of *Lecture Notes in Computer Science*, Springer, 1998, pp. 32–47.

[30] Collberg, C., C. Thomborson, and D. Low, "Manufacturing Cheap, Resilient and Stealthy Opaque Constructs," in *Proceedings of the ACM Symposium on the Principles of Programming Languages*, 1998, pp. 184–196.

[31] Collberg, C., C. Thomborson, and D. Low, "A Taxonomy of Obfuscating Transforms," Technical Report 148, Department of Computer Science, The University of Auckland, 1997.

[32] "Spies Like US," *London Daily Telegraph*, 16th December 1997.

Chapter 3

A survey of steganographic techniques

Neil F. Johnson and Stefan C. Katzenbeisser

Many different steganographic methods have been proposed during the last few years; most of them can be seen as substitution systems. Such methods try to substitute redundant parts of a signal with a secret message (as presented in Section 2.3); their main disadvantage is the relative weakness against cover modifications. Recently, the development of new robust watermarking techniques led to advances in the construction of robust and secure steganography systems. Therefore, some of the methods presented here are strongly related to watermarking techniques of Chapter 6.

There are several approaches in classifying steganographic systems. One could categorize them according to the type of covers used for secret communication. A classification according to the cover modifications applied in the embedding process is another possibility. We want to follow the second approach and group steganographic methods in six categories, although in some cases an exact classification is not possible:

- **Substitution systems** substitute redundant parts of a cover with a secret message;
- **Transform domain techniques** embed secret information in a transform space of the signal (e.g., in the frequency domain);
- **Spread spectrum techniques** adopt ideas from spread spectrum communication;

- **Statistical methods** encode information by changing several statistical properties of a cover and use hypothesis testing in the extraction process;
- **Distortion techniques** store information by signal distortion and measure the deviation from the original cover in the decoding step;
- **Cover generation methods** encode information in the way a cover for secret communication is created.

In the following sections these six categories will be discussed.

3.1   PRELIMINARY DEFINITIONS

Throughout the following sections we want to refer to the cover used in the embedding step as c. We will further assume (without loss of generality) that any cover can be represented by a sequence of numbers c_i of length $\ell(c)$ (i.e., $1 \leq i \leq \ell(c)$). In the case of digital sound this could be just the sequence of samples over time; in the case of a digital image, a sequence can be obtained by vectorizing the image (i.e., by lining up all pixels in a left-to-right and top-to-bottom order). Possible values of c_i are $\{0,1\}$ in the case of binary images or integers greater than 0 and less than 256 in the case of quantized images or sound. We will denote the stego-object by s which is again a sequence s_i of length $\ell(c)$.

Sometimes we have to index all cover-elements c_i; we will use the symbol j for such an index. If the index is itself indexed by some set, we use the notation j_i. When we refer to the j_ith cover-element we mean c_{j_i}. We will refer to a stego-key as k; the structure of k will be explained separately in each steganographic application. The secret message will be denoted by m, the length of m by $\ell(m)$, and the bits forming m by m_i, $1 \leq i \leq \ell(m)$. Unless otherwise stated, we assume that $m_i \in \{0,1\}$.

A color value is normally a three-component vector in a *color space* (a set of possible colors), see [1]. A well-known color space is RGB. Since the colors red, green, and blue are *additive primaries*, every color can be specified as a weighted sum of a red, green, and a blue component. A vector in RGB space describes the intensities of these components. Another space, known as YCbCr, distinguishes between a luminance (Y) and two chrominance (Cb,Cr) components. Whereas the Y component accounts for the brightness of a color, Cb and Cr distinguish between the color grades. A color vector in RGB can be converted to YCbCr using the transform:

$$
\begin{aligned}
Y &= 0.299\,R + 0.587\,G + 0.114\,B \\
Cb &= 0.5 + (B - Y)/2 \\
Cr &= 0.5 + (R - Y)/1.6
\end{aligned}
\tag{3.1}
$$

An *image* C is a discrete function assigning a color vector (of any color space) $c(x, y)$ to every pixel (x, y).

3.2   SUBSTITUTION SYSTEMS AND BITPLANE TOOLS

A number of methods exist for hiding information in various media. These methods range from LSB coding—also known as bitplane or noise insertion tools—manipulation of image or compression algorithms to modification of image properties such as luminance. Basic substitution systems try to encode secret information by substituting insignificant parts of the cover by secret message bits; the receiver can extract the information if he has knowledge of the positions where secret information has been embedded. Since only minor modifications are made in the embedding process, the sender assumes that they will not be noticed by a passive attacker.

3.2.1   Least significant bit substitution

Bitplane tools encompass methods that apply LSB insertion and noise manipulation. These approaches are common in steganography and are relatively easy to apply in image and audio [2–6]. A surprising amount of information can be hidden with little, if any, perceptible impact to the carriers [5, 7, 8].

Sample tools used in this group include StegoDos [9], S-Tools [10], Mandelsteg [11], EzStego [12], Hide and Seek [13], Hide4PGP [14], White Noise Storm [15], and Steganos [16]. The image formats typically used in such steganography methods are lossless and the data can be directly manipulated and recovered. Some of these programs apply compression and encryption in addition to steganography services. These services provide better security of the hidden data. Even so, the bitplane methods are rather brittle and vulnerable to corruption due to small changes to the carrier.

The embedding process consists of choosing a subset $\{j_1, \ldots, j_{\ell(m)}\}$ of cover-elements and performing the substitution operation $c_{j_i} \leftrightarrows m_i$ on them, which exchanges the LSB of c_{j_i} by m_i (m_i can either be 1 or 0). One could also imagine a substitution operation which changes more than one bit of the cover, for instance by storing two message bits in the two least significant bits of one cover-element. In the extraction process, the LSB of the selected cover-elements are extracted and lined up to reconstruct the secret message. This basic scheme is presented in Algorithms 3.1 and 3.2. One problem remains to be solved: in which way should the c_{j_i} be chosen?

In order to be able to decode the secret message, the receiver must have access to the sequence of element indices used in the embedding process. In the simplest

---

Algorithm 3.1 Embedding process: least significant bit substitution

---
for $i = 1, \ldots, \ell(c)$ **do**
   $s_i \leftarrow c_i$
end for
for $i = 1 \ldots, \ell(m)$ **do**
   compute index j_i where to store ith message bit
   $s_{j_i} \leftarrow c_{j_i} \leftrightharpoons m_i$
end for

Algorithm 3.2 Extraction process: least significant bit substitution

---
for $i = 1, \ldots, \ell(M)$ **do**
   compute index j_i where the ith message bit is stored
   $m_i \leftarrow \mathrm{LSB}(c_{i_j})$
end for

---

case, the sender uses all cover-elements for information transfer, starting at the first element. Since the secret message will normally have less bits than $\ell(c)$, the embedding process will be finished long before the end of the cover. In this case, the sender can leave all other cover elements unchanged. This can, however, lead to a serious security problem: the first part of the cover will have different statistical properties than the second part, where no modifications have been made. To overcome this problem, for instance the public domain program PGMStealth enlarges the secret message with random bits—so that $\ell(c) = \ell(m)$—in an attempt to create an equal change in randomness at the beginning and the end of the cover. The embedding process thus changes far more elements than the transmission of the secret would require. Therefore the probability that an attacker will suspect secret communication increases.

A more sophisticated approach is the use of a pseudorandom number generator to spread the secret message over the cover in a rather random manner; a popular approach is the *random interval method* (e.g., [3]). If both communication partners share a stego-key k usable as a seed for a random number generator, they can create a random sequence $k_1, \ldots, k_{\ell(m)}$ and use the elements with indices

$$
\begin{aligned}
j_1 &= k_1 \\
j_i &= j_{i-1} + k_i, \quad i \geq 2
\end{aligned}
\tag{3.2}
$$

for information transfer. Thus, the distance between two embedded bits is determined pseudorandomly. Since the receiver has access to the seed k and knowledge of the pseudorandom number generator, he can reconstruct k_i and therefore the entire sequence of element indices j_i. This technique—which is especially efficient

---

Algorithm 3.3 Embedding process: random interval method

   for $i = 1 \ldots, \ell(c)$ **do**
      $s_i \leftarrow c_i$
   end for
   generate random sequence k_i using seed k
   $n \leftarrow k_1$
   for $i = 1, \ldots, \ell(m)$ **do**
      $s_n \leftarrow c_n \leftrightarrows m_i$
      $n \leftarrow n + k_i$
   end for

Algorithm 3.4 Extraction process: random interval method

   generate random sequence k_i using seed k
   $n \leftarrow k_1$
   for $i = 1, \ldots, \ell(m)$ **do**
      $m_i \leftarrow \text{LSB}(c_n)$
      $n \leftarrow n + k_i$
   end for

---

in the case of stream covers—is illustrated in Algorithms 3.3 and 3.4, which are special cases of the general framework presented in Algorithms 3.1 and 3.2.

3.2.2 Pseudorandom permutations

If all cover bits can be accessed in the embedding process (i.e., if c is a random access cover), the secret message bits can be distributed randomly over the whole cover. This technique further increases the complexity for an attacker, since it is not guaranteed that subsequent message bits are embedded in the same order.

In a first attempt Alice could create (using a pseudorandom number generator) a sequence $j_1, \ldots, j_{\ell(m)}$ of element indices and store the kth message bit in the element with index j_k. Note that one index could appear more than once in the sequence, since we have not restricted the output of the pseudorandom number generator in any way. We call such a case "collision." If a collision occurs, Alice will possibly try to insert more than one message bit into one cover-element, thereby corrupting some of them. If the message is quite short compared with the number of cover-elements, she hopes that the probability of collisions is negligible and that corrupted bits could be reconstructed using an error-correcting code. This is, however, only the case for quite short secret messages. The probability p of at least one collision can be estimated[1] by (provided that $\ell(m) \ll \ell(c)$):

$$p \approx 1 - \exp\left(-\frac{\ell(m)[\ell(m) - 1]}{2\ell(c)}\right)$$

For constant $\ell(c)$, p converges rapidly to 1 as $\ell(m)$ increases. If, for example, a digital image with 600×600 pixels is used as cover and about 200 pixels are selected in the embedding process, p is approximately 5%. On the other hand, if 600 pixels are used for information transfer, p increases to about 40%. We can conclude that only for very short messages the probability of collisions is negligible; if the message size increases, collisions must definitely be taken into account.

To overcome the problem of collisions, Alice could keep track of all cover-bits which have already been used for communication in a set B. If during the embedding process one specific cover-element has not been used prior, she adds its index to B and continues to use it. If, however, the index of the cover-element is already contained in B, she discards the element and chooses another cover-element pseudorandomly. At the receiver side, Bob applies a similar technique.

Another method has been proposed by Aura [18]; he uses the basic substitution scheme of Algorithms 3.1 and 3.2 and calculates the index j_i via a pseudorandom permutation of the set $\{1, \ldots, \ell(c)\}$. Suppose the number $\ell(c)$ can be expressed as a product of two numbers, X and Y (recall that this is always the case for digital images), and h_K is an arbitrary cryptographically secure hash function depending on a key k. Let k_1, k_2 and k_3 be three secret keys. It can then be shown [19, 20] that Algorithm 3.5 outputs a different number j_i for each input i ($1 \leq i \leq XY$), (i.e., it produces a pseudorandom permutation of the set $\{1, \ldots, \ell(c)\}$), provided that the algorithm is evaluated with input $i = 1, \ldots, \ell(c)$.

Alice first splits the stego-key k into three pieces k_1, k_2 and k_3. In the embedding process she stores the ith message bit in the element with index j_i, which is computed according to Algorithm 3.5. Collisions do not occur, since Algorithm 3.5 does not produce duplicate element indices. If Bob has access to the three keys k_1, k_2 and k_3, he is able to reconstruct the positions where Alice embedded the secret

---

1 The problem of calculating p is an instance of the so-called birthday paradox: an urn is filled with n balls, numbered from 1 to n. Suppose that m balls are drawn from the urn with replacement and their numbers are listed. The probability $P(n, m)$ that at least one ball is drawn twice, provided that $m = O(\sqrt{n})$, is given by [17]

$$P(n, m) = 1 - \prod_{i=0}^{m-1}\left(1 - \frac{i}{n}\right) \rightarrow 1 - \exp\left(-\frac{m(m-1)}{2n} + O\left(\frac{1}{\sqrt{n}}\right)\right)$$

Algorithm 3.5 Computing the index j_i using pseudorandom permutations

$v \leftarrow i \operatorname{div} X$
$u \leftarrow i \bmod X$
$v \leftarrow (v + h_{k_1}(u)) \bmod Y$
$u \leftarrow (u + h_{k_2}(v)) \bmod X$
$v \leftarrow (v + h_{k_3}(u)) \bmod Y$
$j_i \leftarrow vX + u$

---

message bits. However, Aura's method needs a considerable amount of computation time, since the chosen hash function must be evaluated $3\ell(m)$ times.

3.2.3   Image downgrading and covert channels

In 1992, Kurak and McHugh [5] reported on a security threat in high-security operating systems. Their fear was that a steganographic technique, called image downgrading, could be used to exchange images covertly. Image downgrading is a special case of a substitution system in which images act both as secret messages and covers. Given a cover-image and a secret image of equal dimensions, the sender exchanges the four least significant bits of the cover's grayscale (or color) values with the four most significant bits of the secret image. The receiver extracts the four least significant bits out of the stego-image, thereby gaining access to the most significant bits of the secret image. While the degradation of the cover is not visually noticeable in many cases, 4 bits are sufficient to transmit a rough approximation of the secret image.

In multilevel-secure operating systems, subjects (processes, users) and objects (files, databases, etc.) are assigned a specific security level; for example, see the famous Bell-LaPadula [21] model. Subjects are normally only allowed to access objects with a lower security level ("no read up"), whereas they are only able to write onto objects with a higher level ("no write down"). Whereas the reason for the first restriction is obvious, the second attempts to prohibit users from making confident information available to subjects with a lower security classification. Information downgrading can be used to declassify or *downgrade* information (hence the name) by embedding classified information into objects with a substantially lower security classification and thus subvert the principle of "no write down." Chapter 4 will look at possible counterstrategies.

3.2.4   Cover-regions and parity bits

We will call any nonempty subset of $\{c_1, \ldots, c_{\ell(c)}\}$ a cover-region. By dividing the cover in several disjoint regions, it is possible to store one bit of information in a whole cover-region rather than in a single element. A *parity bit* of a region I can be calculated by

$$p(I) = \sum_{j \in I} LSB(c_j) \bmod 2 \tag{3.3}$$

In the embedding step, $\ell(m)$ disjoint cover-regions I_i $(1 \leq i \leq \ell(m))$ are selected, each encodes one secret bit m_i in the parity bit $p(I_i)$. If the parity bit of one cover-region I_i does not match with the secret bit m_i to encode, one LSB of the values in I_i is flipped. This will result in $p(I_i) = m_i$. In the decoding process, the parity bits of all selected regions are calculated and lined up to reconstruct the message. Again, the cover-regions can be constructed pseudorandomly using the stego-key as a seed.

Although the method is not more robust than simple bit substitution, it is conjectured to be more powerful in many cases. First, the sender can choose which element should be modified in the cover-region; he can do it in a way that changes the cover statistics least. Furthermore, the probability p_0^* that the parity bit of a cover-region consisting of N randomly chosen elements is zero, is approximately $1/2$, nearly independent of the probability p_0 that the LSB of one randomly selected cover-element is zero, since

$$
\begin{aligned}
p_0^* &= \sum_{i=0}^{\lfloor N/2 \rfloor} \binom{N}{2i} (1 - p_0)^{2i} p_0^{N-2i} \\
&= \frac{p_0^N}{2} \left[\left(1 + \frac{1 - p_0}{p_0} \right)^N + \left(1 - \frac{1 - p_0}{p_0} \right)^N \right] \\
&= \frac{1}{2} \left(1 + (2p_0 - 1)^N \right)
\end{aligned}
\tag{3.4}
$$

Equation (3.4) follows from the fact that $p(I) = 0$ if and only if there is an even number of pixels in the cover-region which have least significant bit 1. Since $(2p_0 - 1)^N \to 0$ if $0 < p_0 < 1$, we can conclude that p_0^* rapidly approaches $1/2$ as N increases, regardless of p_0. This indicates that the effect of the embedding process on the cover can be reduced by increasing N.

3.2.5   Palette-based images

In a palette-based image only a subset of colors from a specific color space can be used to colorize the image. Every palette-based image format consists of two parts: a *palette* specifying N colors as a list of indexed pairs $(i, \mathbf{c}_i)$, assigning a color vector $\mathbf{c}_i$ to every index i, and the actual image data which assign a palette index to every pixel rather than the color value itself. If only a small number of color values are used throughout the image, this approach greatly reduces the file size. Two of the most popular formats are the graphics interchange format (GIF) and the BMP bitmap format. However, due to the availability of sophisticated compression techniques, their use declines.

Generally, there are two ways to encode information in a palette-based image: either the palette or the image data can be manipulated. The LSB of the color vectors could be used for information transfer, just like the substitution methods presented in the last subsections. Alternatively, since the palette does not need to be sorted in any way, information can be encoded in the way the colors are stored in the palette. Since there are $N!$ different ways to sort the palette, there is enough capacity to encode a small message. However, all methods which use the order of a palette to store information, are not robust, since an attacker can simply sort the entries in a different way and destroy the secret message (he thereby does not even modify the picture visibly).

Alternatively, information can be encoded in the image data. Since neighboring palette color values need not be perceptually similar, the approach of simply changing the LSB of some image data fails. Some steganographic applications (e.g., the program EzStego) therefore sort the palette so that neighboring colors are perceptually similar before they start the embedding process. Color values can, for instance, be stored according to their Euclidian distance in RGB space:

$$d = \sqrt{R^2 + G^2 + B^2} \tag{3.5}$$

Since the human visual system is more sensitive to changes in the luminance of a color, another (probably better) approach would be sorting the palette entries according to their luminance component, see (3.1). After the palette is sorted, the LSB of color indices can safely be altered.

Fridrich [22] proposes using a slightly different technique which does not need the palette to be sorted: for every pixel, the set of closest colors (in the Euclidian norm) is calculated. Starting with the closest color, the sender proceeds to find the next-closest color until a color is found where its parity $(R + G + B \bmod 2)$ matches with the secret bit to encode. Once such a color is found, the pixel is changed to this new color.

Yet another steganographic application reduces the total number of color values in a picture to $\lfloor N/2 \rfloor$ using some dithering method, and doubles the entire palette; thereby all doubled entries are slightly modified. After this preprocessing stage, each color value of the dithered image corresponds to two palette entries, from which one is chosen according to a secret message bit (e.g., Mandelsteg [11], S-Tools [10], Hide4PGP [14], and Hide and Seek [13] apply variations of this method).

3.2.6 Quantization and dithering

Dithering and quantization of digital images can be used for embedding secret information. Matsui and Tanaka [23] presented two steganographic systems which operate on quantized images. We briefly review quantization in the context of predictive coding here. In predictive coding, the intensity of each pixel is predicted based on the pixel values in a specific neighborhood; the prediction may be a linear or nonlinear function of the surrounding pixel values. In its simplest form, the difference e_i between adjacent pixels x_i and x_{i+1} is calculated and fed into a quantizer Q which outputs a discrete approximation Δ_i of the difference signal $x_i - x_{i-1}$ (i.e., $\Delta_i = Q(x_i - x_{i-1})$). Thus, in each quantization step a quantization error is introduced. For highly correlated signals we can expect Δ_i to be close to zero, so an entropy coder—which tries to create a minimum-redundancy code given a stochastic model of the data to be transmitted—will be efficient. At the receiver side the difference signal is dequantized and added to the last signal sample in order to construct an estimate for the sequence x_i.

For steganographic purposes the quantization error in a predictive coding scheme can be utilized; specifically, we adjust the difference signal Δ_i so that it transmits additional information. In this scheme, the stego-key consists of a table which assigns a specific bit to every possible value of Δ_i; for instance, the following assignment could be made:

Δ_i	-4	-3	-2	-1	0	1	2	3	4
	0	1	0	1	1	1	0	0	1

In order to store the ith message bit in the cover-signal, the quantized difference signal Δ_i is computed. If Δ_i does not match (according to the secret table) with the secret bit to be encoded, Δ_i is replaced by the nearest Δ_j where the associated bit equals the secret message bit. The resulting values Δ_i are then fed into the entropy coder. At the receiver side, the message is decoded according to the difference signal Δ_i and the stego-key.

Secret information can also be inserted into a signal during a dithering process; see [23] and Baharav and Shaked [24] for details.

Algorithm 3.6 Zhao and Koch's algorithm for data embedding in binary images
for $i = 1, \ldots, \ell(M)$ **do**
  do forever
    pseudorandomly select a new image block B_j
    /* *Test, if block B_i is valid* */
    if $P_1(B_j) > R_1 + 3\lambda$ or $P_1(B_j) < R_0 - 3\lambda$ **then continue**
    if $(c_i = 1$ and $P_1(B_j) < R_0)$ or $(c_i = 0$ and $P_1(B_j) > R_1)$ **then**
      mark block B_j as unusable, i.e. modify block so that
        either $P_1(B_j) < R_0 - 3\lambda$ or $P_1(B_j) > R_1 + 3\lambda$
      continue
    endif
    break
  enddo
  /* *Embed secret message bit in B_j* */
  if $c_i = 1$ **then**
    modify B_j so that $P_1(B_j) \geq R_1$ and $P_1(B_j) \leq R_1 + \lambda$
  else
    modify B_j so that $P_0(B_j) \leq R_0$ and $P_0(B_j) \geq R_0 - \lambda$
  end if
end for

3.2.7   Information hiding in binary images

Binary images—like digitized fax data—contain redundancies in the way black and white pixels are distributed. Although the implementation of a simple substitution scheme is possible (e.g., certain pixels could be set to black or white depending on a specific message bit), these systems are highly susceptible to transmission errors and are therefore not robust.

One information hiding scheme which uses the number of black pixels in a specific image region to encode secret information was presented by Zhao and Koch [25]. A binary image is divided into rectangular image blocks B_i; let $P_0(B_i)$ be the percentage of black pixels in the image block B_i and $P_1(B_i)$ the percentage of white pixels, respectively. Basically, one block embeds a 1, if $P_1(B_i) > 50\%$ and a 0, if $P_0(B_i) > 50\%$. In the embedding process the color of some pixels is changed so that the desired relation holds. Modifications are carried out at those pixels whose neighbors have the opposite color; in sharply contrasted binary images, modifications are carried out at the boundaries of black and white pixels. These rules assure that the modifications are not generally noticeable.

In order to make the entire system robust to transmission errors and other

---

Algorithm 3.7 Extraction process (Zhao and Koch)

---
for $i = 1, \ldots, \ell(M)$ **do**
  do forever
    pseudorandomly select image block B_j
    if $P_1(B_j) > R_1 + 3\lambda$ or $P_1(B_j) < R_0 - 3\lambda$ **then continue**
    break
  enddo
  if $P_1(B_j) > 50\%$ **then**
    $m_i \leftarrow 1$
  else
    $m_i \leftarrow 0$
  end if
end for

---

image modifications, we have to adapt the embedding process. If it is possible that some pixels change color during the transmission process, it could be the case that for instance $P_1(B_i)$ drops from 50.6% to 49.5%, thereby destroying the embedded information. Therefore two threshold values $R_1 > 50\%$ and $R_0 < 50\%$ and a robustness parameter λ, which specifies the percentage of pixels which can change color during transmission, are introduced. The sender assures during the embedding process that either $P_1(B_i) \in [R_1, R_1 + \lambda]$ or $P_0(B_i) \in [R_0 - \lambda, R_0]$ instead of $P_1(B_i) > 50\%$ and $P_0(B_i) < 50\%$. If too many pixels must be changed in order to achieve that goal, the block is marked as "invalid": $P_1(B_i)$ is modified to fulfill one of the two conditions

$$
\begin{aligned}
P_1(B_i) &< R_0(B_i) - 3\lambda \\
P_1(B_i) &> R_1(B_i) + 3\lambda
\end{aligned}
$$

and another block is pseudorandomly chosen for bit i. In the decoding process, invalid blocks are skipped. Otherwise, the information is decoded according to $P_1(B_i)$. The embedding and extraction algorithms are outlined in Algorithms 3.6 and 3.7.

A different embedding scheme, presented by Matsui and Tanaka [23], uses the lossless compression system which is used to encode information in a facsimile document. According to a recommendation of the former Comité Consultatif International Télégraphique et Téléphonique (which is now the International Telecommunication Union) [26], fax images can be coded using a combination of run length (RL) and Huffman encoding. RL techniques utilize the fact that in a binary image successive pixels have the same color with high probability. Figure 3.1 shows one scan line from a fax document; we will indicate positions with changing colors with

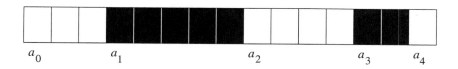

Figure 3.1   One scan line of a binary image.

a_i. Instead of coding the color of every pixel explicitly, RL methods code the positions of color changes (a_i) together with the number $RL(a_i, a_{i+1})$ of successive pixels with the same color starting at a_i. Our hypothetical scan line of Figure 3.1 would be coded by $\langle a_0, 3\rangle, \langle a_1, 5\rangle, \langle a_2, 4\rangle, \langle a_3, 2\rangle, \langle a_4, 1\rangle$. We can thus describe a binary image as a sequence of RL elements $\langle a_i, RL(a_i, a_{i+1})\rangle$.

Information can be embedded into a binary, run-length encoded image by modifying the least significant bit of $RL(a_i, a_{i+1})$. In the encoding process we modify the run lengths of the binary picture so that $RL(a_i, a_{i+1})$ is even, if the ith secret message bit m_i is zero. If, however, $RL(a_i, a_{i+1})$ is odd, m_i is one. This can be achieved, for example, by the following manner: if m_i is zero but $RL(a_i, a_{i+1})$ is odd, we move the position of a_{i+1} one pixel to the left. On the other hand, we move a_{i+1} one pixel to the right, if $m_i = 1$ and $RL(a_i, a_{i+1})$ is even. This insertion technique, however, leads to problems if the run-length $RL(a_i, a_{i+1})$ is one. If the run-length needs to be changed in the embedding process, it could be lost. We therefore have to assure that such a situation will never happen; for example, all RL elements with run-length one could be dropped before starting the embedding process.

3.2.8   Unused or reserved space in computer systems

Taking advantage of unused or reserved space to hold covert information provides a means of hiding information without perceptually degrading the carrier. For example: the way operating systems store files typically results in unused space that appears to be allocated to a file. For example, under Windows 95 operating system, drives formatted as FAT16 (MS-DOS compatible) without compression typically use cluster sizes of 32^2 kilobytes (Kb). This means that the minimum space allocated to a file is 32 Kb. If a file is 1 Kb in size, then an additional 31 Kb is "wasted." This "extra" space can be used to hide information without showing up in the directory. Unused space in file headers of image and audio can also be used to hold "extra" information.

---

2 This depends on the size of the hard drive.

Another method of hiding information in file systems is to create a hidden partition. These partitions are not seen if the system is started normally. However, in many cases, running a disk configuration utility (such as DOS's FDISK) exposes the hidden partition. These concepts have been expanded in a novel proposal of a steganographic file system [27, 28]. If the user knows the file name and password, access is granted to the file; otherwise, no evidence of the file exists in the system.

Protocols in the OSI network model have characteristics that can be used to hide information [29]. TCP/IP packets used to transport information across the Internet have unused space in the packet headers. The TCP packet header has six unused (reserved) bits and the IP packet header has two reserved bits. Thousands of packets are transmitted with each communication channel, which provides an excellent covert communication channel if unchecked. The ease in use and abundant availability of steganography tools has law enforcement concerned in trafficking of illicit material via Web page images, audio, and other files being transmitted through the Internet. Methods of message detection and understanding the thresholds of current technology are necessary to uncover such activities (see Chapter 4).

3.3   TRANSFORM DOMAIN TECHNIQUES

We have seen that LSB modification techniques are easy ways to embed information, but they are highly vulnerable to even small cover modifications. An attacker can simply apply signal processing techniques in order to destroy the secret information entirely. In many cases even the small changes resulting out of lossy compression systems yield to total information loss.

It has been noted early in the development of steganographic systems that embedding information in the frequency domain of a signal can be much more robust than embedding rules operating in the time domain. Most robust steganographic systems known today actually operate in some sort of transform domain.

Transform domain methods hide messages in significant areas of the cover image which makes them more robust to attacks, such as compression, cropping, and some image processing, than the LSB approach. However, while they are more robust to various kinds of signal processing, they remain imperceptible to the human sensory system. Many transform domain variations exist. One method is to use the discrete cosine transformation (DCT) [30–33] as a vehicle to embed information in images; another would be the use of wavelet transforms [34]. Transformations can be applied over the entire image [30], to blocks throughout the image [35, 36], or other variations. However, a trade-off exists between the amount of information added to the image and the robustness obtained [7, 37]. Many transform domain methods are independent to image format and may survive conversion between lossless and lossy formats.

Before we describe transform domain steganographic methods, we will briefly review the Fourier and cosine transforms which can be used to map a signal into the frequency domain. The discrete Fourier transform (DFT) of a sequence s of length N is defined to be

$$S(k) = \mathcal{F}\{s\} = \sum_{n=0}^{N-1} s(n) \exp\left(-\frac{2in\pi k}{N}\right) \tag{3.6}$$

where $i = \sqrt{-1}$ is the imaginary unit. The inverse Fourier transform is given by

$$s(k) = \mathcal{F}^{-1}\{S\} = \sum_{n=0}^{N-1} S(n) \exp\left(\frac{2in\pi k}{N}\right) \tag{3.7}$$

Another useful transform is the DCT, given by

$$
\begin{aligned}
S(k) &= \mathcal{D}\{s\} = \frac{C(k)}{2} \sum_{j=0}^{N} s(j) \cos\left(\frac{(2j+1)k\pi}{2N}\right) \\
s(k) &= \mathcal{D}^{-1}\{S\} = \sum_{j=0}^{N} \frac{C(j)}{2} s(j) \cos\left(\frac{(2j+1)k\pi}{2N}\right)
\end{aligned} \tag{3.8}
$$

where $C(u) = 1/\sqrt{2}$ if $u = 0$ and $C(u) = 1$ otherwise. The DCT has the primary advantage that $\mathcal{D}\{s\}$ is a sequence of real numbers, provided that the sequence s is real. In digital image processing, the two-dimensional version of the DCT is used:

$$
\begin{aligned}
S(u,v) &= \frac{2}{N} C(u)C(v) \sum_{x=0}^{N-1}\sum_{y=0}^{N-1} s(x,y) \cos\left(\frac{\pi u(2x+1)}{2N}\right) \cos\left(\frac{\pi v(2y+1)}{2N}\right) \\
s(x,y) &= \frac{2}{N} \sum_{u=0}^{N-1}\sum_{v=0}^{N-1} C(u)C(v)S(u,v) \cos\left(\frac{\pi u(2x+1)}{2N}\right) \cos\left(\frac{\pi v(2y+1)}{2N}\right)
\end{aligned}
$$

The two-dimensional DCT is the "heart" of the most popular lossy digital image compression system used today: the JPEG system [38, 39] (see Figure 3.2). JPEG first converts the image to be compressed into the YCbCr color space and breaks up each color plane into 8×8 blocks of pixels. Then, all blocks are DCT transformed. In a quantization step all DCT coefficients are divided by some predefined quantization values (see Table 3.1) and rounded to the nearest integer (according to a *quality factor*, the quantization values can be scaled by a constant). The purpose of this process is to modulate the influence of the different spectral components on the

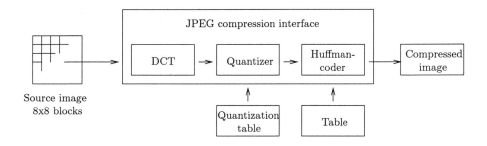

Figure 3.2   Outline of the JPEG image compression algorithm.

(u, v)	0	1	2	3	4	5	6	7
0	16	11	10	16	24	40	51	61
1	12	12	14	19	26	58	60	55
2	14	13	16	24	40	57	69	56
3	14	17	22	29	51	87	80	62
4	18	22	37	56	68	109	103	77
5	24	35	55	64	81	104	113	92
6	49	64	78	87	103	121	120	101
7	72	92	95	98	112	100	103	99

Table 3.1   Quantization values used in the JPEG compression scheme (luminance components).

image. In particular, the influence of the highest DCT coefficients is reduced: they are likely to be dominated by noise and are not expected to contribute significant details to the picture. The resulting quantized DCT coefficients are compressed using an entropy coder (e.g., Huffman [40] or arithmetic coding). In the JPEG decoding step all DCT coefficients are dequantized (i.e., multiplied with the quantization values which had been used in the encoding step). Afterwards an inverse DCT is performed to reconstruct the data. The restored picture will be close to (but not identical with) the original one; but if the quantization values were set properly, there should be no noticeable difference for a human observer.

3.3.1   Steganography in the DCT domain

One popular method of encoding secret information in the frequency domain is modulating the relative size of two (or more) DCT coefficients within one image

---

Algorithm 3.8 DCT–Steg encoding process

---

  for $i = 1, \ldots, \ell(M)$ **do**

    choose one cover-block b_i

    $B_i = \mathcal{D}\{b_i\}$

    if $m_i = 0$ **then**

      if $B_i(u_1, v_1) > B_i(u_2, v_2)$ **then**

        swap $B_i(u_1, v_1)$ and $B_i(u_2, v_2)$

      end if

    else

      if $B_i(u_1, v_1) < B_i(u_2, v_2)$ **then**

        swap $B_i(u_1, v_1)$ and $B_i(u_2, v_2)$

      end if

    end if

    adjust both values so that $|B_i(u_1, v_1) - B_i(u_2, v_2)| > x$

    $b'_i = \mathcal{D}^{-1}\{B_i\}$

  end for

  create stego-image out of all b'_i

---

block. We will describe a system which uses digital images as covers and which is similar to a technique proposed by Zhao and Koch [25].

During the encoding process, the sender splits the cover-image in 8×8 pixel blocks; each block encodes exactly one secret message bit. The embedding process starts with selecting a pseudorandom block b_i which will be used to code the ith message bit. Let $B_i = \mathcal{D}\{b_i\}$ be the DCT-transformed image block.

Before the communication starts, both sender and receiver have to agree on the location of two DCT coefficients, which will be used in the embedding process; let us denote these two indices by (u_1, v_1) and (u_2, v_2). The two coefficients should correspond to cosine functions with middle frequencies; this ensures that the information is stored in significant parts of the signal (hence the embedded information will not be completely damaged by JPEG compression). Furthermore, we can assume that the embedding process will not degenerate the cover heavily, because it is widely believed that DCT coefficients of middle frequencies have similar magnitudes [41]. Since the constructed system should be robust against JPEG compression, we choose the DCT coefficients in such a way that the quantization values associated with them in the JPEG compression algorithm are equal. According to Table 3.1 the coefficients (4,1) and (3,2) or (1,2) and (3,0) are good candidates.

One block encodes a "1," if $B_i(u_1, v_1) > B_i(u_2, v_2)$, otherwise a "0." In the encoding step, the two coefficients are swapped if their relative size does not match with the bit to be encoded. Since the JPEG compression can (in the quantiza-

---

Algorithm 3.9 DCT–Steg decoding process

---

  for $i = 1, \ldots, \ell(M)$ **do**
    get cover-block b_i associated with bit i
    $B_i = \mathcal{D}\{b_i\}$
    if $B_i(u_1, v_1) \le B_i(u_2, v_2)$ **then**
      $m_i = 0$
    else
      $m_i = 1$
    end if
  end for

---

tion step) affect the relative sizes of the coefficients, the algorithm ensures that $|B_i(u_1, v_1) - B_i(u_2, v_2)| > x$ for some $x > 0$, by adding random values to both coefficients. The higher x is, the more robust the algorithm will be against JPEG compression, however, at the expense of image quality. The sender then performs an inverse DCT to map the coefficients back into the space domain. To decode the picture, all available blocks are DCT-transformed. By comparing the two coefficients of every block, the information can be restored. Embedding and extraction algorithms are outlined in Algorithms 3.8 and 3.9.

If the constant x and the location of the used DCT coefficients are chosen properly, the embedding process will not degenerate the cover visibly. We can expect this method to be robust against JPEG compression, since in the quantization process both coefficients are divided by the same quantization values. Their relative size will therefore only be affected in the rounding step.

Perhaps the most important drawback of the system presented above is the fact that Algorithm 3.8 does not discard image blocks where the desired relation of the DCT coefficients cannot be enforced without severely damaging the image data contained in this specific block.

Zhao and Koch [25, 31] proposed a similar system which does not suffer from this drawback. They operate on quantized DCT coefficients and use the relations of three coefficients in a block to store the information. The sender DCT transforms the image block b_i and performs a quantization step to get B_i^Q. One block encodes a "1," if $B_i^Q(u_1, v_1) > B_i^Q(u_3, v_3) + D$ and $B_i^Q(u_2, v_2) > B_i^Q(u_3, v_3) + D$. On the other hand, a "0" is encoded, if $B_i^Q(u_1, v_1) + D < B_i^Q(u_3, v_3)$ and $B_i^Q(u_2, v_2) + D < B_i^Q(u_3, v_3)$. The parameter D accounts for the minimum distance between two coefficients for representing an embedded bit; normally $D = 1$. The higher D is, the more robust the method will be against image processing techniques. Again, the three selected coefficients should be situated in the middle of the spectrum.

In the encoding step, the relations between these three coefficients are changed so that they represent one bit of the secret information. If the modifications required to code one secret bit are too large, then the block is not used for information transfer and marked as "invalid." This is the case, if the difference between the largest and the smallest coefficient is greater than some constant value MD. The higher MD is, the more blocks can be used for communication. In order to allow a correct decoding, the quantized DCT coefficients of an invalid block are changed so that they fulfill one of the two conditions

$$B_i^Q(u_1, v_1) \leq B_i^Q(u_3, v_3) \leq B_i^Q(u_2, v_2) \tag{3.9}$$

or

$$B_i^Q(u_2, v_2) \leq B_i^Q(u_3, v_3) \leq B_i^Q(u_1, v_1) \tag{3.10}$$

Afterwards the block is dequantized and the inverse DCT is applied.

The receiver can restore the information by applying DCT and quantizing the block. If the three selected coefficients fulfill one of the conditions (3.9) or (3.10), the block is ignored. Otherwise the encoded information can be restored by comparing $B_i^Q(u_1, v_1)$, $B_i^Q(u_2, v_2)$, and $B_i^Q(u_3, v_3)$. The authors claim that this embedding method is robust against JPEG compression (with quality factors as low as 50%), since all changes are made after the "lossy" quantization step.

3.3.2   Hiding information in digital sound: phase coding

Embedding secret messages in digital sound is generally more difficult than embedding information in digital images. Moore [42] noted that the human auditory system is extremely sensitive; perturbations in a sound file can be detected as low as one part in 10 million. Although the limit of perceptible noise increases as the noise level of the cover increases, the maximum allowable noise level is generally quite low. It is however known that the human auditory system is much less sensitive to the phase components of sound; this fact has been exploited in numerous digital audio compression systems.

In phase coding [2], a digital datum is represented by a phase shift in the phase spectrum of the carrier signal; the carrier signal c is split into a series of N short sequences, $c_i(n)$ of length $\ell(m)$, a DFT is applied, and a matrix of the phases $\phi_i(k)$ and Fourier transform magnitudes $A_i(k)$ is created. Recall that

$$A_i(k) = \sqrt{\text{Re}[\mathcal{F}\{c_i\}(k)]^2 + \text{Im}[\mathcal{F}\{c_i\}(k)]^2} \tag{3.11}$$

and

$$\phi_i(k) = \arctan \frac{\text{Im}[\mathcal{F}\{c_i\}(k)]}{\text{Re}[\mathcal{F}\{c_i\}(k)]} \tag{3.12}$$

Since phase shifts between consecutive signal segments can easily be detected, their phase differences need to be preserved in the stego-signal. The embedding process thus inserts a secret message only in the phase vector of the first signal segment:

$$\tilde{\phi}_0(k) = \begin{cases} \pi/2 & \text{if } m_k = 0 \\ -\pi/2 & \text{if } m_k = 1 \end{cases} \tag{3.13}$$

and creates a new phase matrix using the original phase differences

$$\tilde{\phi}_1(k) = \tilde{\phi}_0(k) + [\phi_1(k) - \phi_0(k)]$$

$$\cdots$$

$$\tilde{\phi}_N(k) = \tilde{\phi}_{N-1}(k) + [\phi_N(k) - \phi_{N-1}(k)] \tag{3.14}$$

The sender then uses the new phase matrix $\tilde{\phi}_i(k)$ and the original matrix of Fourier transform magnitudes $A_i(k)$ to construct the stego-signal using the inverse Fourier transform. Since $\phi_0(k)$ is modified, the absolute phases of all following segments are changed, while their relative differences are preserved. Before the secret information can be restored, some sort of synchronization must take place. Given the knowledge of the sequence length $\ell(m)$, the receiver is able to calculate the DFT and to detect the phases $\phi_0(k)$.

3.3.3   Echo hiding

Echo hiding [4] attempts to hide information in a discrete signal $f(t)$ by introducing an echo $f(t - \Delta t)$ in the stego-signal $c(t)$:

$$c(t) = f(t) + \alpha f(t - \Delta t) \tag{3.15}$$

Information is encoded in the signal by modifying the delay Δt between the signal and the echo. In the encoding step, the sender chooses either Δt or $\Delta t'$; in the first case, a "0" is encoded in the signal $c(t)$, in the latter case a "1." The delay times Δt or $\Delta t'$ are chosen in a way that the echo signal is not audible for a human observer.

The basic echo hiding scheme can only embed one bit in a signal; therefore a cover signal is divided into $\ell(m)$ blocks prior to the encoding process. Consecutive blocks should be separated by a random number of unused samples so that the detection and extraction of the secret message bits is harder. In each block one secret bit is embedded according to (3.15); in the last step all signal blocks are concatenated.

Before the secret message can be extracted out of the stego-signal, some sort of synchronization must take place; the receiver must be able to reconstruct the $\ell(m)$ signal blocks the sender used to embed one secret message bit. Each signal segment can then be decoded via the autocorrelation function of the signal's cepstrum. Gruhl et al. [4] show that the autocorrelation function shows a spike at the delay time Δt. For a further investigation of echo hiding see Section 7.5.1.

Chang and Moskowitz [43] analyze several methods usable for information hiding in digital sound, among them low-bit coding (LSB), phase coding, spread spectrum techniques (see Section 3.4), and echo hiding. Low-bit coding techniques are not robust, but have the highest data transmission rate. Phase coding provides robustness against resampling of the carrier signal, but has a very low data transmission rate since secret information is encoded only in the first signal segment. On the contrary, spread spectrum and echo hiding perform better in many cases.

3.3.4   Information hiding and data compression

In some cases, information hiding algorithms are incorporated in data compression systems; one can think of a videoconferencing system which allows messages to be hidden in the video stream while it is being recorded. Most research work focussed on information hiding schemes for lossy video or image compression systems, but it should be noted that lossless compression systems can also be used for secret information transfer; Cachin [44] showed how to construct an asymptotically optimal steganographic system by modifying Willems [45] "repetition times" compression algorithm.

Numerous steganographic systems for compressed video or images have been proposed. In the simplest technique, applied by the tool Jpeg-Jsteg [46], information is hidden in the way DCT coefficients in the JPEG compression system (see Section 3.3) are rounded. Since the DCT normally outputs noninteger sequences for integer inputs, the JPEG system must quantize DCT coefficients before the encoding process. Information is hidden by rounding the coefficients either up or down according to the secret message bits. Although such a system is not robust, detection of the cover modifications seems to be difficult. Westfeld and Wolf [47] describe a similar technique. Their system operates on quantized, DCT-encoded blocks of video frames. After distinguishing blocks which are suitable for secret transmission from unusable blocks, the modulo-2 sum of the DCT coefficients of the block is changed in a way that it transmits secret information (see [47] for details). More sophisticated methods combine video compression schemes with spread spectrum. As an example, Hartung and Girod [48, 49] presented an information-hiding scheme operating on precompressed video using their spread spectrum watermarking system (see Section 6.4.1).

3.4   SPREAD SPECTRUM AND INFORMATION HIDING

Spread spectrum (SS) communication technologies have been developed since the 1950s in an attempt to provide means of low-probability-of-intercept and antijamming communications. Pickholtz et al. [50] define spread spectrum techniques as "means of transmission in which the signal occupies a bandwidth in excess of the minimum necessary to send the information; the band spread is accomplished by means of a code which is independent of the data, and a synchronized reception with the code at the receiver is used for despreading and subsequent data recovery." Although the power of the signal to be transmitted can be large, the signal-to-noise ratio in every frequency band will be small. Even if parts of the signal could be removed in several frequency bands, enough information should be present in the other bands to recover the signal. Thus, SS makes it difficult to detect and/or remove a signal. This situation is very similar to a steganography system which tries to spread a secret message over a cover in order to make it impossible to perceive. Since spreaded signals tend to be difficult to remove, embedding methods based on SS should provide a considerable level of robustness. Since the landmark paper by Tirkel et al. [51], spread spectrum methods are of increasing importance in the field of information hiding.

In information hiding, two special variants of SS are generally used: *direct-sequence* and *frequency-hopping* schemes. In direct-sequence schemes, the secret signal is spread by a constant called chip rate, modulated with a pseudorandom signal and added to the cover. On the other hand, in frequency-hopping schemes the frequency of the carrier signal is altered in a way that it hops rapidly from one frequency to the another. SS are widely used in the context of watermarking, as will be shown in Section 6.4.1. One particularly interesting direct-sequence watermarking algorithm, invented by Hartung and Girod [48, 49], which could also be used for steganographic purposes, will be described in Section 6.4.1.

Due to the similarity of SS watermarking and steganography algorithms, we will limit the discussion in this chapter to presenting a mathematical model describing the application of spread spectrum techniques in information hiding and discuss a system called SSIS as a case study.

3.4.1   A spread spectrum model

Smith and Comiskey [52] presented a general framework for spread spectrum steganography. Their approach originally used $N \times M$ grayscale images as covers; however, the work can easily be extended to all cover sets on which a scalar product can be defined. We will assume that Alice and Bob share a set of (at least) $\ell(m)$ orthogonal $N \times M$ images ϕ_i as a stego-key. Alice first generates a stego-message $E(x, y)$ by building the weighted sum

$$E(x, y) = \sum_i m_i \phi_i(x, y) \tag{3.16}$$

The images ϕ_i are orthogonal to each other,

$$\langle \phi_i, \phi_j \rangle = \sum_{x=1}^{N} \sum_{y=1}^{M} \phi_i(x, y) \phi_j(x, y) = G_i \delta_{i,j} \tag{3.17}$$

where $G_i = \sum_{x=1}^{N} \sum_{y=1}^{M} \phi_i^2(x, y)$ and $\delta_{i,j}$ is the Kronecker delta function. Alice then encodes the secret information E in a cover C by building the element-wise sum of both images, creating the stego-cover S:

$$S(x, y) = C(x, y) + E(x, y) \tag{3.18}$$

In the ideal case, C is orthogonal to all ϕ_i, (so $\langle C, \phi_i \rangle = 0$) and Bob can extract the ith message bit m_i by projecting the stego-image S onto the ith basis image ϕ_i:

$$
\begin{aligned}
\langle S, \phi_i \rangle &= \langle C, \phi_i \rangle + \left\langle \sum_j m_j \phi_j, \phi_i \right\rangle \\
&= \sum_j m_j \langle \phi_j, \phi_i \rangle \\
&= G_i m_i
\end{aligned}
\tag{3.19}
$$

Therefore, the secret information can be recovered by calculating $m_i = \langle S, \phi_i \rangle / G_i$. Note that the original cover C is not needed in the decoding phase. In practice, however, C will not be completely orthogonal to all images ϕ_i, so an error term $\langle C, \phi_i \rangle = \Delta C_i$ has to be introduced in (3.19):

$$\langle S, \phi_i \rangle = \Delta C_i + G_i m_i \tag{3.20}$$

We will now show that under reasonable assumptions the expected value of ΔC_i is zero. Let both C and ϕ_i be two independent NM-dimensional random variables. If we assume that all basis images were created using a zero-mean random process and they are independent from the messages to be transmitted, then

$$\mathbf{E}[\Delta C_i] = \sum_{i=1}^{N} \sum_{j=1}^{M} \mathbf{E}[C(x, y)] \mathbf{E}[\phi_i(x, y)] = 0 \tag{3.21}$$

Thus, the expected value of the error term in (3.20) is zero under these assumptions.

The decoding operation therefore consists of reconstructing a secret message by projecting the stego-image S onto all functions ϕ_i yielding an approximative value

$$s_i = \langle S, \phi_i \rangle = \Delta C_i + G_i m_i \tag{3.22}$$

Subject to the conditions stated above, the expected value of ΔC_i is zero, so $s_i \approx G_i m_i$. The final task is to reconstruct m_i from s_i. If we encode secret messages as strings of -1 and 1 instead of simply using binary strings, the values of m_i can be reconstructed using the *sign* function, provided that $G_i \gg 0$:

$$m_i = sign(s_i) = \begin{cases} -1 & \text{if } s_i < 0 \\ 0 & \text{if } s_i = 0 \\ 1 & \text{if } s_i > 0 \end{cases} \tag{3.23}$$

In the case of $m_i = 0$ the encoded information has been lost. In some severe circumstances the quantity $|\Delta C_i|$ could become so large (recall that we have only proved that the expected value is zero) that the recovery of one bit is not possible. However, this case will not happen often and can be coped with by the implementation of an error-correcting code.

The main advantage of using spread spectrum techniques in steganography is the relative robustness to image modifications. Since the encoded information is spread over a wide frequency band it is quite difficult to remove it completely without entirely destroying the cover. In practice, modifications of the stego-cover will increase the value of ΔC_i. These modifications will not be harmful to the embedded message, unless $|\Delta C_i| > |G_i m_i|$.

3.4.2   SSIS: a case study

Marvel et al. [53] presented a steganographic system called SSIS which we will discuss here briefly as a case study. SSIS uses a spread spectrum technique as an embedding function; this mechanism can be described as follows. Before the embedding process, the secret message is encrypted using a conventional symmetric encryption scheme, thereby using a secret key k_1. Furthermore, the encrypted secret message will be encoded via a low-rate error-correcting code (such as a Reed-Solomon code). This step will increase the robustness of the overall steganographic application. The resulting encoded message is then modulated by a pseudorandom sequence produced by a pseudorandom number generator using k_2 as seed. The resulting (random-looking) signal is then input into an interleaver (which uses k_3 as seed) and added to the cover. In a last step, the resulting stego-image is appropriately quantized.

At the receiver side the embedding process is reversed. Since one design goal of SSIS was to provide a *blind* steganographic system—thus, a system in which the original image is not needed in the decoding process—an estimate of the original image is obtained using an image-restoration technique such as an adaptive Wiener filter. Subtracting the stego-image from the cover-image estimate yields an estimate for the modulated and spread stego-message. The resulting bits are then deinterleaved and demodulated (using k_3 and k_2). Due to the poor performance of the Wiener filter, the reconstructed secret message will contain incorrect bits; the stego-system can thus be seen as a form of transmission on a noisy channel. However, the use of an error-correcting code can help to recover corrupted message bits. In a last step, the secret message is decrypted.

3.5 STATISTICAL STEGANOGRAPHY

Statistical steganography techniques utilize the existence of "1-bit" steganographic schemes, which embed one bit of information in a digital carrier. This is done by modifying the cover in such a way that some statistical characteristics change significantly if a "1" is transmitted. Otherwise the cover is left unchanged. So the receiver must be able to distinguish unmodified covers from modified ones.

In order to construct a $\ell(m)$-bit stego-system from multiple "1-bit" stego-systems, a cover is divided into $\ell(m)$ disjoint blocks $B_1, \ldots, B_{\ell(m)}$. A secret bit, m_i, is inserted into the ith block by placing a "1" into B_i if $m_i = 1$. Otherwise, the block is not changed in the embedding process. The detection of a specific bit is done via a test function which distinguishes modified blocks from unmodified blocks:

$$f(B_i) = \begin{cases} 1 & \text{block } B_i \text{ was modified in the embedding process} \\ 0 & \text{otherwise} \end{cases} \tag{3.24}$$

The function f can be interpreted as a hypothesis-testing function; we test the null-hypothesis "block B_i was not modified" against the alternative hypothesis "block B_i was modified." Therefore, we call the whole class of such steganography systems *statistical steganography*. The receiver successively applies f to all cover-blocks B_i in order to restore every bit of the secret message.

The main question which remains to be solved is how such a function f in (3.24) can be constructed. If we interpret f as a hypothesis-testing function, we can use the theory of hypothesis testing from mathematical statistics. Let us assume we can find a formula $h(B_i)$, which depends on some elements of the cover-block B_i, and we know the distribution of $h(B_i)$ in the unmodified block (i.e., the hypothesis holds in this case). We can then use standard procedures to test if $h(B_i)$ equals or exceeds a specific value. If we manage to alter $h(B_i)$ in the embedding process in a way that its expected value is 0 if the block B_i was not modified, and its expected value is much greater otherwise, we could test whether $h(B_i)$ equals zero under the given distribution of $h(B_i)$.

Statistical steganographic techniques are, however, difficult to apply in many cases. First, a good test statistic $h(B_i)$ must be found which allows distinction between modified and unmodified cover-blocks. Additionally, the distribution of $h(B_i)$ must be known for a "normal" cover; in most cases, this is quite a difficult task. In practical implementations many (quite questionable) assumptions are made in order to determine a closed formula for this distribution.

As an example, we want to construct a statistical steganography algorithm out of Pitas' watermarking system [54], which is similar to the Patchwork approach of Bender et al. [2]. Suppose every cover-block B_i is a rectangular set of pixels $p_{n,m}^{(i)}$. Furthermore, let $S = \{s_{n,m}^{(i)}\}$ be a rectangular pseudorandom binary pattern of equal size, where the number of ones in S equals the number of zeros. We will assume that both the sender and receiver have access to S, which represents the stego-key in this application. The sender first splits the image block B_i into two sets, C_i and D_i, of equal size (i.e., he puts all pixels with indices (n, m) into set C where the corresponding key bit $s_{n,m}$ equals zero):

$$
\begin{aligned}
C_i &= \{p_{n,m}^{(i)} \in B_i | s_{n,m} = 1\} \\
D_i &= \{p_{n,m}^{(i)} \in B_i | s_{n,m} = 0\}
\end{aligned}
\tag{3.25}
$$

The sender then adds a value $k > 0$ to all pixels in the subset C_i but leaves all pixels in D_i unchanged. In the last step, C_i and D_i are merged to form the marked image block $\tilde{B}_i$.

In order to extract the mark, the receiver reconstructs the sets C_i and D_i. If the block contains a mark, all values in C_i will be larger than the corresponding values in the embedding step; thus we test the difference of the means of sets C_i and D_i. If we assume that all pixels in both C_i and D_i are independent identically distributed random variables with an arbitrary distribution, the test statistic

$$
q_i = \frac{\overline{C_i} - \overline{D_i}}{\hat{\sigma}_i}
\tag{3.26}
$$

with

$$
\hat{\sigma}_i = \sqrt{\frac{\mathrm{Var}[C_i] + \mathrm{Var}[D_i]}{|S|/2}}
\tag{3.27}
$$

where $\overline{C_i}$ denotes the mean over all pixels in the set C_i and $\mathrm{Var}[C_i]$ the estimated variance of the random variables in C_i, will follow a $N(0, 1)$ normal distribution asymptotically due to the central limit theorem. If a mark is embedded in the image block $\tilde{B}_i$, the expected value of q will be greater than zero. The receiver is thus able to reconstruct the ith secret message bit by testing whether the statistic q_i of block B_i equals zero under the $N(0,1)$ distribution.

3.6   DISTORTION TECHNIQUES

In contrast to substitution systems, distortion techniques require the knowledge of the original cover in the decoding process. Alice applies a sequence of modifications to a cover in order to get a stego-object; she chooses this sequence of modifications in such a way that it corresponds to a specific secret message she wants to transmit. Bob measures the differences to the original cover in order to reconstruct the sequence of modifications applied by Alice, which corresponds to the secret message.

In many applications, such systems are not useful, since the receiver must have access to the original covers. If Wendy also has access to them, she can easily detect the cover modifications and has evidence for a secret communication. If the embedding and extraction functions are public and do not depend on a stego-key, it is also possible for Wendy to reconstruct secret messages entirely. Throughout this section we will therefore assume that original covers can be distributed through a secure channel.

An early approach to hiding information is in text. Most text-based hiding methods are of distortion type (i.e., the arrangement of words or the layout of a document may reveal information). One technique is by modulating the positions of lines and words, which will be detailed in the next subsection. Adding spaces and "invisible" characters to text provides a method to pass hidden information. HTML files are good candidates for including extra spaces, tabs, and linebreaks. Web browsers ignore these "extra" spaces and lines, and they go unnoticed until the source of the Web page is revealed.

3.6.1   Encoding information in formatted text

Considerable effort has been made to construct data-embedding methods for formatted text, which is interpreted as a binary image. Maxemchuk et al. [55–58] presented text-based steganographic schemes which use the distance between consecutive lines of text or between consecutive words to transmit secret information. It should be noted, however, that any steganographic system which uses the text format to transmit information can easily be broken by retyping the document.

In *line-space* encoding, the positions of lines in the document are moved up or down according to secret message bits, whereas other lines are kept stationary for the purpose of synchronization (in the original implementation, information was transmitted in every second line). One secret message bit is encoded in one line that

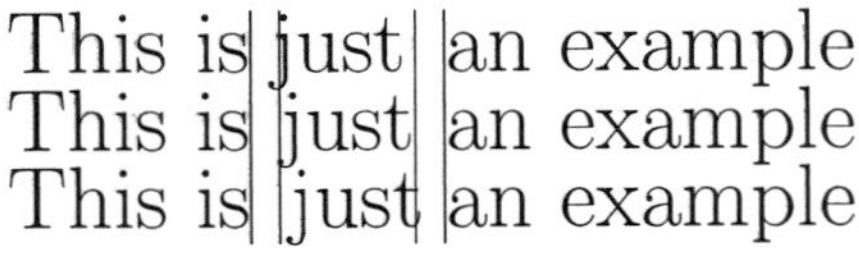

This is| just| |an example
This is| just| |an example
This is| |just| |an example

Figure 3.3   Encoding information in interword spaces (the vertical lines are provided for reference). Data is embedded in the first and third sentences.

is moved; if a line is moved up, a 1 is encoded, otherwise a 0. When decoding a secret message, *centroid detection* can be used; the centroid is defined to be the center of mass of the line about a horizontal axis. Let us denote with Δ_{R+} the distance between the centroids of a shifted line and the next stationary synchronization line above, with Δ_{R-} the distance of centroids between the shifted line and the next stationary line below, and with Δ_{X+} and Δ_{X-} the corresponding centroid distances in the unmodified document. The distance above one line was increased, if

$$\frac{\Delta_{R+} + \Delta_{R-}}{\Delta_{R+} - \Delta_{R-}} > \frac{\Delta_{X+} + \Delta_{X-}}{\Delta_{X+} - \Delta_{X-}} \tag{3.28}$$

Similarly, if

$$\frac{\Delta_{R+} + \Delta_{R-}}{\Delta_{R+} - \Delta_{R-}} < \frac{\Delta_{X+} + \Delta_{X-}}{\Delta_{X+} - \Delta_{X-}} \tag{3.29}$$

the distance above the line was decreased. Note that if the page was scaled by a constant factor during reproduction, this factor cancels out because of the fraction in (3.28) and (3.29). Similarly, changes in vertical print density should affect all centroids in approximately the same way. These properties make line-space encoding techniques resistant to most distortion attacks. For an analysis of this embedding technique see [57].

Another possible embedding scheme in formatted text is *word-space* encoding, illustrated in Figure 3.3. According to a secret message bit, horizontal spaces between selected words of the carrier are altered. Theoretically, it is possible to alter every space between two words; the only limitation is that the sum of all movements in one specific line equals zero so that the line keeps properly aligned.

3.6.2   Distortion of digital images

Distortion techniques can easily be applied to digital images. Using a similar approach as in substitution systems, the sender first chooses $\ell(m)$ different cover-pixels he wants to use for information transfer. Such a selection can again be done using pseudorandom number generators or pseudorandom permutations. To encode a 0 in one pixel, the sender leaves the pixel unchanged; to encode a 1, he adds a random value Δx to the pixel's color. Although this approach is similar to a substitution system, there is one significant difference: the LSB of the selected color values do not necessarily equal secret message bits. In particular, no cover modifications are needed when coding a 0. Furthermore, Δx can be chosen in a way that better preserves the cover's statistical properties. The receiver compares all $\ell(m)$ selected pixels of the stego-object with the corresponding pixels of the original cover. If the ith pixel differs, the ith message bit is a 1, otherwise a 0.

Many variants of the above method could be implemented: similar to the parity bit method presented in Section 3.2.4, the parity bit of a certain image region can be altered or left unchanged in order to encode a 1 or a 0. Furthermore, image processing techniques could be applied to certain image regions so that they are not visible to an observer.

Another image distortion technique, *data embedding*, has been introduced by Sandford et al. [59, 60]. In contrast to all distortion techniques discussed so far, data embedding tries to modify the order of appearance of redundant data in the cover rather than to change values themselves; the embedding process therefore maintains a "pair list" (i.e., a list of pairs of samples whose difference is smaller than a specific threshold). The receiver can reverse the embedding process if he has access to the pair list. This list can be seen as an analogon to a key in cryptography; it normally cannot be restored out of the cover by the receiver (see [59] for details).

3.7   COVER GENERATION TECHNIQUES

In contrast to all embedding methods presented above, where secret information is added to a specific cover by applying an embedding algorithm, some steganographic applications generate a digital object only for the purpose of being a cover for secret communication.

3.7.1   Mimic functions

Due to the explosion of information traffic it can be assumed that it is impossible for a human being to observe all communications around the world; as noted in the conclusion of Chapter 2, such a task can only be done using automated supervision systems which are therefore of increasing importance. These systems check communication by examining keywords and the statistical profile of a message. It is possible, for instance, to distinguish unencrypted from encrypted messages automatically because of their different statistical properties. *Mimic functions*, proposed by Wayner [61], can be used to hide the identity of a message by changing its statistical profile in a way that it matches the profile of any innocent looking text.

It is well known that the English language possesses several statistical properties. For instance the distribution of characters is not uniform (see for instance the appendix of [62] for the frequency distributions of English di- and trigrams). This fact has been exploited in numerous data-compression techniques (e.g., the Huffman coding scheme [40]). Given an alphabet Σ and a probability distribution A, the Huffman coding scheme can be used to produce a minimum-redundancy compression function $f_A : \Sigma \to \{0,1\}^*$, where * denotes the Kleene-Star ($\Sigma^* = \bigcup_{i\geq0}\{x_1 \cdots x_i | x_1, \ldots, x_i \in \Sigma\}$). A mimic function $g : \Sigma^* \to \Sigma^*$ that converts a message whose characters show a probability distribution A to a message which approximately mimics the statistical profile B, can be constructed using two Huffman compression functions:

$$g(x) = f_B^{-1}(f_A(x)) \tag{3.30}$$

Thus, the file x is first compressed using a Huffman scheme with distribution A. This process will create a file of binary strings which can be interpreted as output of a Huffman compression scheme (with distribution B) of a different file. This file can be reconstructed by applying the inverse Huffman compression function f_B^{-1} to the file of binary strings and will act as a stego-object. Since both f_A and f_B are one-to-one, the constructed mimic function will be one-to-one. Wayner showed that this function is optimal in the sense that if f_A is a theoretically optimal Huffman compression function and x is a file of random bits, then $f_A^{-1}(x)$ is the best approximation of the statistical profile A which is one-to-one.

Instead of using distributions of single characters, Huffman coding schemes can be constructed to compress n characters at one time, based on the frequency distribution of n-grams. However, the size of the compression tree created by the Huffman schemes grows exponentially with n. Wayner instead proposed to exploit the intercharacter dependencies by creating Huffman compression functions for every string t of length $n-1$ to encode probabilities for each character which may follow t in the file. A mimic function can be constructed out of the collection of these Huffman compression functions (see [61] for details).

3.7.2   Automated generation of English texts

However, mimic functions can only be used to fool machines. Since the stego-objects are created only according to statistical profiles, the semantic component is entirely ignored. To a human observer the created texts look completely meaningless and are full of grammatical and typographical errors.

To overcome this problem, the use of context-free grammars (CFG) has been proposed; for a theoretical overview of CFG see [63]. Let $G = \langle V, \Sigma, \Pi, S \rangle$ be a CFG, where V is the set of variables, Σ the set of terminal symbols, $\Pi \subseteq V \times (V \cup \Sigma)^*$

the set of productions and $S \in V$ the start symbol. The productions can be seen as a substitution rule; they convert a variable into a string containing terminal or variable symbols. A string $s \in \Sigma^*$ which is defined to be a sequence of terminal symbols is said to be generated by G (formally: $s \in L(G)$) if s can be produced successively from the start symbol S by substituting variables by sequences of terminal or variable symbols according to Π. For example, from the grammar $\langle \{S, A, B, C\}, \{\mathtt{A}, \ldots, \mathtt{Z}, \mathtt{a} \ldots, \mathtt{z}\}, \Pi, S \rangle$ with

$\Pi = \{\ S \rightarrow$ Alice B, $S \rightarrow$ Bob B, $S \rightarrow$ Eve B, $S \rightarrow$ I A,
$\quad A \rightarrow$ am working, $A \rightarrow$ am lazy, $A \rightarrow$ am tired,
$\quad B \rightarrow$ is C, $B \rightarrow$ can cook,
$\quad C \rightarrow$ reading, $C \rightarrow$ sleeping, $C \rightarrow$ working$\}$

the sentences I am lazy, Alice is reading, etc. can be derived. If for every string $s \in L(G)$ there exists exactly one way s can be generated from the start symbol, the grammar is said to be unambiguous.

Unambiguous grammars can be used as a steganographic tool. Wayner [61, 64] proposed an extension to the technique of mimic functions. Given a set of productions, we assign a probability to each possible production for variable V_i. In our example above, we could choose

$\Pi = \{\ S \rightarrow_{0.5}$ Alice B, $S \rightarrow_{0.3}$ Bob B, $S \rightarrow_{0.1}$ Eve B, $S \rightarrow_{0.1}$ I A,
$\quad A \rightarrow_{0.3}$ am working, $A \rightarrow_{0.4}$ am lazy, $A \rightarrow_{0.3}$ am tired,
$\quad B \rightarrow_{0.5}$ is C, $B \rightarrow_{0.5}$ can cook,
$\quad C \rightarrow_{0.5}$ reading, $C \rightarrow_{0.1}$ sleeping, $C \rightarrow_{0.4}$ working$\}$

Let $\Pi_{V_i} = \{\pi_{i,1}, \ldots, \pi_{i,n}\}$ be the set of all productions associated with variable V_i. The sender then constructs a Huffman compression function f_{Π_i} for every set Π_i. In Figure 3.4 possible Huffman trees for Π_S and Π_A are shown. Huffman compression functions can easily be derived out of these trees; for example the production "Eve B" will be encoded as 110, "A am tired" as 11, etc.

For steganographic purposes, the inverse Huffman compression functions will be used. In the encoding step, the sender derives one specific string out of the CFG which will act as the stego-object. Starting from the start symbol S, the leftmost variable V_i is changed by a production. This production is determined by the secret message and the Huffman compression function for Π_{V_i}. Specifically, the Huffman tree is traversed according to the next bits of the secret message until a node of the tree is reached. The start symbol is then substituted by the production which can be found at this node of the tree. This process is iterated (i.e., the leftmost variable is exchanged by a production which is determined by its Huffman tree and the next

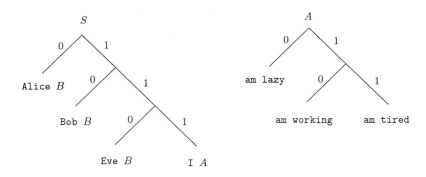

Figure 3.4   Huffman compression functions for Π_S and Π_A.

few message bits), until all message bits are used and the string consists only of terminal symbols. Continuing the previous example, suppose the secret message is 11110. In the first step we traverse the Huffman tree for Π_S and eventually reach the node "I A" by consuming the first three secret message bits. Thus, the start symbol S is replaced by "I A." We now traverse the Huffman tree Π_A and find the replacement "am working" by consuming another two secret message bits. Thus, since the derived string consists of terminal symbols only and all secret message bits were used, the stego-object representing 11110 is the sentence I am working.

In the decoding process, the cover is parsed in order to reconstruct the productions which have been used in the embedding step; this can be accomplished by the use of a parse tree for the given CFG, see [65]. Since the productions uniquely determine the secret message and the underlying grammar is unambiguous, the receiver is able to reconstruct the stego-message.

A similar system has been proposed by Chapman and Davida [66]. Their system consists of two functions, *NICETEXT* and *SCRAMBLE*. Given a large dictionary of words, categorized by different types, and a *style source*, which describes how words of different types can be used to form a meaningful sentence, *NICETEXT* transforms secret message bits into sentences by selecting words out of the dictionary which conform to a sentence structure given in the style source. *SCRAMBLE* reconstructs the secret message if the dictionary which has been used is known. Style sources can either be created from sample natural-language sentences or be generated using CFG.

3.8 CONCLUSION

In this chapter we gave an overview of different steganographic methods which have been proposed in the literature during the last few years. Many flexible and simple methods exist for embedding information in noisy communication channels.

However, covers and messages tend to have unique patterns a steganalyst could exploit. Most of the simple techniques can be broken by careful analysis of the statistical properties of the channel's noise. Images and many other signals were subject to quantization, filters, transformations, format converters, etc. Most of these techniques left some sort of "fingerprints" in the data. All these problems must be addressed when designing a steganographic system; methods which use these properties to break secret communication will be outlined in the next chapter.

REFERENCES

[1] Foley, J., et al., *Computer Graphics, Principles and Practice*, Reading, MA: Addison Wesley, 1990.

[2] Bender, W., D. Gruhl, and N. Morimoto, "Techniques for data hiding," *IBM Systems Journal*, vol. 35, no. 3/4, 1996, pp. 131–336.

[3] Möller, S., A. Pfitzmann, and I. Stirand, "Computer Based Steganography: How It Works and Why Therefore Any Restrictions on Cryptography Are Nonsense, At Best," in *Information Hiding: First International Workshop, Proceedings*, vol. 1174 of *Lecture Notes in Computer Science*, Springer, 1996, pp. 7–21.

[4] Gruhl, D., A. Lu, and W. Bender, "Echo Hiding," in *Information Hiding: First International Workshop, Proceedings*, vol. 1174 of *Lecture Notes in Computer Science*, Springer, 1996, pp. 295–316.

[5] Kurak, C., and J. McHughes, "A Cautionary Note On Image Downgrading," in *IEEE Computer Security Applications Conference 1992, Proceedings*, IEEE Press, 1992, pp. 153–159.

[6] van Schyndel, R. G., A. Tirkel, and C. F. Osborne, "A Digital Watermark," in *Proceedings of the IEEE International Conference on Image Processing*, vol. 2, 1994, pp. 86–90.

[7] Johnson, N. F., and S. Jajodia, "Exploring Steganography: Seeing the Unseen," *IEEE Computer*, vol. 31, no. 2, 1998, pp. 26–34.

[8] Gerzon, M. A., and P. G. Graven, "A High-Rate Buried-Data Channel for Audio CD," *Journal of the Audio Engineering Society*, vol. 43, no. 1/2, 1995, pp. 3–22.

[9] "StegoDos—Black Wolf's Picture Encoder v0.90B," <ftp://ftp.csua.berkeley.edu/pub/cypherpunks/steganography/stegodos.zip>, 1993.

[10] Brown, A., "S-Tools for Windows," <ftp://idea.sec.dsi.unimi.it/pub/security/crypt/code/s-tools4.zip>, 1996.

[11] Hastur, H., "Mandelsteg," <ftp://idea.sec.dsi.unimi.it/pub/security/crypt/code/steg.tar.Z>, 1994.

[12] Machado, R., "EzStego, Stego Online, Stego," <http://www.stego.com>, 1997.

[13] Maroney, C., "Hide and Seek," <ftp://ftp.csua.berkeley.edu/pub/cypherpunks/steganography/hdsk41b.zip>, <http://www.rugeley.demon.co.uk/security/hdsk50.zip>, 1994–1997.

[14] Repp, H., "Hide4PGP," <http://www.rugeley.demon.co.uk/security/hide4pgp.zip>, 1996.

[15] Arachelian, R., "White Noise Storm," <ftp://ftp.csua.berkeley.edu/pub/cypherpunks/steganography/wns210.zip>, 1994.

[16] Hansmann, F., "Steganos, Deus Ex Machina Communications," <http://www.steganography.com/>, 1996.

[17] Menezes, A. J., P. C. van Oorschot, and S. A. Vanstone, *Handbook of Applied Cryptography*, Boca Raton: CRC Press, 1996.

[18] Aura, T., "Practical Invisibility in Digital Communication," in *Information Hiding: First International Workshop, Proceedings*, vol. 1174 of *Lecture Notes in Computer Science*, Springer, 1996, pp. 265–278.

[19] Luby, M., and C. Rackoff, "How to Construct Pseudorandom Permutations from Pseudorandom Functions," *SIAM Journal on Computation*, vol. 17, no. 2, 1988, pp. 373–386.

[20] Naor, M., and O. Reingold, "On the Construction of Pseudorandom Permutations: Luby-Rackoff Revisited," *Journal of Cryptology*, vol. 12, no. 1, 1999, pp. 29–66.

[21] Bell, D. E., and L. J. LaPadula, "Secure Computer Systems: Mathematical Foundations," Mitre Report ESD-TR-73-278 (Vol. I–III), Mitre Corporation, Bedford, MA, Apr. 1974.

[22] Fridrich, J., "A New Steganographic Method for Palette-Based Images," in *Proceedings of the IS&T PICS conference*, Savannah, Georgia, Apr. 1998, pp. 285–289.

[23] Matsui, K., and K. Tanaka, "Video-Steganography: How to Secretly Embed a Signature in a Picture," *IMA Intellectual Property Project Proceedings*, vol. 1, no. 1, 1994, pp. 187–205.

[24] Baharav, Z., and D. Shaked, "Watermarking of Dither Halftoned Images," in *Proceedings of the SPIE 3657, Security and Watermarking of Multimedia Content*, 1999, pp. 307–316.

[25] Zhao, J., and E. Koch, "Embedding Robust Labels into Images for Copyright Protection," in *Proceedings of the International Conference on Intellectual Property Rights for Information, Knowledge and New Techniques*, München, Wien: Oldenbourg Verlag, 1995, pp. 242–251.

[26] "CCITT Recommendation T6: Facsimile Coding Schemes and Coding Control Functions for Group 4 Facsimile Apparatus for Document Transmission," 1984.

[27] Anderson, R. J., R. Needham, and A. Shamir, "The Steganographic File System," in *Proceedings of the Second International Workshop on Information Hiding*, vol. 1525 of *Lecture Notes in Computer Science*, Springer, 1998, pp. 73–82.

[28] "ScramDisk: Free Hard Drive Encryption For Windows 95 & 98," <http://www.scramdisk.clara.net>, 1998.

[29] Handel, T. G., and M. T. Sandford, "Data Hiding in the OSI Network Model," in *Information Hiding: First International Workshop, Proceedings*, vol. 1174 of *Lecture Notes in Computer Science*, Springer, 1996, pp. 23–38.

[30] Cox, I., et al., "A Secure, Robust Watermark for Multimedia," in *Information Hiding: First International Workshop, Proceedings*, vol. 1174 of *Lecture Notes in Computer Science*, Springer, 1996, pp. 185–206.

[31] Koch, E., and J. Zhao, "Towards Robust and Hidden Image Copyright Labeling," in *IEEE Workshop on Nonlinear Signal and Image Processing*, Jun. 1995, pp. 452–455.

[32] Koch, E., J. Rindfrey, and J. Zhao, "Copyright Protection for Multimedia Data," in *Proceedings of the International Conference on Digital Media and Electronic Publishing*, Leeds, UK, Dec. 1994.

[33] Ó Runaidh, J. J. K., F. M. Boland, and O. Sinnen, "Watermarking Digital Images for Copyright Protection," in *Electronic Imaging and the Visual Arts, Proceedings*, Feb. 1996.

[34] Xia, X., C. G. Boncelet, and G. R. Arce, "A Multiresolution Watermark for Digital Images," in *Proceedings of the IEEE International Conference on Image Processing (ICIP'97)*, 1997.

[35] Rhodas, G. B., "Method and Apparatus Responsive to a Code Signal Conveyed Through a Graphic Image," U.S. Patent 5,710,834, 1998.

[36] Swanson, M. D., B. Zhu, and A. H. Tewfik, "Transparent Robust Image Watermarking," in *Proceedings of the IEEE International Conference on Image Processing*, vol. 3, 1996, pp. 211–214.

[37] Langelaar, G., J. van der Lubbe, and R. Lagendijk, "Robust Labeling Methods for Copy Protection of Images," in *Proceedings of the SPIE vol. 3022, Storage and Retrieval for Image and Video Databases V*, 1997, pp. 298–309.

[38] Pennebaker, W. B., and J. L. Mitchell, *JPEG Still Image Compression Standard*, New York: Van Nostrand Reinhold, 1993.

[39] Wallace, G. K., "The JPEG Still Picture Compression Standard," *Communications of the ACM*, vol. 34, no. 4, 1991, pp. 30–44.

[40] Huffman, D. A., "A Method for the Construction of Minimum-Redundancy Codes," *Proceedings of the IRE*, vol. 40, no. 10, 1952, pp. 1098–1101.

[41] Smoot, S., and L. A. Rowe, "DCT Coefficient Distributions," in *Proceedings of the SPIE 2657, Human Vision and Electronic Imaging*, 1996, pp. 403–411.

[42] Moore, B. C. J., *An Introduction to the Psychology of Hearing*, London: Academic Press, 1989.

[43] Chang, L., and I. S. Moskowitz, "Critical Analysis of Security in Voice Hiding Techniques," in *Proceedings of the International Conference on Information and Communications Security*, vol. 1334 of *Lecture Notes in Computer Science*, Springer, 1997, pp. 203–216.

[44] Cachin, C., "An Information-Theoretic Model for Steganography," in *Proceedings of the Second International Workshop on Information Hiding*, vol. 1525 of *Lecture Notes in Computer Science*, Springer, 1998, pp. 306–318.

[45] Willems, F. M., "Universal Data Compression and Repetition Times," *IEEE Transactions on Information Theory*, 1989, pp. 337–343.

[46] Upham, D., "Jpeg-Jsteg, modification of the independent JPEG group's JPEG software (release 4) for 1-bit steganography in JFIF output files," <ftp://ftp.funet.fi/pub/crypt/steganography/>, 1992–1997.

[47] Westfeld, A., and G. Wolf, "Steganography in a Video Conferencing System," in *Proceedings of the Second International Workshop on Information Hiding*, vol. 1525 of *Lecture Notes in Computer Science*, Springer, 1998, pp. 32–47.

[48] Hartung, F., and B. Girod, "Copyright Protection in Video Delivery Networks by Watermarking of Pre-Compressed Video," in *Multimedia Applications, Services and Techniques—ECMAST 97*, vol. 1242 of *Lecture Notes in Computer Science*, Springer, 1997, pp. 423–436.

[49] Hartung, F., and B. Girod, "Watermarking of Uncompressed and Compressed Video,"

Signal Processing, vol. 66, no. 3, 1998, pp. 283–301.

[50] Pickholtz, R. L., D. L. Schilling, and L. B. Milstein, "Theory of Spread-Spectrum Communications—A Tutorial," *IEEE Transactions on Communications*, vol. 30, no. 5, 1982, pp. 855–884.

[51] Tirkel, A. Z., G. A. Rankin, and R. van Schyndel, "Electronic Watermark," in *Digital Image Computing, Technology and Applications—DICTA 93, Macquarie University*, 1993, pp. 666–673.

[52] Smith, J., and B. Comiskey, "Modulation and Information Hiding in Images," in *Information Hiding: First International Workshop, Proceedings*, vol. 1174 of *Lecture Notes in Computer Science*, Springer, 1996, pp. 207–227.

[53] Marvel, L. M., C. G. Bonclet, and C. T. Retter, "Reliable Blind Information Hiding for Images," in *Proceedings of the Second International Workshop on Information Hiding*, vol. 1525 of *Lecture Notes in Computer Science*, Springer, 1998, pp. 48–61.

[54] Pitas, I., "A Method for Signature Casting on Digital Images," in *International Conference on Image Processing*, vol. 3, IEEE Press, 1996, pp. 215–218.

[55] Maxemchuk, N. F., "Electronic Document Distribution," *AT&T Technical Journal*, September/October 1994, pp. 73–80.

[56] Low, S. H., et al., "Document Marking and Identification Using Both Line and Word Shifting," in *Proceedings of Infocom'95*, 1995, pp. 853–860.

[57] Low, S. H., N. F. Maxemchuk, and A. M. Lapone, "Document Identification for Copyright Protection Using Centroid Detection," *IEEE Transactions on Communications*, vol. 46, no. 3, 1998, pp. 372–383.

[58] Low, S. H., and N. F. Maxemchuk, "Performance Comparison of Two Text Marking Methods," *IEEE Journal on Selected Areas in Communications*, vol. 16, no. 4, 1998, pp. 561–572.

[59] Sandford, M. T., J. N. Bradley, and T. G. Handel, "Data Embedding Method," in *Proceedings of the SPIE 2615, Integration Issues in Large Commercial Media Delivery Systems*, 1996, pp. 226–259.

[60] Sandford, M. T., T. G. Handel, and J. M. Ettinger, "Data Embedding in Degenerate Hosts," Technical Report LA-95-4446UR, Los Alamos National Laboratory, 1996.

[61] Wayner, P., "Mimic Functions," *Cryptologia*, vol. XVI/3, 1992, pp. 193–214.

[62] "Basic Cryptanalysis," Headquarters Department of the Army, Field Manual NO 34-40-2, <ftp://ftp.ox.ac.uk/cryptanalysis/basic_cryptanalysis.ps.tar.gz>.

[63] Hopcroft, J. E., and J. D. Ullman, *Introduction to Automata Theory, Languages and Computation*, Reading, MA: Addison Wesley, 1979.

[64] Wayner, P., "Strong Theoretical Steganography," *Cryptologia*, vol. XIX/3, 1995, pp. 285–299.

[65] Aho, A., R. Sethi, and J. Ullman, *Compilers: Principles, Techniques and Tools*, Reading (MA): Addison Wesley, 1986.

[66] Chapman, M., and G. Davida, "Hiding the Hidden: A Software System for Concealing Ciphertext as Innocuous Text," in *Proceedings of the International Conference on Information and Communications Security*, vol. 1334 of *Lecture Notes in Computer Science*, Springer, 1997, pp. 335–345.

Chapter 4

Steganalysis

Neil F. Johnson

Steganography encompasses methods of communication in such a manner that the existence of the messages should be undetected. As indicated in Chapter 3, digital carriers of such messages may resemble innocent images, audio, video, text, or any other digitally represented code or transmission. The hidden message may be plaintext, ciphertext, or anything that can be represented as a stream of bits. Creative methods have been devised in the hiding process to reduce the visible detection of the embedded messages.

Hiding information, where electronic media are used as such carriers, requires alterations of the media properties, which may introduce some form of degradation. If applied to images, that degradation, at times, may be visible to the human eye [1] and point to signatures of the steganographic methods and tools used. These signatures may actually broadcast the existence of the embedded message, thus defeating steganography.

4.1 STEGANALYSIS INTRODUCTION AND TERMINOLOGY

All of the steganography and digital watermarking techniques can be represented in the following simple formula. Assume a measurement of the threshold of human imperceptibility in an image where t is the amount of information in the image that can be manipulated without causing perceptible distortion. The portion of the image that, if manipulated, will produce perceptible distortion is p. The equation of a potential carrier for hidden information (C) is:

$$C = p + t \tag{4.1}$$

The size of t is available to both the user of the steganographic system and to an attacker wanting to disable the hidden information in t. As long as t remains in the imperceptible region, there exists some t' used by the attacker where $C' = p + t'$ and there is no perceptible difference between C and C'. This attack may be used to remove or replace the t region. A variation of this attack is explored in [2] to the aspect of counterfeiting watermarks. If information is added to some media such that the added information cannot be detected, then there exists some amount of additional information that may be added or removed within the same threshold which will overwrite or remove the embedded covert information. Embedding information in more perceptible areas of the carrier makes the hidden information more robust but it may also become perceptible by producing artifacts that advertise the existence of the hidden message. Some amount of distortion and degradation does occur, even though such distortions cannot be detected easily by the human sensory system. The distortion may be anomalous to the "normal" cover, that when discovered may point to the existence of hidden information. Steganography tools vary in their approaches for hiding information. Without knowing which tool is used and which, if any, stego-key (password) is used, detecting the hidden information may become quite complex. However, some of the steganographic approaches have characteristics that act as signatures for the method or tool used.

A goal of steganography is to avoid drawing suspicion to the transmission of a hidden message, so it remains undetected. If suspicion is raised, then this goal is defeated. Steganalysis is the art of discovering and rendering such messages useless.

Attacks and analysis on hidden information may take several forms: detecting, extracting, confusing (counterfeiting or overwriting by an attacker, embedding counterinformation over the existing hidden information), and disabling hidden information. Our objective here is not to advocate the removal or disabling of valid hidden information such as copyrights, but to point out approaches that are vulnerable and may be exploited to investigate illicit hidden information.

Any cover can be manipulated with the intent of disabling or destroying some hidden information whether an embedded message exists or not. Detecting the existence of a hidden message will save time in the disabling phase by processing only those covers that contain hidden information.

Before going further, we should take a look at new terminology with respect to attacks and breaking steganography schemes. These are similar to cryptographic terminology; however, there are some significant differences. Just as a cryptanalyst applies cryptanalysis in an attempt to decipher encrypted messages, the steganalyst is one who applies steganalysis in an attempt to detect the existence of hidden information. In cryptanalysis, portions of the plaintext (possibly none) and portions of the ciphertext are analyzed. In steganalysis, comparisons are made between the cover-object, the stego-object, and possible portions of the message. The end result in cryptography is the ciphertext, while the end result in steganography is the stego-object. The hidden message in steganography may or may not be encrypted. If it is encrypted, then if the message is extracted, cryptanalysis techniques may be applied to further understand the embedded message.

In order to define attack techniques used for steganalysis, corresponding techniques are considered in cryptanalysis. Attacks available to the cryptanalyst are *ciphertext only*, *known plaintext*, *chosen plaintext*, and *chosen ciphertext*. In ciphertext-only attacks, the cryptanalyst knows the ciphertext to be decoded. The cryptanalyst may have the encoded message and part of the decoded message which together may be used for a known plaintext attack. The chosen plaintext attack is the most favorable case for the cryptanalyst. In this case, the cryptanalyst has some ciphertext which corresponds to some plaintext chosen by the cryptanalyst. If the encryption algorithm and ciphertext are available, the cryptanalyst encrypts plaintext looking for matches in the ciphertext. This chosen ciphertext attack is used to deduce the sender's key. The challenge with cryptography is not in detecting that something has been encrypted, but decoding the encrypted message.

Somewhat parallel attacks are available to the steganalyst:

- **Stego-only attack.** Only the stego-object is available for analysis.
- **Known cover attack.** The "original" cover-object and stego-object are both available.
- **Known message attack.** At some point, the hidden message may become known to the attacker. Analyzing the stego-object for patterns that correspond to the hidden message may be beneficial for future attacks against that system. Even with the message, this may be very difficult and may even be considered equivalent to the stego-only attack.
- **Chosen stego attack.** The steganography tool (algorithm) and stego-object are known.
- **Chosen message attack.** The steganalyst generates a stego-object from some steganography tool or algorithm from a chosen message. The goal in this attack is to determine corresponding patterns in the stego-object that may point to the use of specific steganography tools or algorithms.
- **Known stego attack.** The steganography algorithm (tool) is known and both the original and stego-objects are available.

Even given the "best" alternative for the attacker, the embedded message may still be difficult to extract. Sometimes the approach is not to attack the algorithm or images at all, but to attack the password used to encrypt or choose the bits to hide the message. This "brute force" is successful against some tools, but still requires significant processing time to achieve favorable results [3, 4].

4.2   LOOKING FOR SIGNATURES: DETECTING HIDDEN INFORMATION

Unusual patterns stand out and expose the possibility of hidden information. In text, small shifts in word and line spacing may be somewhat difficult to detect by the casual observer [5]. However, appended spaces and "invisible" characters can be easily revealed by opening the file with a common word processor. The text may look "normal" if typed out on the screen, but if the file is opened in a word processor, the spaces, tabs, and other characters distort the text's presentation.

Unused areas on a disk can be used to hide information. A number of disk analysis utilities are available that can report on and filter hidden information in unused clusters or partitions in storage devices. A steganographic file system may be vulnerable to detection through analysis of the system's partition information.

Filters can also be applied to capture TCP/IP packets that contain hidden or invalid information in the packet headers. Internet firewalls are becoming more sophisticated and allow for much customization. Just as filters can be set to determine if packets originate from within the firewall's domain, and the validity of the SYN and ACK bits, the filters can be configured to catch packets that have information in supposed unused or reserved space.

Multimedia provides excellent covers for hidden information. However, distortions may occur from hidden information. Selecting the proper combination of steganography tools and covers is key to successful information hiding. Sounds may become distorted and images may become grossly degraded with even small amounts of embedded information. This "perceptible noise" can give away the existence of hidden information. Audio echoes and shadow signals reduce the chance of audible noise, but they can be detected with little processing.

In evaluating many images used in steganography, characteristics become apparent that point to hidden information. Such characteristics may be unusual sorting of color palettes, relationships between colors in color indexes, or exaggerated "noise." An approach used to identify such patterns is to compare the original cover-images with the stego-images and note visible differences (known cover attack). Minute changes are readily noticeable when comparing the cover- and stego-images. Examples of unique signatures of steganography tools as applied to images are found in [6].

Steganography tools typically hide relatively large blocks of information, where watermarking tools place less information in an image, but the watermark is distributed redundantly throughout the entire image [7]. In any case, these methods insert information and manipulate the images in ways to remain invisible. However, any manipulation to the image introduces some amount of distortion and degradation of some aspect in the "original" image's properties (some basic insertion techniques place information between headers or other "unused" areas that are ignored by image viewers. This avoids degradation to the image, but are detectable in bit analysis).

4.2.1 Palette-based images

To begin evaluating images for additional, hidden information, the concept of defining a "normal" or average image is desirable. Defining a normal image is somewhat difficult when considering the possibilities of digital photographs, paintings, drawings, and graphics. Only after evaluating many original images and stego-images as to color composition, luminance, and pixel relationship do anomalies point to characteristics that are not "normal" in other images. The chosen message and known cover attacks were quite useful in detecting these characteristics. In images that have color palettes or indexes, colors are typically ordered from the most used to the least used, to reduce table lookup time. The changes between color values may change gradually but rarely, if ever, in one bit shifts. Grayscale image color indexes do shift in 1-bit increments, but all the RGB values are the same. Applying a similar approach to monochromatic images other than grayscale, normally two of the RGB values are the same with the third generally being a much stronger saturation of color. Some images such as hand drawings, fractals, and clip art may shift greatly in the color values of adjacent pixels. However, having occurrences of single pixels outstanding may point to the existence of hidden information.

Added content to some images may be recognizable as exaggerated noise. This is a common characteristic for many bit-plane tools when applied to 8-bit images. Using 8-bit images without manipulating the palette will, in many cases, cause color shifts as the raster pointers are changed from one palette entry to another. If the adjacent palette colors are very similar, there may be little or no noticeable change. However, if adjacent palette entries are dissimilar, then the noise due to the manipulation of the LSB is obvious [8]. For this reason, many authors of steganography software stress the use of grayscale images (those with 256 shades of gray) [9]. Grayscale images are special occurrences of 8-bit images and are very good covers, because the grayscale values change gradually from palette entry to palette entry.

In [8], the authors suggest using images with vastly contrasting adjacent palette entries to foil steganography software. In 8-bit images, small changes to pixel values will cause radical color changes in the image that advertise the existence of a hidden message. Without altering the 8-bit palette, changes to the LSB in the raster data may show dramatic changes in the stego-image.

Some of the bit-plane tools attempt to reduce this effect by ordering the palette [10, 11]. Even with a few distinct colors, sorting the palette may not be sufficient to keep from broadcasting the existence of an embedded message. Some tools take this a step further and create new palettes [11–13].[1] Converting an 8-bit image to 24 bit provides direct access to the color values for manipulation and any alteration will most likely be visually undetectable. The disadvantage is that the resulting image is much larger in size. A possible solution is to convert the image back to an 8-bit image after the information is hidden in the LSB. Even if the colors in the image palette change radically, this method may still hide the fact that a message exists.

Since 8-bit images are limited to 256 unique color entries in the image palette, the number of unique colors used by the image must be considered. For example, if a 24-bit image contains 200 unique colors and information is hidden in the LSB then the number of unique colors could easily jump to 300 where we may have two unique colors differing by one bit. Reducing the image to 8-bit again will force the palette into 256 colors. There is a high probability that some of the new colors will be lost.

One method around this is to decrease the number of colors to a value that will maintain good image quality and ensure that the number of colors will not increase beyond 256. This approach applies techniques described in [14, 15] and reduces the number of colors to no less than 32 unique colors. These 32 colors are "expanded" up to eight palette entries by adding adjacent colors in the palette that are very close to the original color [12]. This method produces a stego-image that is so close to the original cover-image that virtually no visual differences are detected. However, this approach also creates a unique pattern which will be explored further.

4.2.2 Image distortion and noise

A method for detecting the existence of hidden messages in stego-images is to look for obvious and repetitive patterns which may point to the identification or signature of a steganography tool or hidden message. Distortions or patterns visible to the human eye are the easiest to detect. An approach used to identify such patterns is to compare the original cover-images with the stego-images and note visible differences

---

1 Hide4PGP [11] provides command line options, which give the user flexibility in determining how image palettes are processed. SysCop [13] changes the stored palette in grayscale images.

(known-cover and known-stego attacks). Without the benefit of using the cover-image, such noise may pass for an integral part of the image and go unnoticed. Some of these "signatures" may be exploited automatically to identify the existence of hidden messages and even the tools used in embedding the messages. With this knowledge base, if the cover-images are not available for comparison, the derived known signatures are enough to imply the existence of a message and identify the tool used to embed the message. However, in some cases recurring, predictable patterns are not readily apparent, even if distortion between the cover- and stego-images is noticeable.

One type of distortion is obvious corruption which is discussed in [1]. A set of test images was created with contrasting adjacent palette entries as prescribed in [8]. Some of the tools, specifically those in the bit-plane set, produce severely distorted and noisy stego-images [10, 16, 17]. These distortions are severe color shifts that advertise the existence of a hidden message. Detecting this characteristic may be automated by investigating pixel "neighborhoods" and determining if a pixel that looks out of place is common to the image, follows a pattern, or resembles noise.

Not all of the bit-plane tools produce this type of image distortion. Several bit-plane programs and those in the transform set embedded information without visible distortion of the stego-image. Even though these tools pass this test, other patterns emerged.

Eight-bit color and grayscale images which have color palettes or indexes are easier to analyze visually. Tools that provide good results "on paper" may have digital characteristics making the existence of a message detectable [12, 13, 17–19]. Unlike the obvious distortions mentioned in [1] or predicted in [8], some tools maintained remarkable image integrity and displayed almost no distortion when comparing the cover- and stego-images on the screen or in print [20]. The detectable patterns are exposed when the palettes of 8-bit and grayscale images are investigated. One method of detecting the existence of a hidden message is accomplished by creating an array of unique pixel values within the image and then sorting by luminance (see (3.1)). This may result in some unusual patterns between the color values.

Some steganography tools adjust the image palette to reduce the noise impact of pointing to different values in the color table [10–14, 16, 17]. An example is to reduce the total number of unique colors to less than 256 for 8-bit images. The new "base" colors are expanded over several palette entries. Sorting the palette by its luminance, blocks of colors appear to be the same [19] or have small variances of only a few bits [12]. Depending upon the distribution of the color entries throughout the image, this could lead to a histogram that contains "twin peaks" for close color values [21] (see Chapter 7 for further discussion of twin peaks). This is a good example of the limits to the human vision system. However, the manners in which the palette entries vary are extremely rare except to a few steganographic techniques. This type of pattern does not occur "naturally." Grayscale and other monochromatic images follow a similar pattern except for each value in the palette all RGB values are identical and increment equally to the next entry, thus the pattern does not follow this example. Nor has it been found that images containing large areas of similar colors produce this pattern. Such images contain similar colors, but the variance in colors is far greater than that represented by a stego-image produced by some steganography tools [11–13, 19]. Another pattern that may occur is the structure of padded values in the image palette (that is, the number of palette entries that are typically unused) [13]. These padded entries are also typically at the end of the color table. Remember, color tables are usually sorted by most frequent to least frequent color. A 256 color approximation of a photograph with black areas rarely has a large number of black palette entries. It is far more common for black areas to actually be a number of different shades near black.

GIF images are common on the Internet and typically consist of 256 distinct colors. If a grayscale image only uses a fraction of the shades available, the color table index still contains 256 shades of gray from white (FF or 255) to black (0). A possible signature of a steganography tool is to reduce the color index to the actual number of colors used. For example, if the cover-image is a GIF grayscale image but only uses nine shades of gray, the image file still has a 256 color index in the file between offset values 0x0D through 0x30C ranging in values from 0 through 255.[2] When SysCop [13] processes the grayscale files, the palette is reduced to the actual colors used in the stego-image. If nine colors are used in the stego-image, then only nine unique RGB triples are in the stego-image file's palette instead of the expected 256 color index.

One steganography tool, Hide and Seek [17], produces an unusual palette by making palette entries divisible by four for all bit values.[3] This is a very unusual occurrence. In processed grayscale images, the 256 shades of gray in the color table increase by sets of four triples from 0 to 252, with incremental steps of 4 (i.e., 0, 4, 8, ..., 248, 252). A key to detecting this when viewing images casually is that the "whitest" values in an image are 252 instead of 255. To date, this signature is unique to Hide and Seek.

In Hide and Seek for Windows 95 (1.0) the cover-images are still limited to 256 colors or grayscale. In previous version of Hide and Seek, GIF images were

---

2 The offset is the number of bits from the beginning of the file. The decimal representation for the hexadecimal values 0x0D and 0x30C is 13 and 780. A typical grayscale color index in a GIF image is from offset 0x0D through 0x30C ranges from 0 to 255.

3 This holds for versions 4.1 and 5.0 of Hide and Seek. The Windows 95 version does not share this characteristic.

used as covers. In the Windows 95 version, BMP images are used due to licensing issues with GIF image compression. No longer do the stego-image palettes produce predictable patterns as in versions 4.1 and 5.0.

4.3 EXTRACTING HIDDEN INFORMATION

As steganography developers and users become more savvy, detection of hidden information will become more challenging. If one cannot detect the possibility of hidden information, then the game of extraction may be lost. Simply embedding information into the LSB of an image provides no protection if the scheme produces artifacts.

Hide4PGP [11] provides a number of options for selecting how the 8-bit palettes are handled or at what bit levels the data is hidden. The default storage area for hidden information is in the LSB of 8-bit images and in the fourth LSB (that is the fourth bit from the right) in 24-bit images. BMP files have a 54-byte header. The raster data in 24-bit images follow this header. Since 8-bit images require a palette, the 1024 bytes following header are used for the palette. Since Hide4PGP embeds a message sequentially in the bit planes, the embedded text can be obtained by extracting the bits used in creating the stego-image. Hiding plaintext and using the default settings in Hide4PGP, we are able to extract the fourth LSB starting at the 54th byte for 24-bit BMP files to recover the embedded message. Extracting the LSB starting at byte 1078 for an 8-bit BMP file reveals the hidden plaintext message. If it so happens that the embedded message is encrypted, then cryptanalysis techniques can be applied in attempts to crack the encryption routine. If the encrypted data has a recognizable header, an attacker will have a step in the right direction for cryptanalysis or brute force attack [1, 22].

Several options are available for selecting the bit levels to hide information. Hiding information in the bit levels produce visible noise in many 8-bit images. As a countermeasure, options to manipulate the image palette were added. These options allow for the duplication palette entries that are more often used or ordering the palette entries by similar colors. By ordering the palette, Hide4PGP pairs similar colors together similar to the approach of [10]. The palette modifications greatly improve the look of the resulting cover-image, but add properties that are unique to this steganography tool and guide the attacker to the possibility of a hidden message. The number of duplicate entries is always an even number. This is a characteristic that can be employed as a signature of Hide4PGP (similar to [23] and [13]).

Using such a steganography technique may also be problematic if the message is encrypted. If the encrypted data has a recognizable header, an attacker will have a step in the right direction for cryptanalysis or brute force attack [1, 6].

4.4   DISABLING HIDDEN INFORMATION

Detecting the existence of hidden information defeats steganography. Methods discussed in Chapter 3 that follow the transform domain produce results which are far more difficult to detect without the original image for comparison. Sometimes it may be desirable to let the stego-object pass along the communication channel, but disable the embedded message [6, 24]. With each method of hiding information, there is a trade-off between the size of the payload (amount of hidden information) that can be embedded, and the survivability or robustness of that information to be manipulated.

Information hidden in text in the forms of appended spaces and "invisible" characters can be easily revealed by opening the file with a word processor. Extra spaces and characters can be quickly stripped from text documents.

Hidden information may also be overwritten. If information is added to some media such that the added information cannot be detected, then there exists some amount of additional information that may be added or removed within the same threshold which will overwrite or remove the embedded covert information (see Section 4.2).

Caution must be used in hiding information in unused space in files or file systems. File headers and reserved spaces are common places to look for "out of place" information. In file systems, unless the steganographic areas are in some way protected (as in a partition), the operating system may freely overwrite the hidden data, since the clusters are thought to be free. This is a particular annoyance of operating systems that do a lot of caching and creating temporary files. Utilities are also available which "clean" or wipe unused storage areas. In wiping, clusters are overwritten several times to ensure data removal. Even in this extreme case, utilities exist that can recover portions of the overwritten information.

As with unused or reserved space in file headers, TCP/IP packet headers can also be reviewed easily. Just as firewall filters are set to test the validity of the source and destination IP addresses, the SYN and ACK bits, the filters can also be configured to catch packets that have information in supposed unused or reserved space. If IP addresses are altered or spoofed to pass covert information, a reverse lookup in a domain name service (DNS) can verify the address. If the IP address is false, the packet can be terminated. Using this technique to hide information is risky as TCP/IP headers may get overwritten in the routing process. Reserved bits can be overwritten and passed along, without impacting the routing of the packet.

If information is passed by manipulating the time-stamps in packets, filters can also overwrite the time-stamps as the packets are routed, thus disabling the hidden information.

The methods discussed here for disabling hidden information are not intended to advocate the removal or disabling of valid information from images, as an illicit behavior, but to evaluate the claims of embedding systems and study the robustness of current methods. Some methods of disabling hidden messages may require considerable alterations to the stego-image (see Chapter 7 for related discussion on watermarks). Disabling embedded messages is fairly easy in cases where bit-plane methods are used since these methods employ the LSB of images which may be changed with compression of small image processes. More effort is required with the transform domain set of data-hiding tools. An objective for many such methods is to make the hidden information an integral part of the image. The only way to remove or disable it is to seriously distort the stego-image, thus rendering the image useless to the attacker.

The disabling or removal of hidden information in images comes down to image processing techniques. For LSB methods of inserting data, simply using a lossy compression technique such as JPEG is enough to render the embedded message useless. Images compressed with such a method are still pleasing to the human eye, but no longer contain the hidden information (see Chapter 3 for an explanation of JPEG compression and its relationship to steganography). With transform domain hiding techniques, more substantial processing is required to disable the readability of the embedded information. Multiple image processing techniques, such as warping, cropping, rotating, and blurring produce enough distortion to disable the embedded message. These combinations of various image processing techniques can be automated and used to test the robustness of information hiding techniques beyond LSB [25, 26]. Examples and evaluation of these tools are found in [6], [27], and Chapter 7. Tools such as these should be used by those considering the investment of information hiding systems as a means to provide a sense of security of the embedded information, just as password cracking tools are used by system administrators to test the strength of user and system passwords. If the password fails, the administrator should notify the password owner that the password is not secure.

A series of image processing tests were devised to evaluate the robustness threshold of the bit-plane and transform tools [6]. These tests will eventually alter the cover to the point that the hidden information cannot be retrieved. This fact may be viewed as a weakness of the "decoder" instead of the "encoder" in some of these tools. The motivation behind these tests is to illustrate what attacks the techniques can withstand and expose common vulnerabilities. Images used in these tests include digital photographs, clip art, and digital art. The digital photographs are typically 24-bit with thousands of colors or 8-bit grayscale. JPEG and 24-bit BMP files make up the majority of the digital photographs. Clip art images have relatively few colors and are typically 8-bit GIF images. Digital art images are not photographs but may have thousands of colors. These images may be 24-bit (BMP or JPEG) or 8-bit images (BMP or GIF). Where necessary, images were converted to other formats as specified by the steganography or watermarking tools.

A number of images from each type were embedded with known messages or watermarks and the resulting stego-images were verified for the message contents. In the robustness testing, the stego-images are manipulated with a number of image processing techniques and checked for the message contents. The tests include: converting between lossless and lossy formats, converting between bit densities (24-bit, 8-bit, grayscale), blurring, smoothing, adding noise, removing noise, sharpening, edge enhancement, masking, rotating, scaling, resampling, warping (asymmetric resampling—similar to the jitter attack [27]), converting from digital to analog and back (printing and scanning), mirroring, flipping, adding bit-plane messages, adding transform messages, and applying the unZign and StirMark tools to test the robustness of watermarking software. A series of tests were also performed to determine the smallest images that can be used successfully to hide data for each tool.

Minor image processing or conversion to JPEG compressed images was sufficient to disable the bit-plane tools. The transform methods survived a few of the image processing tests. Many images were used for each test as results varied between the use of 8-bit, 24-bit, lossless, and lossy image formats.

With any one of the tests, tools that rely on bit-plane methods to hide data failed to recover any messages. The transform domain embedded information survived many of these tests, but failed with combinations of these transformations. Existing tools were also applied to the stego-images to test robustness [25, 26]. The observed success in making the hidden information unreadable is in introducing small geometric distortions to the image then resampling and smoothing. This combines the effects of slight blurring, edge enhancement, and asymmetric resampling or warping. Further discussion on the robustness of watermarks to various attacks can be found in Chapter 7.

Audio and video are vulnerable to similar methods. Manipulation of the signals will alter embedded signals in the noise level (LSB) which may be enough to overwrite or disable the embedded message. Filters can be used in an attempt to cancel out echoes or subtle signals, but this may not be as successful as expected. A possible brute force combination of attacks on echo hiding in audio can be found in [27] (Chapter 7 further discusses the echo hiding attack).

4.5 DISCUSSION AND CONCLUSION

This chapter provided an overview and introduction to steganalysis and identified weaknesses and visible signs of some steganography approaches. This work is a fraction of the steganalysis approach. To date, a general detection technique as applied to digital image steganography has not been devised and methods beyond visual analysis are being explored. Too many images exist to be reviewed manually for hidden messages. We have introduced some weaknesses of steganographic software that point to the possible existence of hidden messages. Detection of these "signatures" can be automated into tools for detecting steganography. Tools for detecting hidden information are promising for future work in steganalysis and for verifying watermarks.

Steganography transmits secrets through apparently innocuous covers in an effort to conceal the existence of a secret. Digital image steganography and its derivatives are growing in use and application. Commercial applications of steganography in the form of digital watermarks and digital fingerprinting are currently being used to track the copyright and ownership of electronic media. Understanding and investigating the limitations of these applications helps to direct researchers to better, more robust solutions. Efforts in devising more robust information hiding techniques are essential to ensure the survivability of embedded information such as copyright and licensing information. Tools that test the survivability of such information are essential for the evolution of stronger techniques. Using these tools and methods introduced in this paper, potential consumers of information hiding tools can see how much (or how little) effort is required to make the embedded information unreadable.

The ease in use and abundant availability of steganography tools has law enforcement concerned with the trafficking of illicit material. Methods of message detection and understanding the thresholds of current technology are under investigation to uncover such activities. Ongoing work in the area of Internet steganography investigates embedding, recovering, and detecting information in TCP/IP packet headers and other network transmissions.

Success in steganographic secrecy results from selecting the proper mechanisms. However, a stego-image which seems innocent enough may, upon further investigation, actually broadcast the existence of embedded information.

Development in the area of covert communications and steganography will continue. Research in building more robust methods that can survive image manipulation and attacks continues to grow. The more information is placed in the public's reach on the Internet, the more owners of such information need to protect themselves from theft and false representation. Systems to recover seemingly destroyed information and steganalysis techniques will be useful to law enforcement authorities in computer forensics and digital traffic analysis [28, 29].

REFERENCES

[1] Kurak, C., and J. McHughes, "A Cautionary Note On Image Downgrading," in *IEEE Computer Security Applications Conference 1992, Proceedings*, IEEE Press, 1992, pp. 153–159.

[2] Craver, S., N. D. Memon, and M. M. Yeung, "Resolving Rightful Ownerships with Invisible Watermarking Techniques," Technical Report RC 20755 (91985), IBM Research Division, 1997.

[3] Flynn, J., "A Journey Within Steganos," <http://www.fravia.org/fly___01.htm>.

[4] "PhotoShop 4.0/Digimarc: Commercial stupidity - Digimarc downfall," <http://www.fravia.org/frogdigi.htm>, 1997. Original post in Learn Cracking IV on <news:tw.bbs.comp.hacker>.

[5] Brassil, J., et al., "Document Marking and Identification Using Both Line and Word Shifting," in *Proceedings of INFOCOM'95*, Apr. 1995, pp. 853–860.

[6] Johnson, N. F., and S. Jajodia, "Steganalysis of Images Created Using Current Steganography Software," in *Proceedings of the Second International Workshop on Information Hiding*, vol. 1525 of *Lecture Notes in Computer Science*, Springer, 1998, pp. 273–289.

[7] Koch, E., J. Rindfrey, and J. Zhao, "Copyright Protection for Multimedia Data," in *Proceedings of the International Conference on Digital Media and Electronic Publishing*, Leeds, UK, Dec. 1994.

[8] Cha, S. D., G. H. Park, and H. K. Lee, "A Solution to the Image Downgrading Problem," in *Computer Security Applications Conference Proceedings*, 1995, pp. 108–112.

[9] Aura, T., "Invisible Communication," Technical report, Helsinki University of Technology, Nov. 1995.

[10] Machado, R., "EzStego, Stego Online, Stego," <http://www.stego.com>, 1997.

[11] Repp, H., "Hide4PGP," <http://www.rugeley.demon.co.uk/security/hide4pgp.zip>, 1996.

[12] Brown, A., "S-Tools for Windows," <ftp://idea.sec.dsi.unimi.it/pub/security/crypt/code/s-tools4.zip>, 1996.

[13] MediaSec Technologies LLC, "SysCop," <http://www.mediasec.com/>, 1994–1997.

[14] Heckbert, P., "Color Image Quantization for Frame Buffer Display," *ACM Computer Graphics*, vol. 16, no. 3, Jul. 1982, pp. 297–307.

[15] Wayner, P., *Disappearing Cryptography*, Chestnut Hill, MA: Academic Press, 1996.

[16] Hansmann, F., "Steganos, Deus Ex Machina Communications," <http://www.steganography.com/>, 1996.

[17] Maroney, C., "Hide and Seek," <ftp://ftp.csua.berkeley.edu/pub/cypherpunks/steganography/hdsk41b.zip>, <http://www.rugeley.demon.co.uk/security/hdsk50.zip>, 1994–1997.

[18] "StegoDos—Black Wolf's Picture Encoder v0.90B," <ftp://ftp.csua.berkeley.edu/pub/cypherpunks/steganography/stegodos.zip>, 1993.

[19] Hastur, H., "Mandelsteg," <ftp://idea.sec.dsi.unimi.it/pub/security/crypt/code/steg.tar.Z>, 1994.

[20] Johnson, N. F., and S. Jajodia, "Exploring Steganography: Seeing the Unseen," *IEEE Computer*, vol. 31, no. 2, 1998, pp. 26–34.

[21] Maes, M., "Twin Peaks: The Histogram Attack on Fixed Depth Image Watermarks," in *Proceedings of the Second International Workshop on Information Hiding*, vol. 1525 of *Lecture Notes in Computer Science*, Springer, 1998, pp. 290–305.

[22] Koch, E., and J. Zhao, "Towards Robust and Hidden Image Copyright Labeling," in *IEEE Workshop on Nonlinear Signal and Image Processing*, Jun. 1995, pp. 452–455.

[23] Arachelian, R., "White Noise Storm," `<ftp://ftp.csua.berkeley.edu/pub/cypherpunks/steganography/wns210.zip>`, 1994.

[24] Anderson, R. J., and F. A. P. Petitcolas, "On The Limits of Steganography," *IEEE Journal of Selected Areas in Communications*, vol. 16, no. 4, 1998, pp. 474–482.

[25] Petitcolas, F. A. P., and M. G. Kuhn, "StirMark," `<http://www.cl.cam.ac.uk/~fapp2/watermarking/stirmark/>`, 1997.

[26] "unZign. Watermarking testing tool," `<http://altern.org/watermark/>`, 1997.

[27] Petitcolas, F. A. P., R. Anderson, and M. Kuhn, "Attacks on Copyright Marking Systems," in *Proceedings of the Second International Workshop on Information Hiding*, vol. 1525 of *Lecture Notes in Computer Science*, Springer, 1998, pp. 218–238.

[28] Johnson, N. F., Z. Duric, and S. Jajodia, "A Role of Digital Watermarking in Electronic Commerce," to appear in in *ACM Computing Surveys*.

[29] Duric, Z., N. F. Johnson, and S. Jajodia, "Recovering Watermarks from Images," Information & Software Engineering Technical Report: ISE-TR-99-04, to appear in *IEEE Transactions on Image Processing*, 1999. `<http://www.ise.gmu.edu/techrep/1999/>`.

Part II

Watermarking and copyright protection

Chapter 5

Introduction to watermarking techniques

Martin Kutter and Frank Hartung

Part I of this book focused on steganography. In Part II, we will deal with watermarking, which is on the one hand closely related to steganography, but is on the other hand based on different underlying philosophies, requirements, and applications, which result in techniques with properties that clearly distinguish them from steganography.

This chapter gives a general introduction to watermarking and the related technologies. The first concern is to clarify unifying and differentiating properties of steganography and watermarking. We will review the historical aspect of digital watermarking and relate it to the common paper watermark. Then we will look at the generic watermarking systems and talk about applications, requirements, and design issues.

5.1 INTRODUCTION

Both steganography and watermarking describe techniques that are used to imperceptibly convey information by embedding it into the cover-data. However, steganography, as introduced in Chapter 3, typically relates to covert point-to-point communication between two parties. Thus, steganographic methods are usually not robust against modification of the data, or have only limited robustness and protect the embedded information against technical modifications that may occur during transmission and storage, like format conversion, compression, or digital-to-analog conversion.

Watermarking, on the other hand, has the additional notion of resilience against attempts to remove the hidden data. Thus, watermarking, rather than steganography principles are used whenever the cover-data is available to parties who know the existence of the hidden data and may have an interest removing it. A popular application of watermarking is to give proof of ownership of digital data by embedding copyright statements. It is obvious that for this application the embedded information should be robust against manipulations that may attempt to remove it. Other applications include data monitoring or tracking, in which the user is interested in monitoring data transmission in order to control royalty payments, or simply track the distribution to localize the data for marketing and sales purposes. Furthermore, digital watermarking may also be used for fingerprinting applications in order to distinguish distributed data sets. Chapter 8 is dedicated to the latter issue.

5.2   HISTORY AND TERMINOLOGY

5.2.1   History

Paper watermarks appeared in the art of handmade papermaking nearly 700 years ago. The oldest watermarked paper found in archives dates back to 1292 and has its origin in the town of Fabriano in Italy which has played a major role in the evolution of the papermaking industry. At the end of the 13th century about 40 paper mills were sharing the paper market in Fabriano and producing paper with different format, quality, and price. At that time paper mills produced raw paper with very coarse surfaces not yet suitable for writing. This raw paper material was given to other artisans who smoothed the paper surface with the help of a hard stone, called calender, to make it suitable for writing. The post-treated paper was then counted, folded, and finally sold to merchants who stored it in huge warehouses for resale with large profits. Competition not only between the 40 paper mills but also between artisans and merchants was very high and it was difficult for any party to keep track of paper provenance and thus format and quality identification. The introduction of watermarks was the perfect method to eliminate any possibility of confusion (see Figure 5.1). After their invention, watermarks quickly spread in Italy and then over Europe and although initially used to indicate the paper brand or paper mill, they later served as indication for paper format, quality, and strength, and were also used as the basis for dating and authenticating paper. A nice example illustrating the legal power of watermarks is a case that happened in France in 1887 [1]. The watermarks of two letters, presented as pieces of evidence, proved that the

Figure 5.1   Monograms figuring TGE RG (Thomas Goodrich Eliensis—Bishop of Ely, England—
and Remy/Remigius Guedon, the papermaker). One of the oldest watermarks found
in the Cambridge area (c. 1550). At that time, watermarks were mainly used to
identify the mill producing the paper; a means of guaranteeing quality. Courtesy of E.
Leedham-Green, Cambridge University Archives, England. Reproduction technique:
beta radiography. Reprinted from [3].

letters had been predated and resulted in the prosecution of a deputy, the release
from office of a police prefect, the downfall of a cabinet, and finally the resignation
of president Grévy. For more information on paper watermarks, watermark history,
and related legal issues the interested reader is referred to [2], an extensive listing
of over 500 references.

The analogy between paper watermarks and digital watermarking is obvious:
paper watermarks in bank notes or stamps inspired the first use of the term "water
mark" [4] in the context of digital data. The first publications that focussed on
watermarking of digital images were published by Tanaka et al. [5] in 1990 and by
Caronni [6] and Tirkel et al. [4] in 1993.

In 1995, the time was obviously right to pick up the topic, and it began to
stimulate increasing research activities. Since 1995, digital watermarking has gained
a lot of attention and has evolved very fast (see Table 5.1), and while there are a
lot of topics open for further research, practical working methods and systems have
been developed, some of which are presented in Chapter 6.

Year	1992	1993	1994	1995	1996	1997	1998
Publications	2	2	4	13	29	64	103

Table 5.1   Number of publications on digital watermarking during the past few years according to INSPEC, Jan. 1999. Courtesy of J.-L. Dugelay [7].

5.2.2   Watermarking terminology

Today, we are of course concerned with digital, rather than analog, communication and media. As in analog media, there is interest in steganographic and watermarking methods that allow the transmission of information hidden or embedded in other data. Several names have been coined for such techniques. However, the terms are often confused, and therefore it is necessary to clarify the differences.

Visible watermarks, as the name says, are visual patterns like logos which are inserted into or overlaid on images (or video), very similar to visible paper watermarks. Visible watermarks are mainly applied to images, for example, to visibly mark preview images available in image databases or on the Web in order to prevent commercial use of such images. The applications of visible watermarks to video is of course also possible and under some circumstances one might even think of embedding an audible watermark into audio. An example of visible watermarking has been developed in the context of the IBM Digital Libraries project [8]. The technique combines the watermark image with the original image by modifying the brightness of the original image as a function of the watermark and a secret key. The secret key determines pseudorandom scaling values used for brightness modification in order to make it difficult for attackers to remove the visible mark. For the rest of this book we will focus on imperceptible watermarks.

Watermarking, as opposed to steganography, has the additional notion of robustness against attacks. Even if the existence of the hidden information is known it should be hard for an attacker to destroy the embedded watermark without knowledge of a key (see Kerckhoffs' principle in Section 1.2.4). A practical implication of the robustness requirement is that watermarking methods can typically embed much less information into cover-data than steganographic methods. Steganography and watermarking are thus more complementary than competitive approaches. In the remainder of this chapter, we will mainly focus on watermarking methods, and not on steganographic methods in general, since they have been covered in the previous chapters.

Fingerprinting and *labeling* are terms that denote special applications of watermarking. They relate to watermarking applications where information such as the creator or recipient of digital data is embedded as watermarks. Fingerprinting

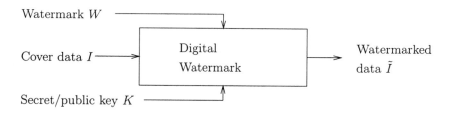

Figure 5.2   Generic digital watermarking scheme.

means watermarking where the embedded information is either a unique code specifying the author or originator of the cover-data, or a unique code out of a series of codes specifying the recipient of the data. More details on fingerprinting are presented in Chapter 8. Labeling means watermarking where the embedded data may contain any information of interest, such as a unique data identifier.

Bitstream watermarking is sometimes used for watermarking of compressed data, for example compressed video.

The term *embedded signatures* has been used instead of "watermarking" in early publications, but is usually not used anymore, since it potentially leads to confusion with cryptographic signatures. Cryptographic signatures serve for authentication purposes. They are used to detect any alteration of the signed data and to authenticate the sender. Watermarks, however, are only used for authentication in special applications, and are usually designed to *resist* alterations and modifications.

Fragile watermarks are watermarks that have only very limited robustness. They are applied to detect modifications of the watermarked data, rather than conveying unerasable information. Fragile watermarks and authentication applications are discussed below in Section 5.4.4.

5.3   BASIC WATERMARKING PRINCIPLES

All watermarking methods share the same generic building blocks: a *watermark embedding system* and a *watermark recovery system* (also called watermark extraction or watermark decoder). Figure 5.2 shows the generic watermark embedding process. The input to the scheme is the watermark, the cover-data and an optional public or secret key. The watermark can be of any nature such as a number, text, or an image. The key may be used to enforce security, that is the prevention of unauthorized parties from recovering and manipulating the watermark. All practical systems employ at least one key, or even a combination of several keys. In combination with a secret or a public key the watermarking techniques are usually

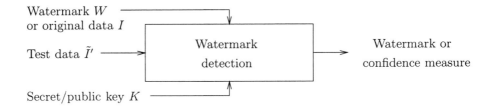

Figure 5.3   Generic watermark recovery scheme.

referred to as secret and public watermarking techniques, respectively. The output of the watermarking scheme is the *watermarked data.*

For real-world robust watermarking systems, a few very general properties, shared by all proposed systems, can be identified. They are:

- **Imperceptibility.** The modifications caused by watermark embedding should be below the perceptible threshold, which means that some sort of perceptibility criterion should be used not only to design the watermark, but also quantify the distortion. As a consequence of the required imperceptibility, the individual samples (or pixels, voxels, features, etc.) that are used for watermark embedding are only modified by a small amount.
- **Redundancy.** To ensure robustness despite the small allowed changes, the watermark information is usually redundantly distributed over many samples (or pixels, voxels, features, etc.) of the cover-data, thus providing a global robustness which means that the watermark can usually be recovered from a small fraction of the watermarked data. Obviously watermark recovery is more robust if more of the watermarked data is available in the recovery process. Robustness criteria will be presented in Chapter 7.
- **Keys.** In general, watermarking systems use one or more cryptographically secure keys to ensure security against manipulation and erasure of the watermark. As soon as a watermark can be read by someone, the same person may easily destroy it because not only the embedding strategy, but also the locations of the watermark are known in this case.

These principles apply to watermarking schemes for all kinds of data that can be watermarked, like audio, images, video, formatted text, 3D models, model animation parameters, and others.

The generic watermark recovery process is depicted in Figure 5.3. Inputs to the scheme are the watermarked data, the secret or public key, and, depending on the method, the original data and/or the original watermark. The output is either the recovered watermark W or some kind of confidence measure indicating how likely it is for the given watermark at the input to be present in the data $\tilde{I}'$ under inspection. Three types of watermarking systems can be identified. Their difference is in the nature and combination of inputs and outputs (from [9]):

- **Private watermarking** (also called nonblind watermarking) systems require at least the original data. *Type I* systems extract the watermark W from the possibly distorted data $\tilde{I}'$ and use the original data as a hint to find where the watermark could be in $\tilde{I}'$. *Type II* systems also require a copy of the embedded watermark for extraction and just yield a "yes" or "no" answer to the question: does $\tilde{I}'$ contain the watermark W? ($\tilde{I}' \times I \times K \times W \rightarrow \{0,1\}$). It is expected that this kind of scheme will be more robust than the others since it conveys very little information and requires access to secret material.
- **Semiprivate watermarking** (or semiblind watermarking) does not use the original data for detection ($\tilde{I}' \times K \times W \rightarrow \{0,1\}$) but answers the same question. Potential applications of private and semiprivate watermarking are for evidence in court to prove ownership, copycontrol in applications such as digital versatile disc (DVD) where the disc reader needs to know whether it is allowed to play the content or not, and fingerprinting where the goal is to identify the original recipient of pirated copies.
- **Public watermarking** (also referred to as *blind* or *oblivious* watermarking) remains the most challenging problem since it requires neither the secret original I nor the embedded watermark W. Indeed, such systems really extract n bits of information (the watermark) from the marked data: $\tilde{I}' \times K \rightarrow W$.

Depending on the application, the input to both generic schemes is usually in the form of uncompressed or compressed data. For obvious reasons the watermarking techniques should exploit the nature of the input. It would not make much sense if a watermarking scheme for MPEG-2 video requires single decompressed video frames to perform the watermarking since this would include a decoding and re-encoding procedure and make the entire watermarking process computationally too expensive. However, it should be noted that for some applications it may be interesting to design watermark detection schemes, which allow for a watermark to be detected regardless of the domain where it was embedded. This is important, for example, in applications requiring resilience to transcoding or change of format.

5.4   WATERMARKING APPLICATIONS

The requirements that watermarking systems have to comply with are always based on the application. Thus, before we review the requirements and the resulting design considerations, we will present some applications of watermarking. For obvious reasons there is no "universal" watermarking method. Although watermarking methods have to be robust in general, different levels of required robustness can be identified depending on the specific application-driven requirements.

5.4.1   Watermarking for copyright protection

Copyright protection is probably the most prominent application of watermarking today. The objective is to embed information about the source, and thus typically the copyright owner, of the data in order to prevent other parties from claiming the copyright on the data. Thus, the watermarks are used to resolve rightful ownership, and this application requires a very high level of robustness. The driving force for this application is the Web which contains millions of freely available images that the rightful owners want to protect. Additional issues besides robustness have to be considered. For example, the watermark must be unambiguous and still resolve rightful ownership if other parties embed additional watermarks. Hence, additional design requirements besides mere robustness apply.

5.4.2   Fingerprinting for traitor tracking

There are other applications where the objective is to convey information about the legal recipient rather than the source of digital data, mainly in order to identify single distributed copies of the data. This is useful to monitor or trace back illegally produced copies of the data that may circulate, and is very similar to serial numbers of software products. This type of application is usually called "fingerprinting" and involves the embedding of a different watermark into each distributed copy. Because the distribution of individually watermarked copies allow collusion attacks (see Chapter 8), the embedded watermarks have to be designed as collusion-secure [10, 11]. Also, for some fingerprinting applications it is required to extract the watermark easily and with a low complexity, for example, for World Wide Web applications where special Web crawlers search for pirated watermarked images. Watermarks for fingerprinting applications also require a high robustness against standard data processing as well as malicious attacks.

5.4.3   Watermarking for copy protection

A desirable feature in multimedia distribution systems is the existence of a copy protection mechanism that disallows unauthorized copying of the media. Copy protection is very difficult to achieve in open systems; in closed or proprietary systems, however, it is feasible. In such systems it is possible to use watermarks indicating the copy status of the data. An example is the DVD system where the data contains copy information embedded as a watermark. A compliant DVD player is not allowed to playback or copy data that carry a "copy never" watermark. Data that carry a "copy once" watermark may be copied, but no further consecutive copies are allowed to be made from the copy [12, 13].

5.4.4 Watermarking for image authentication

In authentication applications, the objective is to detect modifications of the data. This can be achieved with so-called "fragile watermarks" that have a low robustness to certain modifications like compression, but are impaired by other modifications [14, 15]. Furthermore, the robustness requirements may change depending on the data type and application. Nevertheless, among all possible watermarking applications, authentication watermarks require the lowest level of robustness by definition. It should be noted that new approaches have emerged in which data attributes, such as block average or edge characteristics, are embedded and check if the received image still has the same attributes. It is clear that such schemes may require a higher robustness if identification of the modified areas is of interest.

5.5 REQUIREMENTS AND ALGORITHMIC DESIGN ISSUES

Depending on the watermarking application and purpose, different requirements arise resulting in various design issues. Watermark imperceptibility is a common requirement and independent of the application purpose. Additional requirements have to be taken into consideration when designing watermarking techniques:

- **Recovery with or without the original data.** Depending on the application, the original data is or is not available to the watermark recovery system. If the original is available, it is usually advantageous to use it, since systems that use the original for recovery are typically more robust. However, in applications such as data monitoring, the original data is of no use because the goal is to identify the monitored data.
- **Extraction or verification of a given watermark.** There are two inherently equivalent approaches for watermark embedding and recovery. In the first approach, one watermark out of a predefined set of admissible watermarks is embedded, and the watermark recovery tests the watermarked data against the admissible set. The output of the watermark recovery is the index of the embedded watermark or a symbol "no watermark found." In the second approach, the embedded watermark is the modulation of a sequence of

symbols given to the watermark embedding system. In the detection process the embedded symbols are extracted through demodulation.

■ **Robustness.** Robustness of the watermarked data against modifications and/or malicious attacks is one of the key requirements in watermarking. However, as said before, there are applications where it is less important than for others.

■ **Security issues and use of keys.** The conditions for key management differ greatly depending on the application. Obvious examples are public key watermarking systems like DVD versus secret key systems used for copyright protection.

5.5.1 Imperceptibility

One the most important requirements is the perceptual transparency of the watermark, independent of the application and purpose of the watermarking system. Artifacts introduced through a watermarking process are not only annoying and undesirable, but may also reduce or destroy the commercial value of the watermarked data. It is therefore important to design marking methods which exploit effects of the human visual or auditory system in order to maximize the energy of the watermark under the constraint of not exceeding the perceptible threshold. Two problems are related to this issue. The first one is the reliable assessment of the introduced distortion which will be described in Section 5.6. The second problem occurs when processing is applied to the watermarked data. For example, in image watermarking the visibility of the watermark may increase if the image is scaled.

5.5.2 Robustness

The ultimate watermarking method should resist any kind of distortion introduced by standard or malicious data processing. No such perfect method has been proposed so far, and it is not clear yet whether an absolutely secure watermarking method exists at all. Thus, practical systems must implement a compromise between robustness and the competing requirements like invisibility and information rate. Depending on the application purpose of the watermarking methods, the desired robustness therefore influences the design process. For example in image watermarking, if we need a method that is resilient to JPEG compression with high compression factors, it is probably more efficient to employ a method working in a transform domain than to use a method that works in the spatial domain. Similarly, if the method should accommodate generalized geometrical transformations, that is rotation, nonuniform scaling, and shearing, an approach in the spatial domain is probably more suitable. Looking at the distortion that the watermarked data is likely to undergo by either intentional or unintentional modifications, two groups of distortion can be distinguished. The first one contains distortions which can be considered as additive noise to the data whereas the distortion in the second group are due to modifications of the spatial or temporal data geometry with the intent to introduce a mismatch between the watermark and the key used for embedding. These two distortions or attacks are often referred to as *destruction attacks* and *synchronization attacks*, respectively. Finer categorization of attacks were also proposed [16].

Depending on the application and watermarking requirements, the list of distortions and attacks to be considered includes, but is not limited to:

- Signal enhancement (sharpening, contrast enhancement, color correction, gamma correction);
- Additive and multiplicative noise (Gaussian, uniform, speckle, mosquito);
- Linear filtering (lowpass-, highpass-, bandpass filtering);
- Nonlinear filtering (median filtering, morphological filtering);
- Lossy compression (images: JPEG, video: H.261, H.263, MPEG-2, MPEG-4, audio: MPEG-2 audio, MP3, MPEG-4 audio, G.723);
- Local and global affine transforms (translation, rotation, scaling, shearing);
- Data reduction (cropping, clipping, histogram modification);
- Data composition (logo insertion, scene composition);
- Transcoding (H.263 $\rightarrow$ MPEG-2, GIF $\rightarrow$ JPEG);
- D/A and A/D conversion (print-scan, analog TV transmission);
- Multiple watermarking;
- Collusion attacks;
- Statistical averaging;
- Mosaic attacks.

Some of these attacks, and others, are described in Chapter 7. The basic principle is to design watermarking methods, which are robust enough such that successful attacks would also impair the commercial value of the cover-data.

5.5.3 Watermark recovery with or without the original data

Watermarking methods using the original data set in the recovery process usually feature increased robustness not only towards noise-like distortions, but also distortions in the data geometry since it allows the detection and inversion of geometrical distortions. In many applications, such as data monitoring or tracking, access to the original data is not possible. In other applications, such as video watermarking applications, it may be impracticable to use the original data because of the large amount of data that would have to be processed. While most early watermarking techniques require the original data for recovery, there is a clear tendency to devise techniques that do not require the original data set. This is probably due to the larger fields of applications for such techniques.

5.5.4   Watermark extraction or verification of presence for a given watermark

As was said before, two types of watermarking schemes exist: systems that embed a specific information or pattern and check the existence of the (known) information later on in the watermark recovery process, and systems that embed arbitrary information into the data. For example, copyright protection can be achieved with systems verification of the presence of a known watermark. Watermarking schemes embedding arbitrary information are, for example, used for image tracking on the Internet with intelligent agents where it might not only be of interest to discover images, but also to classify them. The embedded watermark can be used as an image identification number or as a pointer to a database entry.

It should be noted that both schemes can be interchanged. A scheme which allows watermark verification can be considered as a one-bit watermark recovery scheme, and can easily be extended to any number of bits by modulation with the arbitrary information to be embedded. The inverse is also true: a watermark recovery scheme can be considered as a watermark verification scheme assuming the embedded information is known.

5.5.5   Watermark security and keys

In most applications, such as copyright protection, the secrecy of embedded information needs to be assured. This and related issues are often referred to as *watermark security*. Applications in which security is not an issue include image database indexing. If secrecy is a requirement, a secret key has to be used for the embedding and extraction process. Two levels of secrecy can be identified. In the highest level of secrecy an unauthorized user can neither read or decode an embedded watermark nor can he detect if a given set of data contains a watermark. The second level permits any user to detect if data is watermarked, but the embedded information cannot be read without having the secret key. Such schemes may, for example, be useful in copyright protection applications for images. As soon as a copyrighted image is opened in a photo editing software program the user is informed by a note indicating that the image is protected.

Such schemes can, for example, contain multiple watermarks, with public and secret keys. It is also possible to combine one or several public keys with a private key and embed a joint public/private watermark [17].

When designing a working overall copyright protection system, issues like secret key generation, distribution, and management (possibly by trusted third parties), as well as other system integration aspects have to be considered as well.

5.5.6   Resolving rightful ownership

In order to successfully resolve rightful ownership, it must be possible to determine who first watermarked a data set in case it contains multiple watermarks. This can be achieved by imposing design constraints, such as the *noninvertibility* of the watermark [18] or using additional functionalities, such as time-stamping. More detail on this issue will be given in Chapter 7.

5.6   EVALUATION AND BENCHMARKING OF WATERMARKING SYSTEMS

Besides designing digital watermarking methods, an important issue addresses proper evaluation and benchmarking. This not only requires evaluation of the robustness, but also includes subjective or quantitative evaluation of the distortion introduced through the watermarking process. In general, there is a trade-off between watermark robustness and watermark perceptibility. Hence, for fair benchmarking and performance evaluation one has to ensure that the methods under investigation are tested under comparable conditions [9, 19].

5.6.1   Performance evaluation and representation

Independent of the application purpose type of data, the robustness of watermarks depends on the following aspects:

- **Amount of embedded information.** This is an important parameter since it directly influences the watermark robustness. The more information one wants to embed, the lower the watermark robustness.
- **Watermark embedding strength.** There is a trade-off between the watermark embedding strength (hence the watermark robustness) and watermark perceptibility. Increased robustness requires a stronger embedding, which in turn increases perceptibility of the watermark.
- **Size and nature of data.** The size of the data has usually a direct impact on the robustness of the embedded watermark. For example, in image watermarking very small pictures do not have much commercial value; nevertheless, a marking software program needs to be able to recover a watermark

from them. This avoids a "mosaic" attack [20] (see Section 7.3.2) on them and allows tiling, used often in Web applications. For printing applications high-resolution images are required but one also wants to protect these images after they are resampled and used on the Web. In addition to the size of the data, the nature of the data also has an important impact on the watermark robustness. Again taking image watermarking as an example, methods featuring a high robustness for scanned natural images have an surprisingly reduced robustness for synthetic, such as computer generated, images.

- **Secret information (e.g., key).** Although the amount of secret information has no direct impact on the perceptibility of the watermark and the robustness of the watermark, it plays an important role in the security of the system. The key space, that is, the range of all possible values of the secret information, must be large enough to make exhaustive search attacks impossible. The reader should also keep in mind that many security systems fail to resist very simple attacks because the system designers did not obey basic cryptographic principles in the design [20, 21].

Taking these parameters into account, we realize that for fair benchmarking and performance evaluation, watermarking methods need to be tested on different data sets. Furthermore, in order to compute statistically valid results the methods have to be evaluated using many different keys and varying watermarks. The amount of embedded information is usually fixed and depends on the application. However, if watermarking methods are to be compared, it has to be assured that the amount of embedded information is the same for all methods under inspection.

As we have seen above, there is a trade-off between the watermark perceptibility and the watermark robustness. For fair evaluation and comparison it is therefore necessary to consider the perceptibility of the watermark in the evaluation process. Evaluating the perceptibility of the watermarks can be done either through subjective tests or a quality metric. When using a subjective test, a testing protocol has to be followed, describing the testing and evaluation procedure. Such tests usually involve a two-step process. In a first round, the distorted data sets are rank ordered from best to worst. In the second round, the subject is asked to rate each data set, describing the perceptibility of the artifacts. This rating, can be based, for example, on the ITU-R Rec. 500 quality rating. Table 5.2 lists the ratings and the corresponding perception and quality. Work done within the European projects OCTALIS (Offer of Content Through Trusted Access Links) has shown that individuals with different experience, for example professional photographers and researchers, generate quite different results in subjective tests on watermarked images. Subjective tests are practical for final quality evaluation and testing, but are not very useful in a research and development environment.

Rating	Impairment	Quality
5	Imperceptible	excellent
4	Perceptible, not annoying	good
3	Slightly annoying	fair
2	Annoying	poor
1	Very annoying	bad

Table 5.2   ITU-R Rec. 500 quality ratings on a scale from 1 to 5.

In such an environment, quantitative distortion metrics are much more efficient and allow fair comparison between different methods as the results do not depend on subjective evaluations. Table 5.3 shows pixel-based difference-distortion metrics commonly used in image and video processing. Most of the shown metrics are also applicable, after adaption of the dimension, to other types of data than images, for example audio. Nowadays, the most popular distortion measures in the field of image and video coding and compression are the *signal-to-noise ratio* (SNR), and the *peak signal-to-noise ratio* (PSNR). They are usually measured in *decibels* (dB): $\text{SNR(dB)} = 10\log_{10}(\text{SNR})$. It is well known that these difference distortion metrics are not very well correlated with the human visual or auditory system. This might be a problem for their application in digital watermarking since sophisticated watermarking methods exploit in one way or the other effects of these systems. Using the above metric to quantify the distortion caused by a watermarking process might therefore result in misleading quantitative distortion measurements. It might be useful, therefore, to use distortion metrics adapted to the human visual and auditory systems. In recent years more and more research concentrates on such adapted distortion metrics [22–25] and it is very probable that future benchmarking of digital watermarking systems employs such quality metrics.

After fixing the parameters and deciding on a distortion metric, the next issue addresses efficient robustness evaluation and visual representation. Table 5.4 lists useful graphs, together with the variable and fixed parameters for comparison. For all evaluation strategies, it is very important to perform the tests using different keys and a variety of data sets (e.g., many different images). The results should then be averaged and plotted. If performance evaluation on individual data sets is desirable for direct performance comparison of two methods for one data set, it is still important that all tests are repeated several times using different keys. In the next paragraphs we will briefly explain the four different graphs. The term *attack* refers to any attack as outlined in Chapter 7 and *robustness* describes the watermark resistance to these attacks. The robustness is usually measured by the *bit-error rate*, defined as the ratio of wrong extracted bits to the total number

Difference distortion metrics	
Average absolute difference	$AD = \dfrac{1}{XY} \sum_{x,y} |p_{x,y} - \tilde{p}_{x,y}|$
Mean squared error	$MSE = \dfrac{1}{XY} \sum_{x,y} (p_{x,y} - \tilde{p}_{x,y})^2$
L^p-norm	$L^p = \left(\dfrac{1}{XY} \sum_{x,y} |p_{x,y} - \tilde{p}_{x,y}|^p \right)^{1/p}$
Laplacian mean squared error	$LMSE = \sum_{x,y} \left(\nabla^2 p_{x,y} - \nabla^2 \tilde{p}_{x,y}\right)^2 / \sum_{x,y} (\nabla^2 p_{x,y})^2$
Signal-to-noise ratio	$SNR = \sum_{x,y} p_{x,y}^2 / \sum_{x,y} (p_{x,y} - \tilde{p}_{x,y})^2$
Peak signal-to-noise ratio	$PSNR = XY \max_{x,y} p_{x,y}^2 / \sum_{x,y} (p_{x,y} - \tilde{p}_{x,y})^2$
Correlation distortion metrics	
Normalized cross-correlation	$NC = \sum_{x,y} p_{x,y}\tilde{p}_{x,y} / \sum_{x,y} p_{x,y}^2$
Correlation quality	$CQ = \sum_{x,y} p_{x,y}\tilde{p}_{x,y} / \sum_{x,y} p_{x,y}$
Others	
Global sigma signal-to-noise ratio	$GSSNR = \sum_{b} \sigma_b^2 / \sum_{b} (\sigma_b - \tilde{\sigma}_b)^2$ where $\sigma_b = \sqrt{\dfrac{1}{n} \sum_{\text{block } b} p_{x,y}^2 - \left(\dfrac{1}{n} \sum_{\text{block } b} p_{x,y}\right)^2}$
Histogram similarity	$HS = \sum_{c=0}^{255} |f_I(c) - f_{\tilde{I}}(c)|$ where $f_I(c)$ is the relative frequency of level c in a 256-levels image.

Table 5.3   Commonly used pixel-based visual distortion metrics. $p_{x,y}$ represents a pixel, whose coordinates are (x, y), in the original, undistorted image, and $\tilde{p}_{x,y}$ represents a pixel, whose coordinates are (x, y), in the watermarked image. $GSSNR$ requires the division of the original and watermarked images into blocks of n pixels (e.g., 4×4 pixels). X and Y are the number of rows and columns, respectively.

Graph type	Parameter			
	Visual quality	*Robustness*	*Attack*	*Bits*
Robustness vs. attack	fixed	variable	variable	fixed
Robustness vs. visual quality	variable	variable	fixed	fixed
Attack vs. visual quality	variable	fixed	variable	fixed
ROC	fixed	fixed	fixed / variable	fixed

Table 5.4   Different graphs and corresponding variables and constants.

of embedded bits, or the *detection-error*, defined by 1 minus the bit-error raised to the power of the number of bits. The term *visual quality* refers to any visual-quality metric appropriate to evaluate the visual distortion due to the watermarking process. In order to illustrate the usefulness of the proposed graphs, samples are shown in Figures 5.4 to 5.7 based on a comparative scenario for two simple image watermarking methods [9]. Both methods employ spread spectrum modulation, but in different domains. One method uses the spatial domain while the other method uses a multiresolution environment (three level wavelet transform with Daubechies 6 tap filters). The systems use a secret key which serves as seed for a pseudorandom number generator used to generate the spread spectrum sequences. As a robustness measure we use the bit-error rate, the metric for the visual quality is the rating proposed by van den Branden Lamprecht and Farrell [22], and the attack is JPEG compression. All tests were performed on the 512×512, 24-bit color version of *lena*. Each test was repeated each time using a randomly chosen key. The watermark length is 100 bits.

The *robustness vs. attack strength graph* is one of the most important graphs relating the watermark robustness to the attack. Usually this graph shows the bit- or detection-error as a function of the attack strength for a given visual quality. Several papers have used this graph, unfortunately without explicitly reporting the visual image quality. This evaluation allows direct comparison of the watermark robustness and shows the overall behavior of the method towards attacks. The *robustness vs. visual quality graph* shows the relationship between the bit- or detection-error and the visual-image quality for a fixed attack. For a given attack, this graph can be used in determining the expected bit-error for a desired visual quality. This might be especially useful determining the minimal visual quality for a desired bit-error rate under a given attack. The *attack vs. visual quality graph* illustrates the maximum allowable attack as a function of the visual quality for a given

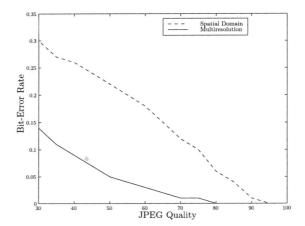

Figure 5.4   Bit-error vs. attack graph for spread spectrum modulation in a spatial and multiresolution environment. The visual quality was fixed to 4.5. It is clearly visible that the multiresolution approach has a higher robustness.

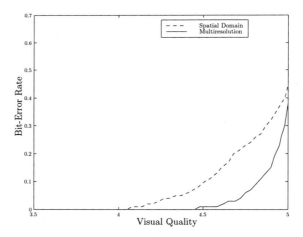

Figure 5.5   Bit-error vs. visual quality graph for spread spectrum modulation in a spatial and multiresolution environment. The attack was fixed to JPEG compression with 75% quality. Again the multiresolution approach shows superior performance.

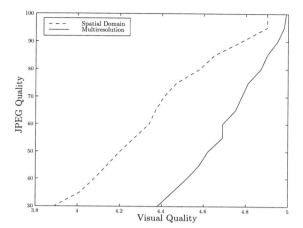

Figure 5.6   Attack vs. visual quality graph for spread spectrum modulation in a spatial and multiresolution environment. The bit-error rate was set to 0.1. The curves clearly show that the multiresolution approach accommodates larger compression ratios for a given visual quality.

robustness. This graph allows immediate evaluation of the allowable watermark attack for given visual qualities. This is especially useful if the visual quality range is given and the corresponding maximal allowable distortion (i.e., watermark attack) needs to be evaluated. Furthermore, this graph is very useful in comparing different watermarking methods since it facilitates immediate robustness comparisons for a given visual image quality at a fixed bit- or detection-error. Given any image, a watermark detector has to fulfill two tasks: decide if the given image is watermarked and decode the encoded information. The former can be seen as hypothesis testing in that the watermark decoder has to decide between the *alternative hypothesis* (the image is watermarked) and the *null hypothesis* (the image is not watermarked). In binary hypothesis testing two kinds or errors can occur: accepting the alternative hypothesis, when the null hypothesis is correct, and accepting the null hypothesis when the alternative hypothesis is true. The first error is often called *type I* error or *false positive* and the second error is usually called *type II* error or *false negative*. Receiver operating characteristic (ROC) graphs [26] are very useful in assessing the overall behavior and reliability of the watermarking scheme under inspection. Usually, in hypothesis testing, a test statistic is compared against a threshold to decide for one or the other hypothesis. Comparing different watermarking schemes with a fixed threshold may result in misleading results. ROC graphs avoid this problem by comparing the test using varying decision thresholds. The ROC graph

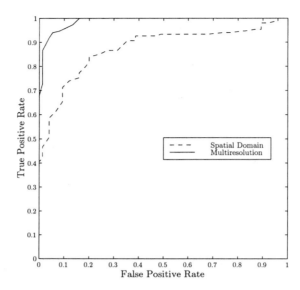

Figure 5.7   ROC graph for spread spectrum modulation in a spatial and multiresolution environment. The curve corresponding to the multiresolution approach is closer to the
top-left corner, which indicates its superior performance.

shows the relation between the *true positive fraction* (TPF) on the y-axis and the
false positive fraction (FPF) on the x-axis. The true positive-fraction is defined as:

$$TPF = \frac{TP}{TP + FN} \tag{5.1}$$

where TP is the number of true-positive test results, and FN is the number false
negative tests. The false-positive fraction is defined as:

$$FPF = \frac{FP}{TN + FP} \tag{5.2}$$

where FP is the total number of false-positive test results, and TN is the number
of true negative test results. In other words, the ROC graph shows TPF-FPF pairs
resulting from a continuously varying threshold. An optimal detector has a curve
that goes from the bottom-left corner to the top-left, and then to the top-right
corner. The diagonal from the bottom-left corner to the top-right corner describes
a detector which randomly selects one or the other hypothesis with equal probability. Hence, the higher the detector accuracy, the more its curve approaches the

top-left corner. Often the integral under the curve is used as a detector performance measure [26]. To generate these graphs, the same number of watermarked and non-watermarked images should be tested. If the overall performance of watermarking methods is to be evaluated, tests should include a variety of attacks with varying parameters.

5.6.2   Watermark removal software and benchmarking

Similar to conditional access and copy prevention mechanisms, the existence of watermarking technology and its potential possibilities have stimulated individuals to come up with attempts to defeat watermarking. Examples are publicly available tools to test the robustness of image watermarking techniques. *Unzign* [27] is a utility that works for images in JPEG format. In version 1.1 Unzign introduces pixel jittering in combination with a slight image translation. Depending on the watermarking technique under investigation, the tool seems to efficiently remove or destroy embedded watermarks. However, besides removing the watermark Unzign version 1.1 often introduces unacceptable artifacts. An improved version 1.2 has been released. Although the artifacts were decreased its watermark destruction capability decreased as well.

StirMark [20, 28, 29] is a tool to test the robustness of image watermarking techniques. It applies minor geometric distortions to images which are described in Section 7.3.1. Applying StirMark only once introduces a practically unnoticeable quality loss in the image. Based on the StirMark utility, a generic benchmark for image watermarking systems has been proposed [9, 19]. The benchmark subjects watermarked images to a variety of attacks to which the watermark should be resistant. The resistance of the methods to groups of attacks is then averaged to allow comparison.

5.7   FUTURE AND STANDARDIZATION

The interest in watermarking technology is high, both from academia and industry. The interest from academia is reflected in the number of publications on watermarking and in the number of conferences on watermarking and data hiding being held. The interest from industry is evident in the number of companies in the field that have been founded within the past few years.

Besides research activities in universities and industry, several international research projects funded by the European Community have the goal to develop practical watermarking techniques. *TALISMAN* [30] (ACTS[1] project AC019, Tracing

---

1 Advanced Communications Technologies and Services.

Authors' Rights by Labeling Image Services and Monitoring Access Network) aims to provide European Union service providers with a standard copyright mechanism to protect digital products against large-scale commercial piracy and illegal copying. The expected output of TALISMAN is a system for protecting video sequences through labeling and watermarking. *OCTALIS* [31] (ACTS project P119, Offer of Content Through Trusted Access Links) is the followup project of TALISMAN and OKAPI [31] (ACTS project 051, Open Kernel for Access to Protected Interoperable Interactive Services) with the main goal to integrate a global approach to equitable conditional access and efficient copyright protection and to demonstrate its validity on large-scale trials on the Internet and EBU (European Broadcasting Union) network.

International standardization consortia are also interested in watermarking techniques. The emerging video-compression standard MPEG-4 (ISO/IEC 14496), for example, provides a framework that allows the easy integration with encryption and watermarking. The DVD industry standard will contain copy control and copy protection mechanisms that use watermarking to signal the copy status of multimedia data, like "copy once" or "do not copy" flags.

Despite all the many efforts that are under way to develop and establish watermarking technology, watermarking is still not a fully mature and understood technology, and a lot of questions are not answered yet. Also, the theoretical fundamentals are still weak, and most systems are designed heuristically.

Another drawback is that fair comparisons between watermarking systems are difficult [9]. As long as methods and system implementations are not evaluated in a consistent manner using sophisticated benchmarking methods, the danger exists that weak and vulnerable systems and de facto standards are produced that result in spectacular failures and discredit the entire concept.

Thus, the expectations into watermarking should be realistic. It should always be kept in mind that every watermarking system involves a trade-off between robustness, watermark data rate (payload), and imperceptibility. The invisible 10000 bit per image watermark that resists all attacks whatsoever is an illusion (realistic numbers are approximately two orders of magnitude lower). Even when designed under realistic expectations, watermarks offer robustness against nonexperts, but may still be vulnerable to attacks by experts.

Although proof of ownership was the initial thrust for the technology, it seems that there will be a long way to go before watermarking will be accepted as a proof in court, and it is likely enough that this may never happen. In copyright-related applications, watermarking must be combined with other mechanisms like encryption to offer reliable protection.

Still, there exist enough applications where watermarking can provide working and successful solutions. Specifically for audio and video it seems that watermarking technology will become widely deployed. The DVD industry standard, as an example, will use watermarking for the copy protection system. Similarly, there exist plans to use watermarking for copy protection for Internet audio distribution. Broadcast monitoring using watermarking is another application that will probably be widely deployed for both audio and video.

Whether the development of watermarking technology will become a success story, or not, is an interesting, but yet unclear question. Watermarking technology will evolve, but attacks on watermarks will as well. Careful overall system design under realistic expectations is crucial for successful applications.

REFERENCES

[1] Emery, O., "Des filigranes du papier," *Bulletin de l'Association technique de l'industrie papetière*, vol. 6, 1958, pp. 185–188.

[2] Weiner, J., and K. Mirkes, *Watermarking*, no. 257 in Bibliographic Series, Appleton, Wisconsin: The Institute of Paper Chemistry, 1972.

[3] Petitcolas, F. A. P., R. J. Anderson, and M. G. Kuhn, "Information Hiding—A Survey," *Proceedings of the IEEE*, vol. 87, no. 7, 1999, pp. 1062–1078.

[4] Tirkel, A., et al., "Electronic Water Mark," in *Proceedings DICTA 1993*, Dec. 1993, pp. 666–672.

[5] Tanaka, K., Y. Nakamura, and K. Matsui, "Embedding Secret Information Into a Dithered Multilevel Image," in *Proceedings of the 1990 IEEE Military Communications Conference*, 1990, pp. 216–220.

[6] Caronni, G., "Ermitteln unauthorisierter Verteiler von maschinenlesbaren Daten," Technical report, ETH Zürich, Switzerland, Aug. 1993.

[7] Roche, S., and J.-L. Dugelay, "Image Watermarking Based on the Fractal Transform," in *Workshop on Multimedia Signal Processing*, IEEE, Los Angeles, California, 7–9 Dec. 1998, pp. 358–363.

[8] Braudaway, G. W., K. A. Magerlein, and F. Mintzer, "Color Correct Digital Watermarking of Images," US patent No. 5,530,759, 1996.

[9] Kutter, M., and F. A. P. Petitcolas, "Fair Benchmarking for Image Watermarking Systems," in *Proceedings of the SPIE 3657, Security and Watermarking of Multimedia Contents*, 1999, pp. 226–239.

[10] Boneh, D., and J. Shaw, "Collusion-Secure Fingerprinting for Digital Data," in *Advances in Cryptology, Proceedings of CRYPTO '95*, vol. 963 of *Lecture Notes in Computer Science*, Springer, 1995, pp. 452–465.

[11] Boneh, D., and J. Shaw, "Collusion-Secure Fingerprinting for Digital Data," *IEEE Transactions on Information Theory*, vol. 44, no. 5, 1998, pp. 1897–1905.

[12] Linnartz, J.-P. M. G., "The 'Ticket' Concept for Copy Control Based on Embedded Signalling," in *Computer Security—5th European Symposium on Research in Computer Security*, vol. 1485 of *Lecture Notes in Computer Science*, Springer, 1998, pp. 257–274.

[13] Bloom, J. A., et al., "Copy Protection for DVD Video," *Proceedings of the IEEE*, vol. 87, no. 7, Jul. 1999.

[14] Schneider, M., and S.-F. Chang, "A Robust Content Based Digital Signature for Image Authentication," in *Proceedings IEEE International Conference on Image Processing 1996*, Lausanne, Switzerland, Sep. 1996.

[15] Xie, L., and G. R. Arce, "A Blind Wavelet Based Digital Signature for Image Authentication," in *Proceedings of the European Signal Processing Conference*, Rhodes, Greece, Sep. 1998.

[16] Hartung, F., J. K. Su, and B. Girod, "Spread Spectrum Watermarking: Malicious Attacks and Counterattacks," in *Proceedings of the SPIE 3657, Security and Watermarking of Multimedia Contents*, 1999, pp. 147–158.

[17] Hartung, F., and B. Girod, "Fast Public-Key Watermarking of Compressed Video," in *Proceedings IEEE International Conference on Image Processing 1997*, vol. 1, Santa Barbara, California, USA, Oct. 1997, pp. 528–531.

[18] Craver, S., et al., "Can invisible watermarks resolve rightful ownerships?" Technical Report RC 20509, IBM Research Devision, Jul. 1996.

[19] Petitcolas, F. A. P., and R. J. Anderson, "Evaluation of copyright marking systems," in *IEEE Multimedia Systems*, Florence, Italy, 7–11 Jun. 1999.

[20] Petitcolas, F. A. P., R. J. Anderson, and M. G. Kuhn, "Attacks on Copyright Marking Systems," in *Proceedings of the Second International Workshop on Information Hiding*, vol. 1525 of *Lecture Notes in Computer Science*, Springer, 1999, pp. 218–238.

[21] Anderson, R. J., "Why Cryptosystems Fail," *Communications of the ACM*, vol. 37, no. 11, Nov. 1994, pp. 32–40.

[22] van den Branden Lambrecht, C. J., and J. E. Farrell, "Perceptual Quality Metric for Digitally Coded Color Images," in *Proceedings of the European Signal Processing Conference*, Trieste, Italy, Sep. 1996, pp. 1175–1178.

[23] Westen, S., R. Lagendijk, and J. Biemond, "Perceptual Image Quality Based on a Multiple Channel HVS Model," in *Proceedings of the IEEE International Conference on Acoustics, Speech, and Signal Processing*, vol. 4, 1995, pp. 2351–2354.

[24] Winkler, S., "A Perceptual Distortion Metric for Digital Color Images," in *Proceedings of the International Conference on Image Processing*, vol. 3, Chicago, IL, Oct. 1998, pp. 399–403.

[25] Winkler, S., "A Perceptual Distortion Metric for Digital Color Video," in *Proceedings of the SPIE 3644, Human Vision and Electronic Imaging*, 1999, pp. 175–184.

[26] Zweig, M. H., and G. Campbell, "Receiver–Operating Characteristics (ROC) Plots: A Fundamental Evaluation Tool in Clinical Medicine," *Clinical Chemistry*, vol. 39, no. 4, 1993, pp. 561–577.

[27] "UnZign watermark removal software," <http://altern.org/watermark/>, 1997.

[28] Petitcolas, F. A. P., and M. G. Kuhn, "StirMark 2," <http://www.cl.cam.ac.uk/~fapp2/watermarking/stirmark/>, 1997.

[29] Petitcolas, F. A. P., and R. J. Anderson, "Weaknesses of Copyright Marking Systems," in *Multimedia and Security—Workshop at ACM Multimedia '98*, 1998, pp. 55–61.

[30] "Talisman," <http://www.cordis.lu/esprit/src/talisman.htm>.

[31] "Octalis," <http://www.cordis.lu/esprit/src/octalis.htm>.

Chapter 6

A survey of current watermarking techniques

Jean-Luc Dugelay and Stéphane Roche

Until now, although existing literature deals with audio and video sources, and explores various security services, the majority of publications in the field of watermarking currently address the copyright of still images. Based on several recent publications related to this most popular facet of watermarking, this chapter discusses the techniques and approaches currently under investigation for data embedding in digital documents.

6.1 INTRODUCTION

Over the past few years, watermarking has emerged as the leading candidate to solve problems of ownership and content authentications for digital multimedia documents (e.g., audio, image, and video). Suppose an owner wants to protect his image rights. For this purpose, he inserts a watermark into the image, hopefully without introducing any visual degradation. When needed, he proves his ownership by retrieving his watermark, despite possible image modifications. It is clear that this type of scenario is based on a robust and invisible signature (for other kinds of watermarks, see Section 5.4). At least, the following three aspects have to be taken into account:

- **Ratio between the information contained in the watermark and in the host signal.** This parameter depends on the nature of the message to be hidden (ID, index or pointer, plain text, logo, etc.)—which itself depends in part on the desired security service—and on the nature of the host signal (text, image, video, sound, etc.).

- **Image degradation due to watermarking.** As in lossy source coding, this criterion is primordial in evaluating the performance of a watermarking system, see Section 5.6.
- **Robustness** of the watermark to "nondestructive" attacks of the image.

In addition to this, as described in Section 5.3, several modes of extraction exist, depending on the necessity to use the original information. Finally, as described in Section 7.4.1 (the "deadlock" problem), some protocol aspects have to be considered in order to design an effective solution. This chapter mainly focuses on the insertion operator, the way of defining it having a decisive effect on watermark properties, for example: visibility, extraction, robustness, and mode of extraction. Since 1992, a wide range of algorithms and techniques have been proposed, emerging from various communities, like steganography, source coding, and communications. Instead of drawing on a collection of paper abstracts that include large overlaps, we present a general outline in which relevant technical key points are introduced according to the current options and solutions proposed in the literature. These major selected key points—which will be detailed in the forthcoming sections—are:

- The selection of pixels or blocks where information will be hidden; in this section, some basic notions of secret and public keys and prediction are addressed.
- The choice of a workspace to perform the hiding operation, for example a spatial domain, or a transform domain such as DCT, Mellin-Fourier, or Wavelet.
- The strategy for formatting the message to be hidden in the host signal (introduction of redundancy, correcting codes).
- The method of merging the message and cover (modulation); the basic idea often consists of imposing a binary relationship between the bits of the message with some selected features of the cover.
- The optimization of the watermark detector. This section mainly deals with operations that are carried out during the extraction process, and that are not dual to those realized during the insertion step (thus, they are not directly deducible from the previous sections). Techniques for compensating some geometrical attacks and blind-mode watermark retrieval are included in this section.
- Concluding this chapter, we will list possible adaptations and extensions of methods from still images to video.

All key points relating to current watermarking techniques are discussed, and draw, when necessary, on a number of related watermarking publications. For readers interested in a specific watermarking scheme and its full description, we list references at the end of the chapter.

6.2 THE CHOICE OF HOST LOCATIONS IN THE COVER: CRYPTOGRAPHIC AND PSYCHOVISUAL ASPECTS

A direct application of Kerckhoffs' principle (see Section 1.2.4) is that the watermarking algorithm should be public and that the full watermark should not be accessible in a straightforward manner in order to prevent casual removal. This is done via the choice of cover-locations where the watermark information will be embedded. In many implementations, a pseudorandom number generator initialized from a secret key determines these locations (one way of doing this was given in Section 3.2.1). This secret key is only known by the owner of the document and correspondingly, he is the only one who can access the watermark in both the insertion and the recovery processes. A more flexible technique allowing public recovery without decreasing the security of the watermark is presented in Section 6.2.2.

Besides security aspects, a good choice of watermark locations is crucial with respect to the visual distortion of the original image. The accuracy of the human visual system varies according to the texture nature of the images. This psychovisual issue of watermark location is discussed in Section 6.2.3.

6.2.1 The Patchwork algorithm

As an example, we will discuss the "patchwork" algorithm, proposed in 1995 by Bender et al. [1]. This algorithm does not as such allow a message to be hidden in a cover, but it simply allows the following binary question to be answered: "Does this person know the key which was used to embed and build a watermark?" In the patchwork algorithm, a secret key is used to initialize a pseudorandom number generator which outputs the locations of the cover which will host the watermark.

The basic version of the patchwork algorithm can be summarized as follows. In the insertion process, the owner selects n-pixel pairs pseudorandomly according to a secret key K_s. He then modifies the luminance values (a_i, b_i) of the n pairs of pixels by using the following formula:

$$\begin{aligned} \tilde{a}_i &= a_i + 1 \\ \tilde{b}_i &= b_i - 1 \end{aligned} \tag{6.1}$$

Thus, the owner simply adds 1 to all values a_i and subtracts 1 from every b_i. In the extraction process, the n-pixel pairs which were used in the encoding step to host the watermark are retrieved, again using the secret key K_s. Then, the sum

$$S = \sum_{i=1}^{n} \tilde{a}_i - \tilde{b}_i \tag{6.2}$$

is computed. If the cover actually contained a watermark, we can expect the sum to be $2n$, otherwise it should be approximately zero. The extraction is based on the statistical assumption

$$\mathbf{E}[S] = \sum_{i=1}^{n} \mathbf{E}[a_i] - \mathbf{E}[b_i] = 0 \tag{6.3}$$

if we randomly choose several pairs of pixels in an image and assume that they are independent and identically distributed. As a consequence, only the owner, who knows the modified locations, can obtain a score close to

$$S \approx 2n \tag{6.4}$$

Since its first appearance, some extensions of this algorithm have been proposed [2, 3] in order to hide a message longer than one bit and increase the robustness of the scheme (one can readily verify that a basic operation such as the translation of one pixel of the image will be sufficient to trap the owner).

6.2.2 Public key cryptography and public watermark recovery

Watermarking algorithms based on a secret key present a major drawback: they do not allow a public recovery of the watermark. In order to overcome this limitation, public key watermarking algorithms have been proposed; such systems consist of two keys: a public and a private one. An image can be watermarked using the private key, whereas the public key is used to verify the mark.

Hartung and Girod [4] introduced the idea of deriving such a public key algorithm from spread spectrum methods. As explained in Section 6.4.1, the direct sequence technique requires the spread sequence S for both spreading and unspreading processes. However, due to the robustness of the encoding, it is possible to reconstruct the original signal without knowledge of the whole spread sequence. Thus, the secret key known only by the owner of the document allows the whole S to be computed, whereas the public key allows only a part of S (S^{pub}) to be computed so that the watermark is kept robust. This portion will, however, suffice to reconstruct the watermark.

In practice, the public spread $\mathcal{S}^{\text{ pub}}$ sequence presents one bit per N equal to the original $\mathcal{S}^{\text{ orig}}$ sequence, whereas all other bits are chosen in a random manner:

$$\mathcal{S}_i{}^{\text{pub}} = \left\{ \begin{array}{ll} \mathcal{S}_i{}^{\text{orig}} & \text{with probability} \frac{1}{N} \\ \text{rand}\{-1, 1\} & \text{otherwise} \end{array} \right. \tag{6.5}$$

Other public key watermarking algorithms are discussed in [5, 6].

6.2.3   Predictive coding for psychovisual watermark management

Predictive models are widely used in source coding, to predict the new value of a signal from its former values. The assumption is that samples or pixels in a neighborhood are highly correlated. This is generally the case, especially in an image where neighboring pixels have related values. So, roughly speaking, predictive coding consists in computing errors between predicted and original values, before encoding these errors in an efficient way. Actually, it is expected that the distribution of errors will be close to zero with a small variance, in which case an efficient binary representation may be obtained using, for instance, Huffman codes.

In the watermarking context, predictive coding is useful for psychovisual reasons. It is well known that the human visual system is less accurate in textured and edge regions, which makes these zones very suitable for watermark locations [7]. On the other hand, human eyes are very sensitive to smooth regions with uniform values, which turn out to be poor candidates for watermark locations. In predictive coding, the error distribution perfectly matches these properties, and the error signal can be used as a modulation carrier for the watermark signal.

Predictive coding is also relevant for watermark systems that do not require the original image [8]. This point is discussed in Section 6.6.

6.3   THE CHOICE OF A WORKSPACE

As we have seen in the case of the patchwork algorithm, the hiding operation can be performed in the spatial domain; nevertheless, this operation is most often carried out in a transform domain. In this section, we first introduce the different spaces proposed in the literature, and second, we present the motivations related to this choice.

6.3.1   Discrete Fourier transform

Widely studied in signal processing, the discrete Fourier transform (DFT) was immediately considered in the field of watermarking in order to offer the possibility of controlling the frequencies of the host signal. It is helpful to select the adequate parts of the image for embedding the watermark in order to obtain the best compromise between visibility and robustness.

Given a two-dimensional signal $f(x, y)$, the DFT is defined to be (see [9] for further description)

$$F(k_1, k_2) = \beta \sum_{n_1=0}^{N_1-1} \sum_{n_2=0}^{N_2-1} f(n_1, n_2) \, \exp(-i2\pi n_1 k_1/N_1 - i2\pi n_2 k_2/N_2) \qquad (6.6)$$

with $\beta = (N_1 N_2)^{-1/2}$ and $i = \sqrt{-1}$. Furthermore, the inverse DFT (IDFT) is given by

$$f(n_1, n_2) = \beta \sum_{k_1=0}^{N_1-1} \sum_{k_2=0}^{N_2-1} F(k_1, k_2) \, \exp(i2\pi k_1 n_1/N_1 + i2\pi k_2 n_2/N_2) \qquad (6.7)$$

The DFT is useful for watermarking purposes in order to perform phase modulation between the watermark and its cover, see Section 6.5.1. This transformation was also applied to split images into perceptual bands, see Section 6.3.5. However, the DFT is more often used in derived forms such as the discrete cosine transform or the Mellin-Fourier transform. The following sections deal with these two transforms.

6.3.2   Discrete cosine transform

In the very early days, the DCT, which was widely studied by the source coding community in the context of JPEG and MPEG [10–12], was also considered to embed a message inside images [13, 14] and videos [7]. For an overview of the DCT see Section 3.3.

The main arguments for using DCT in watermarking are the following. Embedding rules operating in the DCT domain are often more robust to JPEG and MPEG compression; thus the watermark designer can prevent JPEG/MPEG attacks more easily. Furthermore, studies on visibility (i.e., visual distortions) which were previously conducted in the field of source coding can be reused; these studies help to predict the visible impact of the watermark on the cover-image. Last but not least, watermarking in the DCT domain offers the possibility of directly realizing the embedding operator in the compressed domain (i.e., inside a JPEG or MPEG encoder) in order to minimize the computation time.

As described in the following sections, several ways of watermarking via DCT can be considered. First, the DCT coefficients of the image and the DCT coefficients of the watermark can be added [15, 16]. In more subtle algorithms, relationships

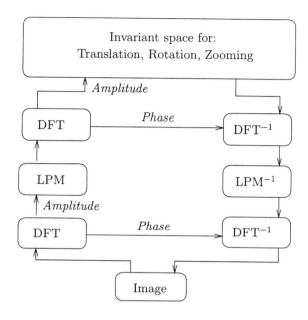

Figure 6.1 Mellin-Fourier transform and its related invariance properties.

between multiple DCT coefficients can be imposed according to the bit values of the watermark [14]. Furthermore, their quantization can be "disturbed" according to the watermark bits [7].

6.3.3 Mellin-Fourier transform

Most watermarking algorithms have problems in extracting the watermark after an affine geometric transformation has been applied on the watermarked object. To overcome this weakness, Ó Ruanaidh et al. [17] have introduced the use of the Mellin-Fourier transform for watermarking.[1]

The transform space of Mellin-Fourier is based on the translation property of the Fourier transform:

$$f(x_1 + a, x_2 + b) \leftrightarrow F(k_1, k_2) \exp\left[-i(ak_1 + bk_2)\right] \qquad (6.8)$$

One can readily verify that only the phase is altered by a translation. As a consequence, if the workspace (i.e., the space in which the watermark will be embedded)

---

1 In [17], they mention that this transformation may also be used in Digimarc's PictureMarc.

is limited to the subspace related to the amplitude of the Fourier transform, it will be insensitive to a spatial shift of the picture. In order to become insensitive to rotation and zoom, let us consider the log-polar mapping (LPM) defined as follows

$$(x,y) \mapsto \begin{cases} x = \exp \rho \, \cos \theta \\ y = \exp \rho \, \sin \theta \end{cases} \text{ with } \rho \in \mathbb{R} \quad \text{and} \quad \theta \in [0, 2\pi] \tag{6.9}$$

It is obvious that the rotation of any element (x, y) in the cartesian coordinate system will result in a translation in the logarithmic coordinate system. In a similar way, a zoom will result in a translation in the polar coordinate system, see Figure 6.1.

Using an adequate modification of the coordinate system, both rotations and zooms can be reduced to a translation. The property of translation invariance can thus be used to construct a space insensitive to any rotation or zoom operations carried out on a watermarked image.

6.3.4   Wavelet domain

Wavelets are becoming a key technique in the ongoing source compression standard JPEG-2000. In several recent publications, this technique has been applied to image watermarking. The positive arguments closely resemble those for advocating DCT for JPEG (i.e. preventing watermark removal by JPEG-2000 lossy compression, reusing previous studies on source coding regarding the visibility of image degradations, and offering the possibility of embedding in the compressed domain). In addition to these criteria, the multiresolution aspect of wavelets is helpful in managing a good distribution (i.e., location) of the message in the cover in terms of robustness versus visibility. Extensive information on wavelet transform and its applications to image processing and coding can be found in [18–21].

Roughly speaking, the wavelet transform consists in a multiscale spatial-frequency decomposition of an image. Figure 6.2 shows the Lena's decomposition with three scale factors. The lowest frequency band at the lowest scale factor is found in the top-left corner (LL_3). At the same resolution level, the block HL_3 contains information about the highest horizontal and lowest vertical frequency band. Similarly, the block LH_3 contains information about the lowest horizontal and the highest vertical frequency band at the lowest scale factor. The same process is repeated for the intermediate and highest resolution levels.

One way to construct these different levels of resolution is to cascade two-channel filter banks and a down-sampling process as suggested in Figure 6.3. The two-channel filter banks must be orthogonal and are defined by the equations

$$H(\omega) \;=\; \sum_k h_k \exp(-j \, k \, \omega) \qquad \text{high pass}$$

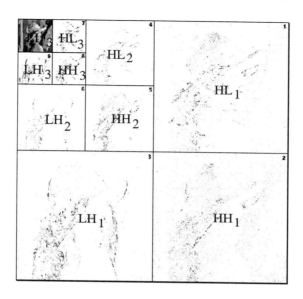

Figure 6.2   Multiscale decomposition. Courtesy of M. Antonini.

$$G(\omega) \;=\; \sum_{k} g_k \exp(-j\,k\,\omega) \qquad \text{low pass} \tag{6.10}$$

Then the iterative process of the decomposition is given by

$$
\begin{aligned}
c_{j-1,k} &= \sum_{n} h_{n-2k} c_{j,n} \\
d_{j-1,k} &= \sum_{n} g_{n-2k} c_{j,n}
\end{aligned}
\tag{6.11}
$$

whereas the iterative reconstruction process is defined by

$$c_{j,n} = \sum_{k} h_{n-2k} c_{j-1,k} + \sum_{k} g_{n-2k} d_{j-1,k} \tag{6.12}$$

There were many attempts in using the wavelet transform in watermarking; we will discuss some schemes briefly. Wang and Kuo [22] suggest a multithreshold wavelet coding scheme allowing significant coefficient searching. They assume that these coefficients do not change much after several signal processing operations. Moreover, if these coefficients lose their fidelity significantly, the reconstructed image

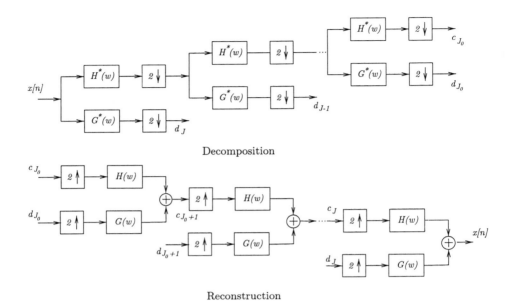

Decomposition

Reconstruction

Figure 6.3   Wavelet transform.

could be perceptually different from the original one. Contrary to the methods which select a predefined set of coefficients (for instance low-frequency coefficients), the resulting method is image dependent. Thus, this method is suitable for textured as well as smooth images.

Kundur et al. [23] describe a watermarking method using wavelet-based fusion. It consists in adding wavelet coefficients of the watermark and the image at different resolution levels. Prior to being added, the wavelet coefficients of the watermark are modulated using a human visual-model constraint based on a measure called saliency [24].

Furthermore, Xia et al. [25] suggest a hierarchical watermark extraction process based on the wavelet transformation. The purpose of such a process is to save computational load if the distortion of the watermarked image is not serious. The basic idea consists in decomposing the received image and the original one (assumed to be known) with the discrete wavelet transform (DWT) into four bands (i.e., only level one). They then compare the watermark added in the HH_1 band and the difference of the DWT coefficients in HH_1 bands of the received and the original images by calculating their cross correlations. If there is a peak in the cross correlations, the

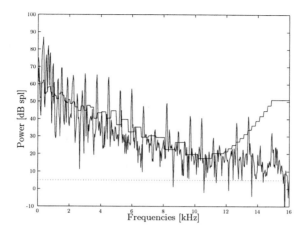

Figure 6.4   Acoustic masking properties. Courtesy of N. Moreau.

watermark is considered detected, otherwise they consider the other bands at the same level (i.e., HL_1, LH_1). In case the watermark still cannot be detected, they compute a new level of the DWT (i.e., level two) and try to detect the watermark again. This process is performed until the watermark is detected or the last level of the DWT has been reached.

Other schemes based on DWT are also proposed in references [25–28].

6.3.5   Split image in perceptual bands

A central requirement of watermarking schemes seems to be the invisibility of the watermark. Delaigle et al. [29] have developed a masking model based on the human visual system in order to minimize the visual impact of a watermark. The ultimate objective is to design an iterative scheme that allows the perceptual model results to be taken into account and then to maintain the watermark below the visibility threshold [30]. This possibility is under investigation for image and video. However, the principle of masking has already been used in the field of audio coding [31], as suggested in Figure 6.4, where energy located in one frequency band may cause that band to mask a neighboring band of lower energy. In the same way, the authors assume that the human visual system splits the visual stimulus into several components [32, 33]. Each component is described according to three parameters:

- The location in the visual field;

- The spatial frequency (computed from the amplitude of the Fourier transform);
- The orientation (computed from the phase of the Fourier transform).

These components are transmitted from the eyes to the cortex through different channels. The masking effect occurs when a channel component is invisible due to a higher energy component in a neighboring channel. Roughly speaking (for more details see [29, 34]), the image is split into several channels using an image analysis technique (e.g., Gabor filters). Then a local energy is computed for each of the channels. Finally, a contrast function depending on the frequency, the orientation, and the location of the channel is computed. This allows a psychovisual mask to be determined so that every signal with an energy below this mask will be invisible.

6.4   FORMATTING THE WATERMARK BITS

This section will address the problem of formatting the watermark bits before the embedding process. Some techniques allow any bitstring to be directly embedded as a watermark, other ones need a transformation of the watermark bits prior to the embedding process.

6.4.1   Spread spectrum

Spread spectrum techniques for watermarking purposes have aroused a lot of interest [35, 36]. The reasons for this are very similar to the arguments for using SS techniques in steganography. Generally, the message used to watermark is a narrow-band signal compared to the wide band of the cover (image). Spread spectrum techniques applied to the message allow the frequency bands to be matched before transmitting the message (watermark) through the covert channel (image). Furthermore, high frequencies are relevant for the invisibility of the watermarked message but are inefficient as far as robustness is concerned, whereas low frequencies are of interest with regard to robustness but are useless because of the unacceptable visible impact. Spread spectrum can reconcile these conflicting points by allowing a low-energy signal to be embedded in each one of the frequency bands. Spread spectrum techniques also offer the possibility of protecting the watermark privacy using a secret key to control a pseudonoise generator.

We will now present the two main spread spectrum methods which we have already mentioned in Section 3.4. More information can be obtained from [37].

Direct-sequence spreading consists of a time modulation of the original signal using a wide-band pseudonoise signal as shown in Figure 6.5. The resulting signal looks like the pseudonoise signal. In particular, the spectrum of the resulting signal

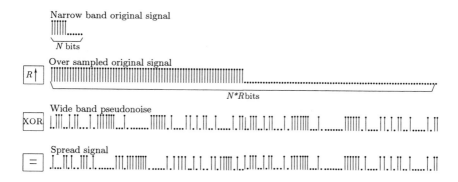

Figure 6.5   Spreading using direct-sequence spread spectrum.

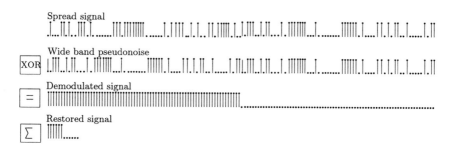

Figure 6.6   Unspreading using direct-sequence spread spectrum.

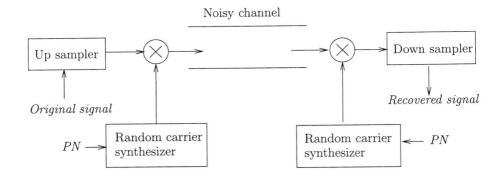

Figure 6.7   Frequency-hopping as a spread spectrum technique.

and the pseudonoise signal are similar, even if the original signal was narrow band. At the receiver, the original signal is reconstructed by demodulation of the received signal using the same pseudonoise signal (see Figure 6.6). The original signal is recovered without error even if some frequencies were dismissed during data transmission because the original information is located in several frequency bands. In *frequency-hopping spread spectrum*, using a random process, the carrier frequency is altered, describing a wide range of frequency values. As a result, the modulated signal has a wide spectrum (see Figure 6.7).

In both approaches, the resynchronization between the received signal and the random signal is the main issue of the recovery process. It requires knowledge of the random process used during the modulation. In particular, for watermarking issues, synchronization problems occur after geometrical attacks are performed on the image.

We will now present a practical watermarking scheme proposed by Hartung et al. [36, 38]. This method is part of a video scheme. Nevertheless, it is also applicable to still images. Let a_j, $(a_j \in \{-1, 1\})$, be a binary signal. From a_i we derive a signal b_i which is a temporal stretching of a_i

$$b_i = a_j, \qquad j\,cr \le i < (j+1)\,cr \tag{6.13}$$

We note by cr the chip rate. Now a modulation is performed between b_i and a pseudonoise signal p_i in order to obtain the watermark signal which will be directly embedded in the image v_i,

$$w_i = \alpha\, b_i\, p_i \tag{6.14}$$

where α is a strength factor controlling the robustness versus visibility trade-off. The final embedding formula is

$$\tilde{v}_i = v_i + \alpha\, b_i\, p_i \tag{6.15}$$

where $\tilde{v}_i$ denotes the watermarked image.

The basic idea of watermark recovery is to demodulate the received signal and to add each signal component corresponding to each piece of binary information:

$$
\begin{aligned}
s_j &= \sum_{i=jcr}^{(j+1)cr-1} p_i\, \tilde{v}_i \\
&= \sum_{i=jcr}^{(j+1)cr-1} p_i\, v_i + \sum_{i=jcr}^{(j+1)cr-1} p_i^2\, \alpha\, b_i
\end{aligned}
\tag{6.16}
$$

Assuming that the p_i signal is zero-mean and is statistically independent with v_i, we can expect s_j to be

$$s_j \approx cr\,\alpha\,a_j \tag{6.17}$$

Thus, a_j is given by

$$a_j = sign(s_j) \tag{6.18}$$

6.4.2   Low frequency watermark design

It is commonly admitted that a watermark must survive all image manipulations that do not damage an image beyond usability. Among these manipulations, many are based on low-pass filtering (e.g., JPEG compression, resizing). This is the reason why many authors [35, 39] advocate designing a low-pass watermark although it creates more visible artifacts by producing patterns with larger features than a high-pass watermark. Braudaway [39] creates a low-pass watermark using the Fourier transform. The process can be described as follows (see also Figure 6.8).

Given the initial watermark $w_{init}(i,j)$, a redundant watermark of the size of the original image, a reduced-size watermark $w_{redu}(i',j')$ is created and its Fourier transform, denoted $W_{redu}(u,v)$, is computed. $W_{redu}(u,v)$ is then padded with zeros until the initial watermark size is reached. Finally, the inverse discrete Fourier transform of $W_{zero-pad}(u',v')$ is computed. The resulting image $w_{low-pass}(i,j)$ is the low-pass watermark; this process assures that only low frequencies will be present in $w_{low-pass}(i,j)$.

6.4.3   Error-correcting codes

Numerous papers [29, 40–42] mention the possibility of using error-correcting codes in order to improve the basic algorithms in terms of watermark robustness. This

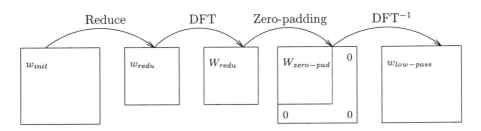

Figure 6.8   Generation of a low-pass watermark.

approach appears natural if one compares the watermarking problem with the transmission of a signal over a noisy channel. This model considers the image as a channel and the different attacks as a noise signal. Error-correcting codes are widely used in channel coding which makes them relevant for watermarking issues. Unfortunately, to the best of our knowledge, only a few papers mention significant results for watermarking systems. This lack of results can be partly explained by the following reasons.

As opposed to the "classical" channel coding applications where the noise signal can generally be efficiently modeled as a Gaussian noise, watermarking applications must take into account several attacks (see Chapter 7) representing a wide range of noises of different natures. The Gaussian assumption is then no longer valid. In this context, it is very difficult to design a unique code that could meet the different requirements coming from different attacks.

Since the support for the watermark is finite and static, especially if you consider a still image, it is sometimes impossible to extend the initial binary flow of the watermark in order to use an error-correcting code. This situation is quite different for video or audio data where watermarks can be spread over several frames, if required. For this purpose, the ratio between the watermark and the image plays an important role.

The use of error-correcting codes for watermarking is still an open problem. It requires the design of error-correcting codes which are very compact and able to take into account many different kinds of noise.

6.5   MERGING THE WATERMARK AND THE COVER

Until now, the original watermark data and the original image have been independently processed to comply with watermarking requirements. This section addresses techniques for merging the watermark and the cover in order to obtain the watermarked image. In particular, the merging step allows the robustness versus visibility trade-off to be managed in relation to the respective energies of the watermark and the image.

6.5.1 Phase modulation

Let $F(I)$ be the DFT of an image I. As I is real, the DFT properties imply that $F(I)$ is complex; $F(I)$ would be real if the image were symmetric. This leads to a magnitude and phase representation of the image.

Ó Ruanaidh and Dowling [43] reported that the phase modulation could be eligible for robust watermarking. Two considerations led them to this conclusion. The first one concerns the importance of phase components on the intelligibility of an image. According to Hayes [44], the phase components of the DFT have more psychovisual impact than magnitude components. As a consequence, if the watermark is introduced in phase components with high redundancy, malicious parties would need to cause unacceptable damage to the quality of the image in order to remove the watermark. The second one is a result of communication theory. It is well known that a phase modulation has superior robustness against noise signals. In addition, Ó Ruanaidh mentions that phase watermarking survives changes of image contrast.

In order to obtain a real watermarked image, phase modulation watermarking must respect the negative symmetry of the DFT-transformed image; thus, if δ is the watermark level, the frequency components can be modified as follows (we use the same notations as in Section 3.3):

$$\phi(k_1, k_2) \quad \leftarrow \quad \phi(k_1, k_2) + \delta \tag{6.19}$$

$$\phi(N_1 - k_1, N_2 - k_2) \quad \leftarrow \quad \phi(N_1 - k_1, N_2 - k_2) - \delta \tag{6.20}$$

A DFT coefficient $F(k_1, k_2)$ will be relevant for watermarking, if its energy is high enough to have a significant impact on the image, that is, if

$$A(k_1, k_2)^2 / \sum_{r_1=1}^{N_1-1} \sum_{r_2=1}^{N_2-1} A(r_1, r_2)^2 > \varepsilon \tag{6.21}$$

This guarantees that attacks against the watermark will cause inacceptable loss of the image quality.

6.5.2 Amplitude modulation

As mentioned in the previous section, amplitude modulation in the Fourier domain does not seem suitable for watermarking purposes, due to the minor contribution of the Fourier amplitude component in the image quality. However, amplitude modulation can be performed successfully directly in the image spatial domain or in part of it. For instance, Kutter et al. [8] propose amplitude modulation of the blue component of an image. Let $I = (R, G, B)$ be a color image, $p = (i, j)$ a random location in the image (see Section 6.2.1), and $m = \{0, 1\}$ a binary digit of the watermark. The new (watermarked) blue component $\tilde{B}$ is derived from B by the following relationship:

$$\tilde{B}_{ij} \leftarrow B_{ij} + (2m - 1)qY_{ij} \qquad (6.22)$$

where Y is the luminance component (see Section 3.1), and q the strength constant balancing the robustness versus visibility trade-off. Note that according to this formula high-luminance values are favored for strong watermarking, assuming that human eyes present less acuteness in high-luminance values.

6.5.3 Merging that preserves the luminance average

This method is based on the classification of image areas by pixel clustering into a set of homogeneous parts. The algorithm presented in [45] can be summarized as follows:

- Select the image blocks that will host the watermark according to a secret key.
- Classify the pixels inside each block either as a member of a high-contrast region or as a member of a low- or mid-contrast region. Hence, for each block, two regions can be defined: R_1 and R_2, for which the mean luminance values are computed.
- Split both R_1 and R_2 into two labelled areas A or B according to a predefined grid. Hence, four subareas have been defined: $R_{1,A}$, $R_{1,B}$, $R_{2,A}$, and $R_{2,B}$ including, respectively, $n_{1,A}$, $n_{1,B}$, $n_{2,A}$ and $n_{2,B}$ pixels associated with the average luminance values $Y_{1,A}$, $Y_{1,B}$, $Y_{2,A}$ and $Y_{2,B}$.
- Let m be the watermark bit to hide in a block. The embedding operation can then be defined by

$$
\begin{aligned}
\text{if } m = 0 \quad \tilde{Y}_{1,A} - \tilde{Y}_{1,B} &= -l \\
\tilde{Y}_{2,A} - \tilde{Y}_{2,B} &= -l \\
\text{if } m = 1 \quad \tilde{Y}_{1,A} - \tilde{Y}_{1,B} &= l \\
\tilde{Y}_{2,A} - \tilde{Y}_{2,B} &= l
\end{aligned}
$$

where l is the embedding level. Since the average luminance values of R_1 and R_2 should be preserved, we can define two other equations:

$$\frac{n_{1,A}\tilde{Y}_{1,A} + n_{1,B}\tilde{Y}_{1,B}}{n_{1,A} + n_{1,B}} = Y_1 \tag{6.23}$$

$$\frac{n_{2,A}\tilde{Y}_{2,A} + n_{2,B}\tilde{Y}_{2,B}}{n_{2,A} + n_{2,B}} = Y_2 \tag{6.24}$$

These equations allow the values of $\tilde{Y}_{1,A}$, $\tilde{Y}_{2,A}$, $\tilde{Y}_{1,B}$ and $\tilde{Y}_{2,B}$ to be computed according to the bit value b of the message to be hidden.

- Each pixel from the same region is then modified by an offset $\delta_{i,j}$

$$\delta_{i,j} = \tilde{Y}_{i,j} - Y_{i,j} \tag{6.25}$$

The first three steps of the extraction are identical to the ones defined for the insertion. Then, we compute $\sigma_1 = \tilde{Y}_{1,A} - \tilde{Y}_{1,B}$ and $\sigma_2 = \tilde{Y}_{2,A} - \tilde{Y}_{2,B}$. Their signs allow the value of the bit b to be deduced. Moreover, their magnitudes can provide some information regarding the accuracy of the retrieval, and as a consequence, a confidence score for each extracted bit. In the context of a copyright application, only some tens of bits are considered. Hence, some redundancies can be added in the message.

6.5.4   Merging based on DCT coefficient quantization

As mentioned in Section 6.3.2, the DCT domain seems to be relevant for watermarking. In this section we describe one way to combine the DCT coefficients from the image and the watermark. This method is based on a constrained quantization of the original DCT coefficients. The insertion part of the algorithm proposed in 1995 by Koch and Zhao [13, 14] can be outlined as follows.

Given a sequence of bits m to be hidden in a picture, the sender selects (according to a secret key) k blocks of size 8×8 in the image. If not already done, the DCT coefficients $\{a_{i,j}\}_{i,j=1,\dots,8}$ of each selected block are computed. The owner then looks at the relationship between two DCT coefficients of one block and the next watermark bit. If needed, he makes a modification in order to impose a specific relationship between the selected two coefficients. More precisely, for all watermarking bits $k = 1, \dots, \ell(m)$, do the following: if $(m_k = 1$ and $(a_{1,2})_k > (a_{2,1})_k)$ or $(m_k = 0$ and $(a_{1,2})_k < (a_{2,1})_k)$, the desired relation is already enforced and no modifications are needed. Otherwise, the two DCT coefficients are exchanged to satisfy the corresponding relations. If required, the owner computes the inverse DCT for all modified image blocks.

Because of these modifications, one image block hosts exactly one watermark bit. To retrieve the mark, the relations between the coefficients $(a_{1,2})_k$ and $(a_{2,1})_k$ are examined. The kth bit of the watermark is assumed to be zero, if $(a_{1,2})_k < (a_{2,1})_k$, and one otherwise.

Unfortunately, the proposed algorithm can generate visible artifacts. Several improvements were proposed in order to optimize this approach, including the way of selecting blocks (i.e., if the owner is not able to enforce the desired relation without making visible changes, several image blocks are not used for embedding watermark bits), the number of DCT coefficients to be considered (three instead of only two) and the way of modifying the DCT coefficient values.

6.5.5   Merging based on block substitution in fractal coding

This approach, based on fractal coding, was proposed by Puate et al. [46]. We will first briefly review fractal image coding here.

Let I_{orig} be the image to be compressed, I_0 an arbitrary initial image, I and J two generic images, and $d(I, J)$, a distortion measure which measures the dissimilarity between images. A transformation τ that maps an image into another is said to be contractive if: $d(\tau(I), \tau(J)) < \sigma\, d(I, J)$ with $0 < \sigma < 1$, where σ is the contractivity of σ. Then $\tau^n(I_0)$ converges to an attractor I_a as n approaches infinity, where I_a is independent of I_0. The collage theorem states that if there exists a transformation τ such that, $d(I_{\text{orig}}, \tau(I_{\text{orig}})) < \varepsilon$ and τ is contractive with contractivity σ, then $d(I_{\text{orig}}, I_a) < \varepsilon/(1 - \sigma)$. The task of the encoder is to determine a transformation τ (an "IFS code") for which $\tau(I_{\text{orig}})$ is as similar as possible to I_{orig}, subject to a limitation on the number of bits needed to specify τ. The IFS code τ is transmitted to the decoder which then computes the attractor I_a as the reconstructed image. The reconstruction error is upper-bounded by the collage theorem.

In Jacquin's approach [47], the encoder finds the transformation τ from the original image I_{orig} as a sum of affine transformations τ_i, one for each range block R_i, each of which maps a particular domain block into the corresponding range block R_i. The domain and range are partitioned at different resolutions; typically with square range blocks of size $B \times B$ and domain blocks of size $2\,B \times 2\,B$ (generally B is 8 pixels). For each range block, the encoder searches for the best collage match from a suitably transformed and selected domain block. For this search, candidate domain blocks are transformed in three steps, by performing subsampling, isometry, and scale and shift operations on the block luminance values, as shown in Figure 6.9.

To decode an image, the received IFS code τ is applied to an arbitrary initial image I_0 to form an image I_1. The process is repeated to obtain I_2 from I_1, and so on, until it reaches I_a. Typically, fewer than ten iterations are needed for convergence. More information regarding fractal image encoding can be found in [47, 48].

For watermarking purposes, the key idea is to impose an additional constraint regarding the search window during the matching. For example, instead of scanning the whole image, two parts can be defined, as shown in Figure 6.10. According to

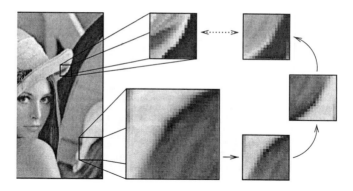

Figure 6.9   Fractal coding: an example of matching between range block and domain block via a rotation and an invert luminance transformation

the bit value of the message to be hidden, only one of them will be considered. More precisely, the insertion process can be outlined as follows:

- Given m, a sequence of bits to be hidden, with a redundancy U;
- For each bit m_k, select U-range blocks (randomly chosen *via* a secret key, only known to the user);
  - If $(m_k = 1)$ then R_k is encoded by searching its candidate domain block D_i in local searching regions type 0 (see Figure 6.10);
  - otherwise (i.e., $m_k = 0$), R_k is encoded by searching D_k in local searching regions of type 1;
- The remaining range blocks R_k are encoded by searching for D_k in the union of the search regions of type 1 and type 0, as in the case of "classical" fractal image coding;
- Compute the attractor.

The extraction process consists of two steps:

- From the attractor and each signed block $\tilde{R}_k$ (indicated via the secret key), find its associated domain block $\tilde{D}_k$; if $\tilde{D}_k$ belongs to region of type 1, then a "1" was embedded, otherwise a "0" has been embedded;
- For each bit m_k, the final decision is taken by considering the majority of "0" or "1" in the set of U responses.

This approach exploits the fact that an attractor is invariant, that is to say, it can be encoded without error (i.e., using the same IFS code apart from some blocks

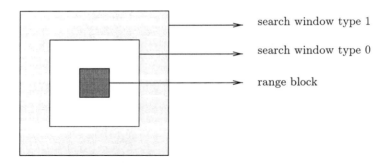

Figure 6.10   Search windows used in fractal coding.

for which multiple solutions could exist). Nevertheless, for the majority of attacks, this property is no longer verified.

6.6   OPTIMIZATION OF THE WATERMARK RECEIVER

Most of the receiver operations are directly derived from the insertion algorithm; however, others are specific to the recovery process. These operations are the core of this section. They allow the watermark detection robustness to be improved by taking into account possible luminance values or geometrical manipulations.

6.6.1   Image prefiltering

Many embedding algorithms rely on a statistical assumption about the host signal. To make this assumption as reliable as possible during the retrieval process, the watermarked image is filtered before starting the extraction of the message [49]. To continue the example given in Section 6.4.1, the authors [38] proposed to carry out the extraction from a filtered version $\tilde{v}'$ instead of $\tilde{v}$. In the context of amplitude modulation (see Section 6.5.2), Kutter suggests that it is more suitable to perform the watermark recovery from a Gaussian signal with a zero average and a small variance. Such a signal can be obtained from a convolution between the watermarked image and the following mask given in [50]:

$$h = \frac{1}{12} \begin{bmatrix} 0 & 0 & 0 & -1 & 0 & 0 & 0 \\ 0 & 0 & 0 & -1 & 0 & 0 & 0 \\ 0 & 0 & 0 & -1 & 0 & 0 & 0 \\ -1 & -1 & -1 & 12 & -1 & -1 & -1 \\ 0 & 0 & 0 & -1 & 0 & 0 & 0 \\ 0 & 0 & 0 & -1 & 0 & 0 & 0 \\ 0 & 0 & 0 & -1 & 0 & 0 & 0 \end{bmatrix}$$

6.6.2 Phase-correlation maxima for reorientation and resizing

An easy way of overcoming some geometrical attacks such as rotation or zoom would be to apply inverse transformations of all possible attacks, with more or less accuracy. Then, the retriever would have to define which reverse transformation provided the best result. The choice of the correct (or at least an adequate) transformation to apply on the watermarked image is often suggested by a knowledge of the original documents (i.e., one knows the original image or the embedded watermark).

In order to take into account possible reorientations and resizing of the watermarked image, two strategies have emerged. The first one, presented in Section 6.3.3, is to embed the watermark in a scale-rotation invariant space. The second one, presented here, consists of an *a posteriori* estimation of the geometrical transformation of the attacked image and then the application of the reverse transform before recovering the mark. In other words, the first approach is preventive whereas the second one is curative. The main advantage of the last approach compared to the preventive methods is that it does not decrease the watermark capacity by restricting the choice of watermark locations to an invariant subspace, which could be small. This advantage has to be balanced by the difficulty of performing an efficient transformation estimation as required in the curative approach. Such an approach is proposed by Braudaway [39]. His method is based on phase-correlation maxima and requires either a fragment of the original image or the original watermark as a reference plane. The plot of a three-dimensional grid of phase-correlation maximum is performed. Axes of the grid correspond to the horizontal-scale factor, the vertical-scale factor, and the angle of rotation of the correlation reference plane relative to the watermarked image (possibly manipulated). This three-dimensional grid allows the greatest phase-correlation maximum to be determined. The coordinates of this maxima give the values of the horizontal-scale factor, the vertical-scale factor, and finally the angle of rotation.

6.6.3   Adaptive threshold improving decision robustness

Most of the decision process concerning the bit-value recovery is performed by comparing the extracted value to a threshold. Unfortunately, due to attacks on the watermarked image, the optimum threshold is different from the insertion and extraction stages. Kutter [8] suggests introducing constant bits in the watermark allowing a new optimum threshold to be computed during the extraction.

6.7   EXTENSIONS FROM STILL IMAGES TO VIDEO

The general trade-off (ratio, visibility, and robustness) included in a watermarking algorithm is (of course) significantly modified when considering video instead of images. The modification of the ratio between the information contained in a given watermark and in the host signal becomes less critical. Nevertheless, because of the temporal dimension, the visual distortion due to watermarking is even more difficult to manage. Also, the list of possible attacks increases; for example, a video watermarking scheme has to consider some possible frame-rate conversions. Above all, the problem of the complexity of computation is now primordial when real-time watermarking is desired. Most studies on watermarking have mainly concerned still images, so far. Hence, more than audio and image, video watermarking remains an open problem. Some basic questions such as: "Would a video watermarking strategy perform better if it included a time-varying strategy?" are currently under investigation. In any case, most of the basic ideas defined for still images can also be used for moving pictures. For example, the method in [51] based on the addition of DCT coefficients from the host signal and the watermark can be realized on JPEG streams as well as on I frames from MPEG streams (as proposed in [36, 52]). Nevertheless, some new problems related to the temporal dimension of videos have to be overcome. In this particular case, as underlined by the authors, there is a possible drift problem. In short, some distortions introduced when embedding I frames can also damage neighboring P and B frames due to the motion compensation module included in the MPEG video encoder/decoders [53].

6.7.1   Motion vector quantization

In a similar way to the previously presented approaches based on the perturbation of DCT coefficients of images, Jordan [54] suggests that the motion vector quantization be disturbed according to the bits of the message, in order to embed a message inside a video MPEG stream. As seen in the previous sections, several possibilities have been presented to impose a relationship between watermark information and image features. In [7], instead of using the closest integer to quantify the value of a given float DCT coefficient, the authors consider the closest even integer when the bit of the message to be hidden is "0" and the closest odd integer when the bit of the message to be hidden is "1." For video, in [54], the authors suggest that the quantization of the motion parameters be disturbed in the same manner.

6.8 CONCLUDING REMARKS

In this chapter, based on several key points of watermarking, a wide range of techniques have been presented. Due to the variety of aimed applications (copyright but also integrity, nonrepudiation), the unlimited possible attacks, the different nature of host signals (audio, image, video) which can be considered, the complex trade-off between visibility and robustness, and the different modes of watermark extraction, one of the major challenges of watermarking is the ability to evaluate and compare the performances of the schemes found in the literature. The next chapter is dedicated to this important and difficult aspect of watermarking.

REFERENCES

[1] Bender, W., D. Gruhl, and N. Morimoto, "Techniques for Data Hiding," in *Proceedings of the SPIE 2420, Storage and Retrieval for Image and Video Databases III*, 1995, pp. 164–173.

[2] Langelaar, G. C., J. C. A. Van der Lubbe, and R. L. Lagendijk, "Robust Labeling Methods for Copy Protection of Images," in *Proceedings of SPIE 3022, Storage and Retrieval for Image and Video Databases V*, 1997, pp. 298–309.

[3] Pitas, I., and T. H. Kaskalis, "Applying Signatures on Digital Images," in *IEEE Workshop on Nonlinear Signal and Image Processing*, Thessaloniki, Greece, Oct. 1995, pp. 460–463.

[4] Hartung, F., and B. Girod, "Fast Public-Key Watermarking of Compressed Video," in *International Conference on Image Processing*, Santa Barbara, California, Oct. 1997.

[5] Wong, P. W., "A Public Key Watermark for Image Verification and Authentication," in *Proceedings of the International Conference on Image Processing*, vol. 1, Chicago, Illinois, Oct. 1998.

[6] Memon, N., and P. W. Wong, "Buyer-seller Watermarking Protocol Based on Amplitude Modulation and the El Gamal Public-Key Cryptosystem," in *Proceedings of the SPIE 3657, Security and Watermarking of Multimedia Contents*, 1999, pp. 289–294.

[7] Matsui, K., and K. Tanaka, "Video-steganography: How to Secretly Embed a Signature in a Picture," *Journal of the Interactive Multimedia Association Intellectual Property Project*, vol. 1, no. 1, 1994, pp. 187–206.

[8] Kutter, M., F. Jordan, and F. Bossen, "Digital Signature of Color Images Using Amplitude Modulation," in *Proceedings of the SPIE 3022, Storage and Retrieval for Image and Video Databases V*, 1997, pp. 518–526.

[9] Pratt, W. K., *Digital Image Processing*, New York: Wiley, 1991.

[10] Wallace, G. K., "The JPEG Still Picture Compression Standard," *Communications of the ACM*, vol. 34, no. 4, 1991, pp. 40–44.

[11] Pennebaker, W. B., and J. L. Mitchell, *JPEG Still Image Data Compression Standard*, New York: Van Nostrand Reinhold Company, 1992.

[12] Rao, K. R., and P. Yip, *Discrete Cosine Transform: Algorithms, Advantages, Applications*, New York: Academic Press, 1990.

[13] Koch, E., and J. Zhao, "Towards Robust and Hidden Image Copyright Labeling," in *IEEE Workshop on Nonlinear Signal and Image Processing*, Thessaloniki, Greece, Oct. 1995, pp. 452–455.

[14] Zhao, J., "A WWW Service to Embed and Prove Digital Copyright Watermarks," in *Proceedings of the European Conference on Multimedia Applications, Services and Techniques*, 1996, pp. 695–709.

[15] Johnson, N. F., and S. Jajodia, "Exploring Steganography: Seeing the Unseen," *IEEE Computer*, vol. 31, no. 2, 1998, pp. 26–34.

[16] Johnson, N. F., and S. Jajodia, "Steganalysis of Images Created Using Current Steganography Software," in *Proceedings of the Second International Workshop on Information Hiding*, vol. 1525 of *Lecture Notes in Computer Science*, Springer, 1998, pp. 273–289.

[17] Ó Ruanaidh, J. J. K., and T. Pun, "Rotation, Translation and Scale Invariant Digital Image Watermarking," in *Proceedings of the International Conference on Image Processing*, vol. 1, Santa Barbara, California, Oct. 1997, pp. 536–539.

[18] Mallat, S., *A Wavelet Tour of Signal Processing*, London: Academic Press, 1998.

[19] Vetterli, M., and J. Kovačević, *Wavelets and Subband Coding*, Englewood Cliffs: Prentice Hall, 1995.

[20] Antonini, M., et al., "Image Coding Using Wavelet Transform," *IEEE Transactions on Image Processing*, vol. 1, no. 2, 1992, pp. 205–220.

[21] Daubechies, I., *Ten Lectures on Wavelets*, SIAM Press, 1992.

[22] Wang, H.-J., and C.-C. J. Kuo, "Image Protection via Watermarking on Perceptually Significant Wavelet Coefficients," in *Proceedings of the IEEE Multimedia Signal Processing Workshop*, Redondo Beach, California, Dec. 1998, pp. 279–284.

[23] Kundur, D., and D. Hatzinakos, "A Robust Digital Image Watermarking Method Using Wavelet-Based Fusion," in *Proceedings of the International Conference on Image Processing*, vol. 1, Santa Barbara, California, Oct. 1997, pp. 544–547.

[24] Wilson, T. A., S. K. Rogers, and L. R. Myers, "Perceptual-Based Hyperspectral Image Fusion Using Multiresolution Analysis," *Optical Engineering*, vol. 34, 1995, pp. 3154–3164.

[25] Xia, X.-G., C. G. Boncelet, and G. R. Arce, "Wavelet Transform Based Watermark for Digital Images," *Optics Express*, vol. 3, no. 12, 1998, pp. 497–511.

[26] Kundur, D., and D. Hatzinakos, "Digital Watermarking Using Multiresolution Wavelet Decomposition," in *Proceedings of the IEEE International Conference on Acoustics, Speech and Signal Processing*, vol. 6, 1998, pp. 2969–2972.

[27] Swanson, M. D., B. Zhu, and A. Tewfik, "Multiresolution Scene-Based Video Watermarking Using Perceptual Models," *IEEE Journal on Selected Areas in Communications*, vol. 16, no. 4, 1998, pp. 540–550.

[28] Zeng, W., B. Liu, and S. Lei, "Extraction of Multiresolution Watermark Images for Claiming Rightful Ownership," in *Proceedings of the SPIE 3657, Security and Watermarking of Multimedia Contents*, 1999, pp. 404–414.

[29] Delaigle, J.-F., C. De Vleeschouwer, and B. Macq, "Watermarking Using a Matching

Model Based on the Human Visual System," École thématique CNRS GDR-PRC ISIS: Information Signal Images, Marly le Roi, 1997.

[30] Bartolini, F., et al., "Mask Building for Perceptually Hiding Frequency Embedded Watermarks," in *Proceedings of the International Conference on Image Processing*, vol. 1, Chicago, Illinois, USA, Oct. 1998, pp. 450–454.

[31] Moreau, N., *Techniques de compression des signaux*, Collection technique et scientifique des télécommunications, Masson, 1995.

[32] Westen, S., R. Lagendijk, and J. Biemond, "Perceptual Image Quality Based on a Multiple Channel HVS Model," in *Proceedings of the IEEE International Conference on Acoustics, Speech and Signal Processing*, vol. 4, 1995, pp. 2351–2354.

[33] Winkler, S., "A Perceptual Distortion Metric for Digital Color Images," in *Proceedings of the International Conference on Image Processing*, vol. 1, Chicago, Illinois, USA, Oct. 1998, pp. 399–403.

[34] Goffin, F., et al., "A Low Cost Perceptive Digital Picture Watermarking Method," in *Proceedings of the SPIE 3022, Storage and Retrieval for Image and Video Databases V*, 1997, pp. 264–277.

[35] Cox, I., et al., "Secure Spread Spectrum Watermarking for Multimedia," Technical report, NEC Research Institute, 1995.

[36] Hartung, F., and B. Girod, "Digital Watermarking of MPEG-2 Coded Video in the Bitstream Domain," in *Proceedings of the IEEE International Conference on Acoustics, Speech, and Signal Processing*, vol. 4, Munich, Germany, Apr. 1997, pp. 2621–2624.

[37] Pickholtz, R. L., D. L. Schilling, and L. B. Millstein, "Theory of Spread Spectrum Communications—A Tutorial," *IEEE Transactions on Communications*, vol. 30, no. 5, 1982, pp. 855–884.

[38] Hartung, F., and B. Girod, "Digital Watermarking of Raw and Compressed Video," in *Proceedings of the European EOS/SPIE Symposium on Advanced Imaging and Network Technologies*, Berlin, Germany, Oct. 1996.

[39] Braudaway, G. W., "Protecting Publicly-Available Images with an Invisible Image Watermark," in *Proceedings of the International Conference on Image Processing*, Santa Barbara, California, Oct. 1997.

[40] Delaigle, J.-F., et al., "Digital Images Protection Techniques in a Broadcast Framework: Overview," in *Proceedings of the European Conference on Multimedia Applications, Services and Techniques*, Louvain-la-Neuve, Belgium, May 1996, pp. 711–728.

[41] Darmstaedter, V., et al., "A Block Based Watermarking Technique for MPEG-2 Signals: Optimization and Validation on Real Digital TV Distribution Links," in *Proceedings of the European Conference on Multimedia Applications, Services and Techniques*, May 1998.

[42] Hernández, J. R., et al., "The Impact of Channel Coding on the Performance of Spatial Watermarking for Copyright Protection," in *Proceedings of the IEEE International Conference on Acoustics, Speech and Signal Processing*, vol. 5, 1998, pp. 2973–2976.

[43] Ó Ruanaidh, J. J. K., W. J. Dowling, and F. M. Boland, "Phase Watermarking of Digital Images," in *Proceedings of the IEEE International Conference on Image Processing*, vol. 3, Sep. 1996, pp. 239–242.

[44] Hayes, M. H., "The Reconstruction of a Multidimensional Sequence," *IEEE Transactions on Acoustics, Speech and Signal Processing*, Apr. 1992, pp. 140–154.

[45] Bruyndonckx, O., J.-J. Quisquater, and B. Macq, "Spatial Method for Copyright Labeling of Digital Images," in *Nonlinear Signal Processing Workshop*, Thessaloniki, Greece,

1995, pp. 456–459.

[46] Puate, J., and F. Jordan, "Using Fractal Compression Scheme to Embed a Digital Signature into an Image," in *Proceedings of the SPIE 2915, Video Techniques and Software for Full-Service Networks*, 1996, pp. 108–118.

[47] Jacquin, A. E., "Image Coding Based on a Fractal Theory of Iterated Contractive Image Transformations," *IEEE Transactions on Image Processing*, vol. 1, no. 1, 1992, pp. 18–30.

[48] Fisher, Y. (ed.), *Fractal Image Compression: Theory and Application*, New York: Springer-Verlag, 1995.

[49] Depovere, G., T. Kalker, and J.-P. M. G. Linnartz, "Improved Watermark Detection Reliability Using Filtering Before Correlation," in *Proceedings of the International Conference on Image Processing*, vol. 1, IEEE Signal Processing Society, Chicago, Illinois, USA, Oct. 1998.

[50] Kutter, M., "Watermarking Resisting to Translation, Rotation and Scaling," in *Proceedings of the SPIE 3528, Multimedia Systems and Applications*, 1998, pp. 423–431.

[51] Barni, M., et al., "Robust Watermarking of Still Images for Copyright Protection," in *Proceedings of the 13th International Conference on Digital Signal Processing*, vol. 2, Santorini, Greece, Jul. 1997, pp. 499–502.

[52] Swanson, M. D., B. Zhu, and A. H. Tewfik, "Data Hiding for Video-in-Video," in *Proceedings of the International Conference on Image Processing*, vol. 1, Santa Barbara, CA, 1997, pp. 676–679.

[53] Riley, M. J., and I. E. G. Richardson, *Digital Video Communications*, Artech House, 1997.

[54] Jordan, F., and T. Vynne, "Motion Vector Watermarking," Laboratoire de Traitement des Signaux École Polytechnique Fédérale de Lausanne, Patent, 1997.

Chapter 7

Robustness of copyright marking systems

Scott Craver, Adrian Perrig, Fabien A. P. Petitcolas

7.1 ROBUSTNESS REQUIREMENTS

Robustness of the watermark to removal is typically achieved via computation time and image quality trade-offs, by forcing an attacker to inflict an unreasonable amount of damage on marked content, or to spend an unreasonable amount of computer time to reverse-engineer the mark.

An initial attempt at defining robustness in this context may be found in a recent request for proposals for audio-marking technology from the International Federation for the Phonographic Industry (IFPI) [1]. The goal was to find a marking scheme that would generate evidence for antipiracy operations, track the use of recordings by broadcasters and others, and control copying. The IFPI robustness requirements are as follows:

- The marking mechanism should not affect the sonic quality of the sound recording;
- The marking information should be recoverable after a wide range of filtering and processing operations, including two successive D/A and A/D conversions, steady-state compression or time expansion of 10%, data compression techniques such as MPEG and multiband nonlinear amplitude compression, adding additive or multiplicative noise, adding a second embedded signal using the same system, frequency response distortion of up to 15 dB as applied by bass, mid and treble controls, group delay distortions and notch filters;

- There should be no other way to remove or alter the embedded information without sufficient degradation of the sound quality as to render it unusable;
- Given a signal-to-noise level of 20 dB or more, the embedded data channel should have a bandwidth of 20 bps after error correction, independent of the signal level and type (classical, pop, speech).

The requirements for marking still pictures, videos, and general multimedia objects, are similar; few attempts to quantify them exist (e.g. [2]).

An attacker wants to eliminate (or degrade) the effectiveness of the content owner's mark, which was inserted to protect the owner's claims, and control the watermarked content. As in computer security, a system is only as strong as its weakest link. An attack is considered successful if the attacker disrupts *any* stage of the watermark life cycle; thus, the content owner and the watermarking software have to ensure that each stage is sufficiently secure against attacks.

Watermark researchers recognize several general classes of attacks on watermarking schemes, each attack exploits a different stage of the watermarking process. To give an idea of the diversity of the existing body of attacks, only the first class of attacks involves an attempt to remove or diminish the presence of the watermark. The remaining classes of attacks use subtler tricks to destroy the watermark's usefulness without necessarily damaging it. Hence, straightforward robustness is necessary but not sufficient to guarantee security.

We divide the landscape of watermark attacks into four regions, as outlined by Craver et al. [3]: robustness attacks, presentation attacks, interpretation attacks, and legal attacks. Robustness attacks involve *signal diminishment*, and they are the most intuitively obvious attacks of the four. Such attacks run the gamut from innocent operations, such as compression, to surgical assaults on the watermark with general-purpose image processing programs, or specifically tailored attack programs. Presentation attacks exploit *watermark detector failure*: rather than unmarking a marked object, we skew it in such a way that the watermark passes by a detector unnoticed. Interpretation attacks usually succeed by *counterfeiting marks*, creating situations in which the original watermarker cannot be determined, in which the original mark no longer *means* anything. Finally, *court of law attacks* take advantage of legal issues—some of them are detailed in Chapter 9—largely beyond the reach of engineering.

A thorough examination of these attacks raises several design issues we feel are pivotal to their prevention. Consumer standards have a powerful effect on robustness which some ignore at their own risk: "Unreasonably damaged" media must appear unreasonably damaged to customers, not merely to professional photographers and filmmakers. On the other hand, "invisible" marks must be invisible not merely to customers, but to experts with sophisticated statistical arsenals. Architectural flaws in watermarking tools and watermark detectors, their design too easily left to the engineers, can render watermarking schemes useless; sometimes these flaws in implementation hint at severe problems lurking in the design.

Once a robust watermarking technology is in place and in use, one powerful attack will compromise the property of everyone who previously trusted it, and this damage cannot be undone with more technology: poorly marked media will already be published and distributed at the speed of light on the Internet. We cannot stress enough the importance of understanding and considering *now*, before deployment, each of these security threats, and the attacks which illustrate them.

7.2 SIGNAL DIMINISHMENT

Removing a watermark by simply degrading the content is the most blunt of all possible attacks. Creators of watermarking schemes have these attacks in mind when attempting to engineer robustness. Schemes are designed to survive common operations such as compression, cropping, blurring, and even printing and rescanning, perhaps in hopes that the scheme will be robust to unanticipated operations as well. Unfortunately, an attacker has a large arsenal of image processing operations to use for an attack—a brief analysis of any scheme often reveals a mild operation which obliterates the mark.

7.2.1 Noise and overmarking

One interesting way to add subtle noise is to simply add another watermark. Here is an operation which is designed to cause little quality degradation, conveniently implemented in software by the very people whom the attacker is attempting to outwit.

In examining the watermark-degrading quality of the watermark itself, we highlight some important differences between private and public watermarking schemes, as defined in Section 5.3. For our purposes, a public mark is much easier than a private mark to obliterate by overwriting with a second mark. In steganographic terms, the secret information in a private mark can be said to implement a *selection channel*, literally hiding the mark in one of a great deal of possible locations. This typically allows two marks, each embedded with a different secret key, to reside in distinct locations without causing much damage to one another. The public mark, however, must be placed in a single location which every detector knows. Two marks are thus more likely to occupy the same "space" in a piece of digital content.

Some public marking programs, such as Digimarc Corporation's PictureMarc embedder, recognize this problem, and refuse to let a user insert a watermark if one already exists. There are many ways in which this can be circumvented, from damaging the watermark to hacking the actual software product [4]. One could even reimplement the watermarking algorithm, possibly publishing the source code for others to use. The amount of effort to do so, however, may be a sufficient deterrent to foil many cases of image theft, especially since patent law can be used to discourage anyone from publishing source code. Even common hacking tools, in the threat models of some, are uncommon enough that casual theft is prevented. An interesting problem, then, is to find a simple, painless way to circumvent such measures; if this countermeasure can be defeated with a handful of common operations available in a standard image processing program, the attack becomes viable enough for even the casual image thief.

Here's an example which uses the layering functionality of Adobe Photoshop. We take an image, watermarked using the Digimarc plug-in for Photoshop, and find ourselves unable to insert our own watermark. Successive blurring can be performed until the old watermark is unreadable, but the required blurring is so extreme that this cannot be considered a successful attack. However, we can take this blurred image, watermark it ourselves with maximum strength, and simply overlay it, with a transparency of 30% (this amount will vary with the image used and the strength of the underlying watermark) on top of the original image. This is trivially accomplished in Adobe Photoshop by duplicating the background image into a layer, blurring and watermarking that layer, setting its transparency and flattening the image. The result looks only mildly blurred, an effect which can be remedied with a sharpen filter, contains our new mark with very high strength, while the old mark is not detectable any more.

7.2.2   Compression

JPEG compression is currently the most widely used compression algorithm for still images. When preparing images for Web publication, images are resized and compressed to meet layout and bandwidth requirements. Unfortunately, lossy compression tends to remove less visible high-frequency components and keeps only the lower ones. This interferes with digital image watermarking schemes, which embed information into the same high frequencies to minimize the distortions introduced.

Therefore, it has been suggested that watermarks should be placed in the perceptually significant components of the image despite the potential distortions introduced [5]. These can leave visible artifacts.

7.2.3   User quality standards

Robustness is the main goal of a digital watermarking scheme, and so a great deal relies on the actual meaning of this term. A scheme is generally considered robust if an "unreasonable" amount of damage to "quality" is inflicted to remove a watermark successfully, or possibly if an "unreasonable" amount of time is spent by the attacker to do so. But this places the definition of robustness, the defining characteristic of all successful marking schemes, on a foundation of fuzzy and variable terms. How do we define quality? How much is too much quality loss?

One of the vulnerabilities of watermarking technology is the degree of quality degradation which users are willing to accept, for it is this quality standard which defines the true usefulness of degraded content, and thus the degree of damage that a watermark must survive. Web page designers are willing to subject their images to JPEG compression and scaling to save memory and download times, and users are willing to see their favorite films reduced to a 250-line resolution on a video cassette, perhaps with the edges of the screen cropped to fit their television. This is obviously not content degraded beyond its usefulness or monetary value.

It is dangerously easy to define quality, and thus robustness, in terms of the standards of media creators. These are the people who will actually use watermark software, and so their definitions of quality already set limits on the damage inflicted by watermark *insertion*. Watermark software makers must think twice before considering a certain degree of down-sampling, compression, or color quantization to be "unreasonable," for simply putting content in print, on tape, or on television should not be declared unreasonable.

Another point to consider is the amount of degradation in relation to the degradation caused by a mark's insertion. Some watermark software products produce a noticeable amount of noise. If a content creator is willing to accept a large degree of noise, then it is fair to say that, in the application domain for which that content is targeted, a much larger amount of noise may be accepted by users. Thus, a watermark embedder cannot be made more robust simply by increasing the strength of its embedding. If this is done, it might only be used in domains where the extra noise caused by the embedding is acceptable, and thus domains in which marks need to resist substantial degradation.

7.2.4   Averaging

When a large sample of images is available, an attacker can average them to produce an image without a detectable mark. This could be applied easily in video applications where the same mark, W, is added to successive images $\{I_i\}_{i=1,n}$ of a video sequence as described by Cox and Linnartz [6]. If f is a feature extraction function (which describes where the watermark shall be added), the addition of these n-watermarked frames in this feature domain is $nW + \sum_{i=1}^{n} f(I_i)$ whose expected value for large values of n is nW. The attacker can use this idea to generate a rough estimate of the watermark and remove it from the frames. The obvious countermeasure is to embed more than one watermark and make them dependent on the image. The reader can refer to Cox et al. [6] for a more subtle solution.

Averaging can also be applied against fingerprinting. This will be later detailed in Chapter 8, but for now it is sufficient to think of a fingerprint as a serial number. The general scenario that was mentioned in the introduction is that the merchant of the images embeds a unique number for each customer to thus trace infringers. In this case this image is the same but the watermarks are different so watermarked images add up to $nf(I) + \sum_{i=1}^{n} W_i$ whose expected value for large values of n is simply $nf(I)$. Possible countermeasures are proposed in Chapter 8.

7.2.5   Specifically designed attacks

By knowing the details of a watermarking algorithm, an attacker can invent an attack specifically designed to obliterate that kind of watermark. For instance, while a scheme which embeds the watermark by changing predefined frequencies in the Fourier domain might be difficult to remove by changing pixels in the image, an attacker knowing the scheme would also transform the image into the Fourier domain and remove the watermark by changing the same frequencies.

Nonlinear filtering against spread spectrum based watermarking systems is another example of specific attack. But since many marking schemes are based on spread spectrum techniques, the attack described by Langelaar, Lagendijk, and Biemond [7] has broad implications. The general idea is to separate a given watermarked image $\tilde{I}$, into two components, $\hat{I}$ and $\hat{W}$, such that the estimate $\hat{I}$ of the original image does not contain the watermark anymore. Langelaar et al. have found experimentally that the 3×3 median filter gives good separation results when applied to the methods of Bender et al. [8] and Pitas and Kaskalis [9] and use it for a rough estimation of the watermark: $\tilde{I} - \mathrm{med}_{3\times3}(\tilde{I})$. Before it can be subtracted from $\tilde{I}$, this estimate has to be refined because it still contains edge information and some values might be too large. Consequently Langelaar et al. suggest filtering it through a high-pass filter and truncate the output values to the range $[-2, 2]$. The estimated original is given by:

$$\begin{cases} \hat{I} &= \tilde{I} - \hat{W} \\ \hat{W} &= a\mathrm{H}_{3\times3}(\tilde{I} - \mathrm{med}_{3\times3}(\tilde{I}))|_{[-2,2]} \end{cases} \tag{7.1}$$

where a is an amplification factor determined experimentally.

Still more specific attacks exist. Section 7.2.1 described how to remove specific watermarks and Section 7.5.2 describes an attack to fixed depth image watermarks. As watermarking is increasingly used, we can expect more publications on how to break various schemes, similar to the field of cryptanalysis which analyzes weaknesses in cryptography.

At this point we would also like to remind the reader of Kerckhoffs' principle (see Section 1.2.4). There are many reasons that back this principle: today's tools to reverse-engineer binary code are quite sophisticated, many people have access to the source code in a company, and the time-span for developing and implementing a new watermarking algorithm is quite long. If we are to imagine a future in which watermarking becomes a popular security technology upon which many rely, scenarios such as a cleaning lady who "borrows" a backup tape or notebook of an engineer, installs a Trojan horse into the system, become increasingly plausible.

For these reasons, published algorithms under the scrutiny of watermarking experts are more trustworthy in the long run. Attacks geared to a given watermarking algorithm can be assumed inevitable, and we cannot tell if a scheme will survive such attacks unless the algorithm is publicly known.

7.3 WATERMARK DETECTOR FAILURE

One does not necessarily need to remove a watermark to make it useless. The content can be manipulated in such a way that the detector cannot find a valid watermark. Such attacks are called *presentation attacks* and are best illustrated by *geometrical distortions* attacks and *mosaic* attack.

7.3.1 Distortion attacks

Although many watermarking systems survive basic manipulations—that is, manipulations that can be done easily with standard tools (e.g., [10])—they do not cope with combinations of them and especially minor random geometric distortions.

StirMark is a testing tool for watermarking systems that applies such distortions to images [11]. If A, B, C, and D are the corners of the image, a point M of the said image can be expressed as $M = \alpha(\beta A + (1-\beta)D) + (1-\alpha)(\beta B + (1-\beta)C)$ where $0 \leq \alpha, \beta \leq 1$ are the coordinates of M relative to the corners (see Figure 7.1). The distortion is done by moving the corners by a small random amount in both directions. The new coordinates of M are given by the previous formula, keeping (α, β) constant but using the new corners. Note that this transformation is invertible. Consequently it does not remove the mark per se but prevents some systems from detecting or recovering their marks.

More distortions—still unnoticeable—can be applied to a picture (see Figure 7.2). In addition to the general bilinear property explained previously, a slight deviation is applied to each pixel, which is greatest at the center of the picture and almost null at the borders. In the current implementation, the shape of this embossment is simply a sine wave. If (x, y) are the coordinates of a pixel with $0 \leq x \leq X$ and $0 \leq y \leq Y$, then the modified pixel has coordinates (x', y') where

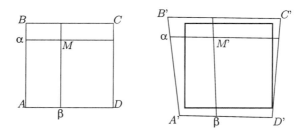

Figure 7.1   Random bilinear distortions applied by StirMark 1.

$x' = x + \lambda \sin(\pi y/Y)$ and $y' = y + \lambda \sin(\pi x/X)$. On top of this a higher frequency displacement of the form $\delta = \lambda \sin(\omega_x x) \sin(\omega_y y)(1 + n(x, y))$, where n is a random number, is added: $x'' = x' + \delta_1$ and $y'' = y' + \delta_2$.

All these distortions combined together with a mild JPEG compression do not remove the watermark per se. They prevent the detector from finding it; they desynchronize the detector. This suggests that the real problem is not so much inserting the marks as recognizing them afterwards. These small random geometric distortions can also be applied to video, provided that the random parameters are saved; otherwise, a wobbling effect appears when the video is played. However, this exploits only one aspect of video and better attacks should also take into account the time dimension of videos. StirMark can also perform a default series of tests which serve as a benchmark for image watermarking [10, 12].

One might try to increase the robustness of a watermarking system by trying to foresee the possible transformations used by pirates—although it might be harder if they are random. One might then use techniques such as embedding multiple versions of the mark under suitable inverse transforms; for instance Ó Ruanaidh and Pereira suggest using the Mellin-Fourier transform (see Section 6.3.3) to cope with rotation and scaling [13]. One can also use the fact that distortions are locally almost linear (equivalent to translation and rotation) and use a block-based detection algorithm. Alternatively, when the original image is available it suffices to approximate an inverse to the random distortions; Davoine et al. [14] showed recently that this can be done using triangular meshes.

7.3.2   Bitrate limitation

In Section 5.6.1 we showed the trade-off between the bitrate of the watermarking system and the robustness of this system to various attacks. It should also be clear that the larger the image the easier it is to hide a few bits of information in it. The

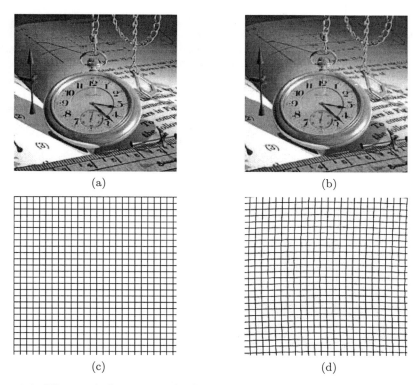

$$(a) \qquad\qquad (b)$$

$$(c) \qquad\qquad (d)$$

Figure 7.2   When applied to images, the distortions introduced by StirMark are almost unnoticeable: "Watch" before (a) and after (b) StirMark with default parameters. For comparison, the same distortions have been applied to a grid (c & d). *Pocket Watch on a Gold Chain.* Copyright image courtesy of Kevin Odhner (jko@home.com).

converse is also true and is the basis of the "mosaic attack": an image can be too small to contain a watermark.

This point is emphasized by a "presentation" attack, which is of quite general applicability. It possesses the initially remarkable property that a marked image can be unmarked and yet still be rendered pixel for pixel in exactly the same way as the marked image by a standard browser.

The attack was motivated by a fielded automatic system for copyright piracy detection, consisting of a watermarking scheme plus a Web spider (or Web crawler) that downloads pictures from the net and checks whether they contain a watermark. It consists of chopping up an image into a number of smaller subimages, which are embedded in a suitable sequence in a Web page. Common Web browsers render juxtaposed subimages stuck together, so they appear identical to the original image (see Figure 7.3). This attack appears to be quite general; all marking schemes require the marked image to have some minimal size (one cannot hide a meaningful mark in just one pixel). Thus by splitting an image into sufficiently small pieces, the mark detector will be confused [15]. The best that one can hope for is that the minimal size could be quite small and the method might therefore not be very practical.

7.3.3   Unanticipated collisions and false alarms

A *false alarm* occurs when a watermark detector detects a mark in an image although this mark was not inserted beforehand. If the image already contains another watermark, we call this event a *watermark collision*. A collision most commonly occurs if both parties use the same watermarking scheme.

Both false alarms and watermark collisions may cause problems when resolving ownership over an image. Since the detection of a watermark implies image ownership, a false alarm can be used to claim copyright infringement against the innocent image publisher. Alternatively, false alarms can be used to call into question the meaning of legitimate watermarks. In the case of a watermark collision, the image contains apparently two watermarks; one could not ask for a more effective display of the unreliability of a watermarking scheme. Readers interested by the study of false alarms in watermarking systems are referred to a paper by Linnartz [16].

These concerns may seem paranoid, but false alarms have already been observed with today's commercially available watermarking systems. Images marked with a watermarking scheme developed by Holliman [17] were found to trigger a well-known existing watermarking product, even though the two are embedded using different principles. This fact is alarming when one considers that automated spiders are already crawling the Web and looking for marked images.

An interesting question to ask is: Given an arbitrary image I and a watermark

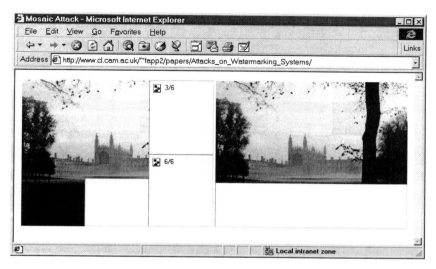

Figure 7.3   Screen-shot of a Web browser while downloading an image after the *mosaic attack*. This attack chops a watermarked image into smaller images which are stuck back together when the browser renders the page. Software that reads a JPEG picture and produces a corresponding mosaic of small JPEG images as well as the necessary HTML code automatically is available. In some cases downloading the mosaic is even faster than downloading the full image! In this example we used a 350 × 280-pixel image watermarked using PictureMarc 1.51. *King's College Chapel.* Courtesy of J. Thompson, Jet Photographic, Cambridge.

detection function D, can we find a secret key k such that the image appears to contain a watermark inserted with key k, such that $D(I, k) = yes$? Any watermarking technique used commercially should make it computationally infeasible to find such a key k. It must also be computationally infeasible to do a sensitivity analysis of function D on individual pixels of image I (see Section 7.4.2). Otherwise, we could choose a random key k and change pixels until the image contains the desired watermark.

We have seen that designing a watermarking scheme bears many trade-offs: one of them is between error correction and unanticipated collisions. On the one hand any algorithm needs strong error correction to achieve high robustness. On the other hand, the probability of watermark collision increases as the error correction becomes stronger. Some schemes compute the correlation of the watermark to a database of watermarks [5, 18]. This method is vulnerable to false alarms and collisions if we have a large number of users because the probability of a false alarm or collision rises with the number of users and images.

7.4   COUNTERFEITING MARKS

So far, we have seen two classes of watermarking attacks. *Signal diminishment* attacks seek to damage the watermark without unreasonably harming the marked content, while *presentation* attacks merely "misalign" the content in such a way that an automated detector fails to locate the watermark.

A successful signal diminishment attack means, quite literally, that the watermarking scheme is not robust to some "reasonable" operation whereas a successful presentation attack does not exploit any such weaknesses in the watermarking scheme. Some presentation attacks exploit the unavoidable weakness of all schemes to extremely damaging (yet invertible) operations, such as extreme cropping or reversal of pixel values; but the true weakness exploited by all presentation attacks is the natural and incurable brainlessness of Web spiders and automated detectors (relative, perhaps, to the natural intelligence of the human Web surfer, for whom a mouse click in an applet window is a trivial task).

One important lesson to be learned from the presentation attack is that, as is usually the case in computer security, an attack is successful if it disrupts any of the steps in the watermarking process, from insertion to distribution to eventual detection. A defense is only successful if every stage is secured, and nowhere is this more clearly illustrated than in the case of automated watermark detection: all the robustness in the world is foiled by the simple act of chopping an image to bits on a Web page.

With this in mind, we may ask if other stages in the watermarking process are prone to attack. The answer is an emphatic yes, as we will now illustrate with the concept of a *protocol* attack.

7.4.1   Protocol attack

As described previously, many private watermarks survive the insertion of a second mark, since the mark is stored in a manner or a location which is kept secret, with enough "room" for marks that an attacker must inflict an unreasonable amount of damage to the content in order to lay waste to every possible hiding place within. One may be tempted to ask, then, if one can simply add a second watermark, and claim ownership of marked content. The reason this fails is that the original content creator has a piece of truly original content, hopefully hidden away from attackers. This original contains no watermarks, whereas the attacker's supposed original contains the first watermark and not the second, clearly establishing an order of insertion.

In general, a dispute over multiple watermarks could be resolved by each party searching for his watermark within the other's original. It would certainly be very

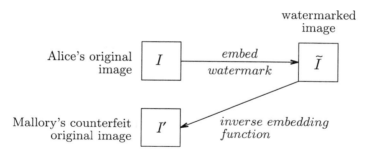

Figure 7.4 Counterfeit original. Alice watermarks an image I to get $\tilde{I}$, which she makes public. Mallory computes an image I' such that he gets $\tilde{I}$ when he watermarks it.

strange if each original was a watermarked version of the other original! If appropriately symmetric in terms of watermark strength, this would prevent either party from establishing ownership, obliterating the effectiveness of the watermark. It turns out that this very situation can be engineered for some watermarking methods by a clever attacker.

Ideally, the original content creator would add a mark w to an image I, yielding a marked image $\tilde{I} = I + w$. This image $\tilde{I}$ is distributed to customers, and when a suspect image I' is found, the difference $I' - I$ is computed, which should equal w if I' and $\tilde{I}$ are the same, and which would be very close to w if I' was derived from $\tilde{I}$, and the scheme robust. A correlation function $c(w, x)$ is used to determine the similarity between the original watermark w and the extracted datum x. In essence, then, the watermark is found in the *difference* between two images. Numerous watermarking schemes are based on this model, although it should be added that this attack has been shown to work in schemes which do not utilize originals [19].

In Figure 7.4, Alice, the content creator, adds a watermark w to an image I to get $\tilde{I} = I + w$, which is then distributed on the Internet. Mallory, hoping to steal the image for himself *subtracts*, rather than adds, a second watermark x to get an image $\tilde{I}' = \tilde{I} - x = I + w - x$. Now, Mallory claims I' rather than $\tilde{I}$ to be his original image, and hauls Alice into court for violating *his* copyright. When originals are compared, Alice will find that her mark w is present in Mallory's image I':

$$I' - I = w - x, \quad c(w - x, w) = 1 \tag{7.2}$$

Since two marks can survive in the same image, the subtraction of x should not greatly hurt the presence of w. So, Mallory has not successfully removed Alice's mark. However, Mallory can show

$$I - I' = x - w, \quad c(x - w, x) = 1 \tag{7.3}$$

In other words, Mallory's mark is present in Alice's original image, despite the fact that Alice has kept it locked away. Empirical data collected by Craver et al. [19] for the watermarking scheme described by Cox et al. [20] shows that this attack works, and that the relative strengths of the two watermarks are virtually identical. There is no real evidence that either party was the image's originator.

This attack works by subtracting a mark rather than adding one, and so relies on the invertibility of a watermarking scheme. A good way to fix this is to make the watermark insertion method a one-way function h of the original image. In these noninvertible schemes, it is practically impossible for Mallory to subtract his mark x, for $x = h(I')$ could not be computed until I' is known and I' could not be computed from $\tilde{I}$ until x is known. As long as h is difficult to invert, I' is difficult to compute.

For example, [19] illustrates a modification of the scheme in [20], in which a bitstring derived from the original image is used to control the method of watermark insertion. A watermark is a vector of real numbers $w = \{w_0, w_1, \ldots, w_n\}$, and a hash of the original image is used to generate a string of bits $b_0, b_1, \ldots, b_n$. Each element w_i can be inserted by two different methods, and the value of b_i indicates which method. If one attempts to detect a watermark using a different bitstring than the one used for insertion, the detector fails. In this scheme, Mallory is unable to simply subtract a watermark from an image. Because the kind of watermark to be subtracted is a one-way function of the original image, Mallory's watermark must be a one-way function of the counterfeit original resulting from the mark's removal. In other words, Mallory must somehow guess a bitstring $\{b_i\}$ and a mark x, such that when x is removed from an image using the control string $\{b_i\}$ the resulting image *hashes* to $\{b_i\}$. With a one-way hash, this kind of prediction should be impossible. This is, therefore, a noninvertible watermarking scheme.

Noninvertibility, however, is merely a necessary condition for avoiding this protocol attack. Even if $\tilde{I}'$ cannot be computed, it can be approximated if a one-way hash function is applied incorrectly. Let us use the aforementioned watermarking scheme as an example. While we know of no way to efficiently compute the image I', Mallory is nevertheless able to perform the protocol attack on this implementation. He simply subtracts x using a control string of all zeros ($b = \{0, 0, \ldots, 0\}$) to create an image I'_0, and then subtracts again with a string of all ones to create an image I'_1. These are then averaged to produce the final image $\tilde{I}'$. It turned out that whatever control string $b = h(I')$ was used, the watermark detector could find x.

The situation is illustrated in Figure 7.5. Here, Mallory computes an image I' which approximates $\tilde{I} - x$ as closely as possible. $\tilde{I}' = I' + x$ is now different from $\tilde{I}$.

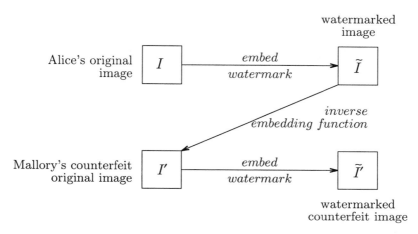

Figure 7.5   Forging a watermark: the four-image case. Mallory can compute any image I' (of reasonable quality) and watermark x such that x is present in $\tilde{I}$, even if watermarking I' with x yields an image different from $\tilde{I}$, the counterfeit attack is still successful.

7.4.2   Oracle attack

In most applications an attacker has access to a detector. This detector can be a piece of software shipped with a major image processing package or an electronic circuit embedded into consumer electronics such as DVD. Even if the attacker does not know much about the watermark embedding method, he can still use the information returned by the detector to remove the watermark by applying small changes to the image until the decoder cannot find it anymore [21].

This attack is analyzed in detail by Linnartz [22]. The attacker starts by constructing an image that is very close to the decision threshold of the detector: modifying this image very slightly should make the detector switch from "watermark present" to "watermark absent" with probability close to 0.5. Note that the constructed image does not need to resemble to the original. This can be achieved by slightly blurring repeatedly the image until the detector fails to find a watermark, or by replacing progressively pixels by gray.

The second step analyzes the sensitivity of the detector to modification of each pixel. The luminance of a given pixel is increased or decreased until the detector changes its output. This is repeated for each pixel. From this analysis the attacker can devise a combination of pixels and modifications such that the distortions in the image are minimized and the effect of the modifications on the detector are maximized, that is that the watermark is not detected.

A possible countermeasure is to randomize the detection process [22]. Rather than having only one decision threshold for the hypothesis testing, two thresholds may be used. Between the thresholds the detector returns a random answer, below the first threshold "present," say, and above the second threshold "absent." This kind of randomized decision rule would greatly impede any process relying on subtle modifications to a barely watermarked image.

One could also make the decoding process computationally expensive. Neither approach is really satisfactory, however, in the absence of tamper-resistant hardware. Unless a breakthrough is made, applications that require the public verifiability of a mark (such as DVD) appear doomed to operate within the constraints of the available tamper-resistance technology, or to use a central "mark reading" service.

One final possibility hinges upon the meaning of the digital watermark. If the presence of a mark is meant to indicate to a recording device that one is attempting an unauthorized copy, then said device may have an excuse to disable itself, or even send a silent warning of a copy attempt. If an attacker is forced to take a DVD recorder to a shop to have it reenabled after every five attempts (say) to record marked data, oracle attacks would be both difficult and noticeable to authorities.

7.4.3   Custom-tailored oracle attack

The oracle attack only works for public watermarks, but even in the presence of purely private watermarks, the *custom-tailored oracle attack* is possible [21]. The only requirement for the attack is that the attacker possesses the watermark embedding and detection algorithm.

The attacker inserts his own watermark once or multiple times into the image, using the same method as the copyright owner. The attacker uses his own watermark as a probabilistic strength indicator for the private watermark. The normal oracle attack is then used until all the newly inserted watermarks are removed. Considering that the original watermark gets weaker when the image is changed in a random manner, it is also weakened when inserting other watermarks. So we can assume that the strength of the newly inserted marks provide an upper bound for the strength of the original watermark. Therefore when all the new marks are removed, then with high probability, the original private watermark will be removed as well.

7.5   DETECTION OF THE WATERMARK

The previous attacks were fairly general and considered the embedding algorithm unknown. There are some cases, though, where enough details about the embedding and detection are available to the attacker and where the hiding process is relatively simple. In such cases the hidden information can be detected and later removed.

7.5.1   An attack on "echo hiding"

The "obvious" attack against echo hiding (presented in Section 3.3.3) is to detect the echo and then remove it by simply inverting the convolution formula; the problem is to detect the echo without knowledge of either the original object or the echo parameters. It appears that the technique used in the legitimate system can also be used by the attacker but requires a bit more work: the detector used in the echo hiding system is based on *cepstrum alanysis;* the attack uses the same detection function but combines it with brute force search.

The underlying idea of cepstrum analysis is presented by Bogert et al. [23] and is as follows: suppose that we are given a signal $y(t)$ which contains a simple single echo (i.e., $y(t) = x(t) + \alpha x(t - \Delta t)$). If we note Φ_{xx}, the power spectrum of x then $\Phi_{yy}(f) = \Phi_{xx}(f)(1 + 2\alpha \cos(2\pi f \Delta t) + \alpha^2)$ whose logarithm is approximately $\log \Phi_{yy}(f) \approx \log \Phi_{xx}(f) + 2\alpha \cos(2\pi f \Delta t)$. This is a function of the frequency f and taking its power spectrum raises its "quefrency" Δt, that is the frequency of $\cos(2\pi \Delta t f)$. The autocovariance of this later function emphasizes the peak that appears at "quefrency" Δt.

Better results are given if one uses a slightly modified version of the cepstrum: $C \circ \Phi \circ \ln \circ \Phi$ where C is the autocovariance function $(C(x) = E((x - \overline{x})(x - \overline{x})^*))$, Φ the power spectrum density function and $\circ$ the composition operator. Experiments on random signals as well as on music show that this method returns quite accurate estimators of the delay when an artificial echo has been added to the signal. In the detection function only echo delays between 0.5 and 3 milliseconds are considered. Below 0.5 ms the function does not work properly and above 3 ms the echo becomes too audible. Incidentally, in the original echo hiding system, the echo delays are chosen between 0.5 and 2 ms and the best relative amplitude of the echo is around 0.8 ms [24].

7.5.2   The "twin peaks" attack

In some cases the image to be watermarked has certain features that help a malicious attacker gain information about the watermark itself. An example of such features is where a picture, such as a cartoon, has only a small number of distinct colors, giving clear peaks in the color histogram (see Figure 7.6). The *twin peaks* attack takes advantage of this to recover simple spread spectrum watermarks. We shall illustrate this attack only in the case of grayscale images. The reader is referred to Maes [25] for a detailed explanation of the attack in the case of color images.

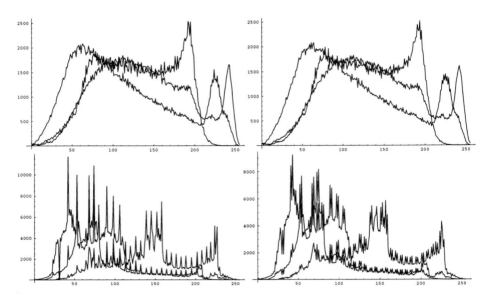

Figure 7.6   The color histograms of baboon (upper) and monarch (lower), of the original (left) and watermarked (right) images, respectively. All three-color components are plotted within the same figure. Courtesy of M. Maes.

As we have seen in Section 6.4.1, a simple example of digital watermarking based on spread spectrum ideas is to add or subtract randomly a fixed value d to each pixel value. So each pixel's value has a 50% chance to be increased or decreased. Let n_k be the number of pixels with gray value k and suppose that for a particular gray value k_0 the dth neighboring colors do not occur, so $n_{k_0-d} = n_{k_0+d} = 0$. Consequently, the expected numbers of occurrences after watermarking are: $\hat{n}_{k_0-d} = \hat{n}_{k_0+d} = n_{k_0}/2$ and $\hat{n}_{k_0} = 0$. Hence, using a set of similar equations, it is possible in certain cases to recover the original distribution of the histogram and the value of the embedded watermark.

7.6   SYSTEM ARCHITECTURE ISSUES

The attacks we considered so far are based on signal processing but these are not the only issue. In this section we discuss watermarking weaknesses which result from system designs which fail to take real-world issues into account, such as human factors, user interfaces, and implementation weaknesses.

7.6.1   Human factors

The typical user usually has only a limited understanding of the underlying mechanisms of image watermarking and does not want to spend hours of training to use one function of his image processing software. Watermarking should behave like a "black box" where the user enters the original image and by some magic the box outputs the watermarked image. No specific user understanding should be necessary.

Usually artists and designers are the creators of images that require copyright protection. The observation that artists do not like to degrade their work deliberately by inserting a watermark leads us to believe that they will either insert a weak watermark[1] or not insert anything at all. Security is not always a strong enough argument to convince artists to lower the image quality.

7.6.2   User interface

Considering the human factors described above, we can see that the user interface (UI) becomes a crucial component of a security architecture. Whitten and Tygar demonstrate how a flawed PGP user interface can limit the security of the system [26]. The UI should present the user with a clear model of the effects of watermarking and protect him from misuse. It needs to iron out users misconceptions about the watermarking technique.

Since watermark embedding programs come with image processing applications, the user might accidentally remove the watermark by working on the image. In current applications, for example PictureMarc in Adobe Photoshop, this issue is not addressed and it might not be clear to the user that the watermark is weakened by changing colors in the image, cropping the borders, or other operations. Clearly the UI should protect the user from accidental removal or weakening of the watermark. One possible improvement is to include a watermark strength indicator on the screen, so the user sees how the watermark reacts to image transformations. Ideally the watermark embedding should be the last step before publishing the image. Therefore the software could delay the embedding until the user wants to save the image. Similarly when loading the image, the watermark could be extracted and the user would always work with an unwatermarked image. The watermarking would become an operation transparent to the user.

---

1 Today's watermarking schemes present a trade-off between watermark strength and image degradation.

7.6.3   Implementation weaknesses

Most attacks on fielded cryptographic systems have come from the opportunistic exploitation of loopholes that were found by accident; cryptanalysis was rarely used, even against systems that were vulnerable to it [27]. We cannot expect copyright marking systems to be any different and this pattern was followed in the first attack to be made available on the Internet against the most widely used picture-marking scheme. This attack [4] exploited weaknesses in the implementation rather than the underlying marking algorithms, even though these are weak—the marks can be made unusable using StirMark (see Section 7.3.1).

In this system, each user has an ID and a two-digit password, which are issued when he registers with the watermarking software provider. The correspondence between ID and passwords is checked when inserting a watermark. This check supposedly prevents an attacker from embedding a watermark with a given ID. Unfortunately, a design flaw allows an attacker to break this system using two different methods.

The first method to break the system is to use a debugger to break into the software and disable the password checking mechanism. This attack is documented and available on the Internet [4]. In the second method, the secret password which corresponds to a given ID is only two numerical digits long, hence there are only a hundred possibilities. Assuming that it takes a human user two seconds to try out a password, it would take only a hundred seconds on average to find the secret password of any user ID! Not to mention how easily this process could be automated. We note in passing that IDs are public, so either password search or disassembly can enable any user to be impersonated.

A deeper examination of the program also allows a villain to change the ID, thus the copyright, of an already marked image as well as the type of use (such as adult versus general public content). Before embedding a mark, the program checks whether there is already a mark in the picture, but this check can be bypassed fairly easily using the debugger with the result that it is possible to overwrite any existing mark and replace it with another one.

Exhaustive search for the personal code can be prevented by making it longer, but there is no obvious solution to the disassembly attack. If tamper-resistant software [28] cannot give enough protection, then one can always have an online system in which each user shares a secret embedding key with a trusted party and uses this key to embed some kind of digital signature. Observe that there are two separate keyed operations here: the authentication (which can be done with a signature) and the embedding or hiding operation.

7.6.4   Automated spider limitations

In Section 7.3.2 we discussed the mosaic attack which prevents a Web spider from detecting a watermark in an image found on the Web, even though the image presentation has not been changed in a perceptible way. Unfortunately, there are many more issues when a Web spider searches the Internet for stolen images.

The first problem is bandwidth: crawling the Internet requires high bandwidth. This makes it impossible for an individual user to search the Web for copyright infringement of his own images. Therefore this user needs to register with a public crawling service to look for his images. If he uses private watermarks, he will also need to register his private key with the spider. This opens many key management and security problems.

Now let's look into the entire crawling life cycle and analyze possible problems we might run into. Imagine that Alice is an artist and she created valuable images for which she holds a copyright. After inserting her private watermark, she registers with Mallory's to detect copyright infringements and gives him her private key.[2] In this scenario, Mallory has stolen Alice's images and presents them proudly on his Web page. Since Mallory knows that Alice holds the copyright for these images, he has programmed his Web server not to serve stolen images to Web spiders. Assuming that there will not be a large number of companies which crawl the Web, this defense is easy to accomplish. In order to prevent suspicion, the server can return an arbitrary image to a request for a stolen image issued by a Web spider.

Another drawback of Web spiders is access-controlled Web sites or pay sites. The spider will not gain access to the images without authenticating itself or paying for the information. We do not know of any laws which would allow spiders or government agents to search access-controlled sites for investigation purposes for free. Even in presence of such a law, the Web server could detect such a user and present a phony Web to the agent. Unfortunately, access-controlled (pay) sites are the sites whose infringement most directly damages the content creator, because these are the sites making money from the creator's works. If the spider had to purchase the images using a credit card before it could examine them, it might even become a target, providing "guaranteed sales" to a Web site. These problems present high barriers for any Web spiders to overcome.

Java applets or ActiveX controls mobile objects which can be embedded to display a picture inside the browser and thus they present yet another big problem for

---

2 At this point we would like to note that this scenario would not be a problem if there existed a watermarking algorithm analog to public key cryptography. Each user would then have a private key to embed a watermark, which everybody could verify using the corresponding public key. Unfortunately this method does not exist and the problem is sometimes referred to as "the holy grail of watermarking."

spiders. The applet could even descramble the picture in real time. Defeating such techniques would entail rendering the Web page, detecting pictures, and checking whether they contain a mark.

In addition, Mallory could even have Alice's image on his Web page without actually "stealing" the image. Through HTML, Mallory can refer to the image on Alice's server directly without copying the image into his own Web space. The viewer's browser would then download the Web page from Mallory's server and the image from Alice's server. We believe that Alice will have a difficult case for claiming copyright infringement, since the image can only be found on her server.

We have now seen many ways in which Web spiders can be prevented from finding stolen images. We can now present the problems which arise after a case of copyright infringement has been detected.

7.7 COURT OF LAW ATTACKS

7.7.1 Foreign server

The first scenario is the following: in a country that does not adhere to the Berne convention on copyright protection (see Chapter 9), Mallory sets up his Web server distributing copyrighted images, music, etc. There is no way to prevent him from doing this "illegal" distribution as the country does not provide the legal basis for prosecution. All forms of intellectual property share this common problem. The past has shown that such scenarios are not far-fetched. In fact, recent incidents prove that this attack is quite common.[3] The situation gets worse as the Internet expands its range with high-speed connections to countries that are "traditionally" known for copyright infringement. If these countries do not change their laws, this problem cannot be solved trivially by technical means.

7.7.2 Spoofing attack

The legal enforcement of copyright infringement in countries that enforce the Berne convention of copyright protection is not a simple task either. It is difficult to prove copyright infringement in court. The complication is that Alice cannot just claim "Mallory distributed my copyrighted image on his Web server." We need sound evidence for the fraud. For example, an impartial witness could provide for a resolution. But the problem here is that Web servers do not send nonrepudiable responses. Therefore how can the witness really know where the data came from?

---

3 Examples include servers in Indonesia that distribute copyrighted music in high fidelity. Another example was given in [29]: Warner Bros. was hunting bootleggers who were distributing Madonna's forthcoming album "Ray of Light" over the Internet.

In a possible scenario let us say that Mallory tries to convince Alice that Bob stole her image. But Bob is a good person and would not steal any images. So Mallory needs to trick Alice. One simple way to trick her is by domain name server (DNS) spoofing; when Alice accesses <http://www.bob.com/image.gif> on Mallory's machine, Mallory's DNS lookup function replies with a wrong address for www.bob.com, namely one of Mallory's servers, which will then deliver the "stolen" image to Alice's browser.

In another case where Mallory really did steal Alice's image, Alice files a law suit. But during this process, Mallory will surely remove the stolen image from the server. In the case where Alice first consults a notary to look at Mallory's Web site to confirm that the stolen image really is stored there, Mallory might refuse to send the image to notaries. This would certainly be difficult to achieve but it would be technically feasible by excluding data delivery to certain domains.

These attacks show that the legal system needs to be extended to prevent such scenarios.

7.8 CONCLUSION

We have described a number of attacks on information hiding systems, which show strong weaknesses in many existing watermarking schemes. Through these attacks, we have shown that desynchronization is a very efficient tool against most marking techniques. This led us to suggest that detection, rather than embedding, is the core problem of digital watermarking. We also showed how very simple attacks that were not expected by the software designers can fool some marking systems (e.g., "mosaic" attack) and how lazy implementation and pressure from marketing people and clients lead to unsatisfactory implementation. Although this sounds very familiar (e.g., [27, 30]), it is not very surprising since nobody knows what "robustness" means in the context of digital marking.

Understanding these attacks—and the ones to come—will help designers of copyright marking systems to propose better schemes. This has already been proven by the introduction of new technologies like templates and by some attempts to survive random geometric distortions.

Watermarking has introduced a new paradigm where signal processing, computer security, cryptography, law, and business converge to protect the rights of photographers, digital artists, singers, composers, in short, copyright holders. The view of a senior executive at a California-based record label is significant of the expectations surrounding digital watermarking: *"Sooner or later, any encryption system can be broken. We need watermarking technologies to tell us who did it"* [31].

But the state-of-the-art is still far from achieving what has been promised by the industry; lack of standardization, interoperability issues, and lack of a set of precise and realistic requirements for watermarking systems still severely hinder the development of copy protection mechanisms. Strong digital watermarking and fingerprinting may exist (in the signal processing sens), but until this is proved, the attacks presented in this chapter tend to show the contrary.

REFERENCES

[1] "Request for Proposals—Embedded Signalling Systems," International Federation of the Phonographic Industry, 54 Regent Street, London W1R 5PJ, 1997.

[2] Kutter, M., and F. A. P. Petitcolas, "A Fair Benchmark for Image Watermarking Systems," in *Proceedings of the SPIE 3657, Security and Watermarking of Multimedia Contents*, 1999, pp. 226–239.

[3] Craver, S., B.-L. Yeo, and M. Yeung, "Technical Trials and Legal Tribulations," *Communications of the ACM*, vol. 41, no. 7, Jul. 1998, pp. 44–54.

[4] Anonymous, "Learn Cracking IV—Another Weakness of PictureMarc," posted by <zguan.bbs@bbs.ntu.edu.tw> on <news:tw.bbs.comp.hacker>, mirrored on <http://www.cl.cam.ac.uk/~fapp2/watermarking/image_watermarking/ digimarc_crack.html>, 1997. Includes instructions to override any Digimarc watermark using PictureMarc.

[5] Cox, I. J., et al., "Secure Spread Spectrum Watermarking for Images, Audio and Video," in *International Conference on Image Processing*, IEEE, Lausanne, Switzerland, 16–19 Sep. 1996, pp. 243–246.

[6] Cox, I. J., and J.-P. M. G. Linnartz, "Some General Methods for Tampering with Watermarks," *IEEE Journal of Selected Areas in Communications*, vol. 16, no. 4, May 1998, pp. 587–593.

[7] Langelaar, G. C., R. L. Lagendijk, and J. Biemond, "Removing Spatial Spread Spectrum Watermarks by Non-linear Filtering," in *9th European Signal Processing Conference*, Island of Rhodes, Greece, 8–11 Sep. 1998, pp. 2281–2284.

[8] Bender, W., et al., "Techniques for Data Hiding," *IBM Systems Journal*, vol. 35, no. 3 and 4, 1996, pp. 313–336.

[9] Pitas, I., "A Method for Signature Casting on Digital Images," in *International Conference on Image Processing*, vol. 3, Sep. 1996, pp. 215–218.

[10] Petitcolas, F. A. P., and R. J. Anderson, "Evaluation of Copyright Marking Systems," in *IEEE Multimedia Systems*, Florence, Italy, 7–11 Jun. 1999, pp. 574–579.

[11] Petitcolas, F. A. P., R. J. Anderson, and M. G. Kuhn, "Attacks on Copyright Marking Systems," in *Proceedings of the Second International Workshop on Information Hiding*, vol. 1525 of *Lecture Notes in Computer Science*, Springer, 1998, pp. 218–238.

[12] Petitcolas, F. A. P., "Attaques et évaluation des filigranes numériques," in *Cinquièmes journées d'études et d'échanges sur la compression et la représentation des signaux audiovisuels (CORESA '99)*, Centre de recherche et développement de France Télécom (Cnet), EURÉCOM, Conseil Général des Alpes-Maritimes and Télécom Valley, Sophia-Antipolis, France, 14–15 Jun. 1999.

[13] Ó Ruanaidh, J. J. K., and S. Pereira, "A Secure Robust Digital Image Watermark," in *International Symposium on Advanced Imaging and Network Technologies—Conference*

on *Electronic Imaging: Processing, Printing and Publishing in Colour*, Europto, International Society for Optical Engineering, European Optical Society, Commission of the European Union, Directorate General XII, Zürich, Switzerland, May 1998.

[14] Davoine, F., et al., "Watermarking et résistance aux déformations géométriques," in *Cinquièmes journées d'études et d'échanges sur la compression et la représentation des signaux audiovisuels (CORESA '99)*, Centre de recherche et développement de France Télécom (Cnet), EURÉCOM, Conseil Général des Alpes-Maritimes and Télécom Valley, Sophia-Antipolis, France, 14–15 Jun. 1999.

[15] Petitcolas, F. A. P., "2Mosaic," `<http://www.cl.cam.ac.uk/~fapp2/watermarking/image_watermarking/>`, 1997.

[16] Linnartz, J.-P., T. Kalker, and G. Depovere, "Modeling the False Alarm and Missed Detection Rate for Electronic Watermarks," in *Proceedings of the Second International Workshop on Information Hiding*, vol. 1525 of *Lecture Notes in Computer Science*, Springer, 1998, pp. 329–343.

[17] Holliman, M., Personal communication, 1999.

[18] Ó Ruanaidh, J. J. K., W. J. Dowling, and F. M. Boland, "Watermarking Digital Images for Copyright Protection," *IEE Proceedings on Vision, Signal and Image Processing*, vol. 143, no. 4, Aug. 1996, pp. 250–256.

[19] Craver, S., et al., "Resolving Rightful Ownerships with Invisible Watermarking Techniques: Limitations, Attacks, and Implications," *IEEE Journal of Selected Areas in Communications*, vol. 16, no. 4, May 1998, pp. 573–586.

[20] Cox, I., et al., "Secure Spread Spectrum Communication for Multimedia," Technical report, N.E.C. Research Institute, 1995.

[21] Perrig, A., *A Copyright Protection Environment for Digital Images*, Diploma dissertation, École Polytechnique Fédérale de Lausanne, Lausanne, Switzerland, Feb. 1997.

[22] Linnartz, J.-P. M. G., and M. van Dijk, "Analysis of the Sensitivity Attack Against Electronic Watermarks in Images," in *Proceedings of the Second International Workshop on Information Hiding*, vol. 1525 of *Lecture Notes in Computer Science*, Springer, 1998, pp. 258–272.

[23] Bogert, B. P., M. J. R. Healy, and J. W. Tukey, "The Quefrency Alanysis of Time Series for Echoes: Cepstrum, Pseudo-Autocovariance, Cross-Cepstrum and Saphe Cracking," in *Symposium on Time Series Analysis*, New York, New York, USA: John Wiley & Sons, Inc., 1963, pp. 209–243.

[24] Gruhl, D., W. Bender, and A. Lu, "Echo Hiding," in *Information Hiding: First International Workshop, Proceedings*, vol. 1174 of *Lecture Notes in Computer Science*, Springer, 1996, pp. 295–315.

[25] Maes, M., "Twin Peaks: The Histogram Attack on Fixed Depth Image Watermarks," in *Proceedings of the Second International Workshop on Information Hiding*, vol. 1525 of *Lecture Notes in Computer Science*, Springer, 1998, pp. 290–305.

[26] Whitten, A., and J. D. Tygar, "Why Johnny Can't Encrypt: A Usability Evaluation of PGP 5.0," in *8th USENIX Security Symposium*, August 1999.

[27] Anderson, R. J., "Why Cryptosystems Fail," *Communications of the ACM*, vol. 37, no. 11, Nov. 1994, pp. 32–40.

[28] Aucsmith, D., "Tamper Resistant Software: An Implementation," in *Information Hiding: First International Workshop, Proceedings*, vol. 1174 of *Lecture Notes in Computer Science*, Springer, 1996, pp. 317–333.

[29] Wilson, D. L., "Copyright vs. the right to copy," *San Jose Mercury News*, February 28

1998. <http://www.mercurycenter.com/business/center/copy030198.htm>.

[30] Anderson, R. J., "Liability and Computer Security: Nine Principles," in *Computer Security—Third European Symposium on Research in Computer Security*, vol. 875 of *Lecture Notes in Computer Science*, Springer, 1994, pp. 231–245.

[31] Yoshida, J., "Digital Watermarking Showdown Between ARIS and BlueSpike," EETimes on-line, 1999. Quotation of a senoir executive at a California-based record label.

Chapter 8

Fingerprinting

Jong-Hyeon Lee

8.1 INTRODUCTION

Fingerprints are characteristics of an object that tend to distinguish it from other similar objects. They have various applications, but in this chapter, we will show how they can be used for copyright protection of data. The techniques we are interested in do not rely on tamper-resistance and hence do not prevent users from making copies of the data, but they enable the owner to trace authorized users distributing them illegally. In the case of encrypted satellite television broadcasting, for instance, users could be issued a set of keys to decrypt the video streams and the television station could insert fingerprint bits into each packet of the traffic to detect unauthorized uses. If a group of users give their subset of keys to unauthorized people—so that they can also decrypt the traffic—at least one of the key donors can be traced when the unauthorized decoder is captured [1]. In this respect, fingerprinting is usually discussed in the context of the *traitor tracing* problem.

Fingerprints have another application: they can also be used as a means of high-speed searching. For example, the Cambridge University Library uses a fingerprint code with six characters to search periodicals. If the title consists of one word, one just needs to keep the first six characters. Otherwise, the first three characters of the first word of the periodical title and three initial characters of the following words in the title are used [2]. For instance, "Computer & Communications Security Reviews," can be found simply using "comcsr." Similar ideas but more complicated techniques involving hashes are also used in database searching. Usually, cryptographic techniques are not used for such purposes. In both cases, the underlying concept is similar but the aspects and detailed techniques are different.

Fingerprinting refers to the process of adding fingerprints to an object or of identifying fingerprints that are already intrinsic to an object. The next sections present examples of fingerprints, the terminology and requirements for fingerprinting, a classification of fingerprints, research history, and a brief survey of important fingerprinting schemes.

8.2   EXAMPLES OF FINGERPRINTING

Fingerprinting has been used for centuries and we may find several classical examples of it. We list typical examples of fingerprinting before the computer era. These examples will provide inspiration about what fingerprinting is and why it is needed.

Human fingerprints: It is known that each fingerprint has a different pattern that distinguishes it from others. For investigation purpose, human fingerprints are collected from prisoners and criminals. Since it is an easy means of identification, some countries adopt it in the citizen's identification card (e.g., Korea and France). The Korean resident identification card contains a human fingerprint, and French citizens must give their fingerprints when requesting a new national identification. Human fingerprints are also used for access control as shown in several spy movies. During World War II, the American Office of Strategic Services (OSS) used the fist of their agents to identify them [3]. Similar biometrics means such as human iris patterns and voiceprints are used for the same purpose. A British building society has been operating a large number of human iris scanning test systems on automated teller machines and will adopt this technology for customer identification on their automated teller machines rather than a typed password [4].

Fired bullet: Each weapon has its own type of fired bullet depending on both the manufacturer and the type of weapon. Typewriters are similar; each typewriter has its own typesets.

Serial number: Serial numbers on manufactured products are unique for each product and can be used to distinguish between them.

Coded particles of explosives: Some explosives are manufactured with tiny coded particles that can be found after an explosion. By examining the particles, the manufacturer, type, and manufactured time can be identified.

Maps: Sometimes maps have been drawn with slight deliberate variations from reality to identify copies.

Since fingerprints on digital data are easy and inexpensive means of copyright protection, the demand on fingerprinting in computers and communication is getting stronger. We can find several examples of fingerprints in the computer era.

Prefix of email address: On mailing systems supporting IETF RFC 754 [5], it is possible to add a prefix to usual email addresses. This can be useful when registering with an on-line service. For example, Bob (`Bob@foo.org`) can register `Mallory+Bob@foo.org` at Mallory's site. Then if he receives an unsolicited message to this address, he can infer that Mallory passed the address to some bulk mailer.

PGP public keys: PGP (Pretty Good Privacy) is one of the most widely used public key packages [6] and fingerprints for PGP public keys are used as one of the most important methods of identification. In PGP, the fingerprint is the MD5 [7, pp. 436–441] hash of public key bits including the public modulus and encryption exponent [8]. This fingerprint is almost unique, and can be used as an identifier in directories of keys such as the Global Internet Trust Register [9]. This register includes PGP fingerprints and key length as identifiers for public keys.

Digital audio/video: It has been suggested to use fingerprints to check out piracy of video data. In a pay-TV broadcast system, fingerprinting is applied to trace illegal subscribers [1].

Documents: As copyright protection means, fingerprinting is used in documents to discourage copying [10, 11].

Fingerprints are also embedded in computer programs, multimedia data, data streams, etc.

8.3 TERMINOLOGY AND REQUIREMENTS

A *mark* is a portion of an object and has a set of several possible states; a *fingerprint* is a collection of marks; a *distributor* is an authorized provider of fingerprinted objects to users; an *authorized user* is an individual who is authorized to gain access to a fingerprinted object; an *attacker* is an individual who gains unauthorized access to fingerprinted objects; and a *traitor* is an authorized user who distributes fingerprinted objects illegally.

To help understand this terminology, let us think about a case of image distribution; the image producer deliberately puts tiny errors into each distributed copy. These errors are the marks and the collection of all these errors is the fingerprint. The producer of the image is the distributor, and the buyer the user. A group of users may compare their images and find deliberate errors, then they may give or sell this information to others so that they can make illegal copies (such an attack is called a *collusion* attack). In this example, a group of users who give the information of errors are the traitors and the people who make illegal copies are the attackers.

The general threat model in fingerprinting is as follows: the distributor's goal is to identify the users whom the attacker has compromised and the attacker's goal is to prevent his identification by the distributor.

While fingerprinting in itself provides only detection and not prevention, the ability to detect illegal use may help deter individuals from committing these acts. Requirements of fingerprinting for copy tracing and copy reduction include collusion tolerance as well as all requirements of watermarking:

- Collusion tolerance: even if attackers have access to a certain number of copies (objects), they should not be able to find, generate, or delete the fingerprint by comparing the copies. In particular, the fingerprints must have a common intersection.
- Object quality tolerance: the marks must not significantly decrease the usefulness or quality of the object.
- Object manipulation tolerance: if an attacker tampers the object, the fingerprint should still be negotiable, unless there is so much noise that makes the object useless. In particular, the fingerprint should tolerate lossy data compression.

8.4 CLASSIFICATION

Fingerprinting can be classified by the objects to be fingerprinted, detection sensitivity, fingerprinting methods, and generated fingerprints. These four categories are not exclusive. The taxonomy we adopt is based on Wagner [12].

8.4.1 Object-based classification

The nature of the objects is a primitive criterion, since it may provide a customized way to fingerprint the object. There are two categories in object-based classification: digital fingerprinting and physical fingerprinting. If an object to be fingerprinted is in digital format so that computers can process fingerprints, we call it *digital fingerprinting*.

If an object has its own physical characteristics that can be used to differentiate it from others, we speak of *physical fingerprinting*. Human fingerprints, iris patterns, voice patterns, and coded particles of some explosives are of this type.

8.4.2 Detection-sensitivity-based classification

The sensitivity level of a fingerprinting scheme against illegal use is another criterion. Based on the detection sensitivity against violation, we classify fingerprinting into three categories: *perfect fingerprinting*, *statistical fingerprinting*, and *threshold fingerprinting*.

If any alteration to the objects that makes the fingerprint unrecognizable must also make the object unusable, we speak of perfect fingerprinting. Thus the fingerprint generators can always identify the attacker by one misused object. Statistical fingerprinting is less strict. Given many sufficiently misused objects to examine, the fingerprint generators can gain any desired degree of confidence that they have correctly identified the compromised user. The identifier is, however, never certain. Threshold fingerprinting is a hybrid type of the above two. It allows a certain level of illegal uses, say threshold, but it identifies the illegal copy when the threshold is reached. Thus it is allowed to make copies of an object less than the threshold, and the copies are not detected at all. When the number of copies exceeds the threshold, the copier is traced.

8.4.3 Fingerprinting method-based classification

Primitive methods for fingerprinting such as recognition, deletion, addition, and modification have also been used as another classification criterion. If the fingerprinting scheme consists of recognizing and recording fingerprints that are already part of the object, it is of *recognition* type; examples are human fingerprints and iris patterns. In *deletion*-type fingerprinting, some legitimate portion of the original object is deleted. If some new portion is added to the object, it is of *addition type*. The additional part can be either sensible or meaningless. When a change to some portion of the object is made, it is of *modification* type; examples are maps with variations.

8.4.4 Fingerprint-based classification

We may identify two types of fingerprints: discrete fingerprinting and continuous fingerprinting. If the generated fingerprint has a finite value of discontinuous numbers, the fingerprint is called *discrete*. Examples include hash values of digital files. If the generated fingerprint has a continuous value and essentially there is no limit to the number of possible values, the fingerprint is called *continuous*. Most physical fingerprints are of this type.

8.5 RESEARCH HISTORY

Before the emergence of computers, only physical fingerprinting had been studied and developed. With the increasing importance of digital data, there is a strong desire to use fingerprinting to protect intellectual properties, because it requires light-weight cryptographic capability but satisfies the purpose. Examples of digital data to be fingerprinted include documents, images, movies, sounds, executables, and so on.

As with other cryptographic techniques, there are some known problems to be solved. When fingerprinting digital data, one must consider the problem of collusions. Suppose a digital image is distributed with fingerprints. If a group of users who got it compare their copies, they can easily discover all the marks. The users can then remove these marks, interpolate gaps, and resell the image without worrying about being traced.

This problem of collusions was first discussed by Blakley et al. [13] and a solution against larger collusions was presented by Boneh and Shaw [14]. Low and Maxemchuk [15] presented a collusion analysis in their model for general multiparty cryptographic protocols.

Traitor tracing is the equivalent of fingerprinting for cryptologic keys. It was introduced by Chor et al. [1] for broadcast encryption. When the data (e.g., a pay-TV movie) is broadcast in encrypted form, and only the decryption keys are sold, a different key is sold to each pay-TV subscriber. Furthermore, the encryption scheme is adapted so that all keys can be used to decrypt the same ciphertext. Since the decryption key is different for each subscriber, the pay-TV company can trace the user who made illegal copies of his key.

Recently, several studies enhance the functionality of fingerprinting schemes in various ways (e.g., asymmetric fingerprinting and anonymous fingerprinting). Asymmetric fingerprinting was introduced by Pfitzmann and Schunter [14]. Unlike conventional fingerprinting schemes, only the buyer of a fingerprinted object knows the data with the fingerprint. When a merchant finds the copy, he can nevertheless identify the buyer and prove to third parties that this buyer bought the copy from him. Pfitzmann [16, 17] also proposed a traitor-tracing scheme using asymmetric fingerprinting. Anonymous fingerprinting was introduced by Pfitzmann and Waidner [18] as an analogy of the blind signature for fingerprinting. It uses a trusted third party, called the registration center, to identify buyers suspected of behaving illegally. Thus the merchant is not able to identify him without help of the registration center. By using the registration center the merchant can eliminate the need for the distributor to keep detailed records binding fingerprints to users. We will outline these schemes in the next section.

8.6 FINGERPRINTING SCHEMES

In this section, we list important achievements in fingerprinting and summarize statistical fingerprinting, traitor tracing, collusion-secure fingerprinting, asymmetric fingerprinting, and anonymous fingerprinting.

8.6.1 Statistical fingerprinting

In 1983, Wagner [12] introduced statistical fingerprinting based on hypothesis tests. The detailed procedure is as follows: suppose there are n real data values $v_1, v_2, \ldots, v_n$ and m users. We assume there are a sufficiently large number of data values so that we can test statistical hypotheses. To qualify for use in statistical fingerprinting, it must be able to find a value $\delta_j > 0$ for each v_j such that the δ_j-neighborhood of v_j does not intersect with some neighborhood of v_i, for each $i \neq j$. Then, each user receives a number in the closed interval $[v_j - \delta_j, v_j + \delta_j]$ that is different from other users' numbers. Approximately half of the data values received by users are in $[v_j, v_j + \delta_j]$ and the remaining half are in $[v_j - \delta_j, v_j]$. The version of the jth datum sent to user i is denoted v_{ij}.

Suppose the data has been misused some way, and that the distributor can extract the values $v_1', v_2', \ldots, v_n'$ from the illegal copy he found. For each i with $1 \leq i \leq m$, we want to test the hypothesis that user i is the source of the returned values. In order to do so, we examine the likelihood

$$L_{ij} := \frac{v_j' - v_{ij}}{\delta_j}, \quad 1 \leq j \leq n \tag{8.1}$$

for a given i; that is, $(L_{ij})_{1 \leq j \leq n}$ are the normalized differences between the returned values and the values given to user i.

For a given i, we consider the means of $(L_{ij})_{1 \leq j \leq n}$ over two disjoint subsets. Let μ_i^h be the mean of those L_{ij} such that v_{ij} is the higher of the two versions of v_j sent to different users and μ_i^l be the mean of those L_{ij} such that v_{ij} is the lower of the two versions. Then $\mu_i^h \leq 0$ and $\mu_i^l \geq 0$. Let $\mu_i := \mu_i^l - \mu_i^h$.

Suppose the attacker made no alteration to the values before they returned as v_j'. If the attacker got the data from user i, then $\mu_i = \mu_i^h = \mu_i^l = 0$. If he got it from someone else, then we expect

$$\mu_i^h \approx -0.5, \quad \mu_i^l \approx 0.5, \quad \text{and} \quad \mu_i^l - \mu_i^h \approx 1 \tag{8.2}$$

Thus if no alteration was made, the attacker should be identified immediately unless n is very small.

When the attacker alters the returned values, $\mu_i^h \approx 0$ might no longer be valid even for large n, since the attacker might alter these values according to some distribution with nonzero mean. However, it can be assumed that the attacker cannot tell which values were the larger of the two possible versions and which were the smaller. Thus for large enough n, if user i is the source of the attacker's value, one expects that μ_i can be close to zero. On the other hand, if user i is not the source of the attacker's values, we expect

$$\mu_i = \mu_i^l - \mu_i^h \approx 1 \tag{8.3}$$

for large n.

As a result, one can use the following algorithm. For each i, calculate the difference μ_i of the two means as above. If for some i, μ_i is close to zero and for all other $k \neq i$, μ_k is close to one, then there is evidence for the hypothesis that the user i is the source of the misused data. By checking the value μ_i for all i, it is possible to identify which user leaked the information.

Since this fingerprinting scheme is based on hypothesis tests, we may raise the confidence level of hypothesis tests, however the hypothesis never becomes a certainty.

8.6.2   Collusion-secure fingerprinting

In 1995, Boneh and Shaw [14, 19] introduced *c-secure codes* to obtain collusion-secure fingerprinting. They pointed out that collusions are the most significant problems in fingerprinting schemes, and they provided a clear solution for collusion-tolerant fingerprinting.

Let Σ be an alphabet of size s representing s different states of the marks. The letters in Σ can be the integers 1 to s. Given an l-bit word $x \in \Sigma^l$ and an index set $I = \{i_1, \ldots, i_r\} \subseteq \{1, \ldots, l\}$, we denote by $x|_I$ the word $x_{i_1} x_{i_2} \cdots x_{i_r}$ where x_i is the ith letter of x. We call $x|_I$ the restriction of x to the positions in I. A set $\Gamma = \{x^{(1)}, \ldots, x^{(n)}\} \subseteq \Sigma^l$ is called a (l, n)-code. The codeword $x^{(i)}$ will be assigned to user u_i, for $1 \leq i \leq n$. Let C be a coalition of users; a coalition is a set of users involved in making illegal copies. If the words assigned to users in C match in their ith position out of $\{1, \ldots, l\}$, we say that position i is *undetectable* for C; that is, $x_i^{(u_1)} = x_i^{(u_2)} = \cdots = x_i^{(u_c)}$ for $C = \{u_1, \ldots, u_c\}$. Suppose the ith mark is detectable by the coalition. The coalition can generate an object in which the mark is in an unreadable state so that the police cannot determine which state an unreadable mark is in. We denote a mark in an unreadable state by "?". Let R be the set of undetectable positions for C. Then the *feasible set* of C is defined as

$$F(C) = \{x \in (\Sigma \cup \{?\})^l : \; x|_R = x^{(u)}|_R\}$$

for some user u in C. Hence the feasible set contains all words which match the coalition's undetectable bits.

We would like to construct codes with the following property: no coalition can collude to frame a user not in the coalition. When we limit the size of the coalition to c users, we call such codes *c-frameproof codes*. Formally, a c-frameproof code Γ is defined as a code satisfying $F(W) \cap \Gamma = W$ for $W \subset \Gamma$ of size at most c. Over the binary alphabet $\Sigma = \{0, 1\}$, we define the (n, n)-code $\Gamma_0(n)$ containing all n-bit binary words with exactly one 1. We can prove that $\Gamma_0(n)$ is n-frameproof.

Suppose a distributor marks an object with a code Γ and a coalition C of users colludes to generate an illegal object marked by some word x and then distribute this new object. We would like to detect a subset of the coalition when an illegal object is found; that is, we would like to construct a tracing algorithm to detect it. A code Γ is said to be *totally c-secure* if there is a tracing algorithm A satisfying the following condition: if a coalition C of at most c users generates a word x then $A(x) \in C$; that is, the tracing algorithm A on input x must output a member of the coalition C that generated the word x. Hence an illegal copy can be traced back to at least one member of the guilty coalition. We regard the tracing algorithm A as a function $A : \{0, 1\}^n \longrightarrow \{1, \ldots, n\}$, where n is the number of users. We describe how such a tracing algorithm can be constructed.

Suppose a coalition C of c users creates an illegal copy of an object. Fingerprinting schemes that enable us to capture a member of coalition C with probability at least $1 - \varepsilon$ are are called *c-secure codes with ε-error*. Formally, Γ_r is c-secure with ε-error if there is a tracing algorithm A such that if a coalition C of at most c users generates a word x then $Pr[A(x) \in C] > 1 - \varepsilon$ where the probability is taken over by the random bits r and the random choices made by the coalition. In a construction of collusion-secure codes, we can obtain a tracing algorithm which given a word x generated by some coalition C, outputs a member of C with probability $1 - \varepsilon$.

Let c_m be a column of height n in which the first m bits are one and the rest are zero. The code $\Sigma_0(n, d)$ consists of all columns $c_1, \ldots, c_{n-1}$, each duplicates d times. The amount of duplication determines the error probability ε. Let $x^{(1)}, \ldots, x^{(n)}$ denote the codewords of $\Gamma_0(n, d)$. Before the distributor embeds the codewords of $\Sigma_0(n, d)$ in an object, he makes the following random choice: he randomly picks a permutation $\pi \in S_l$, where S_l is the full symmetric group of all permutations on l letters. User u_i's copy of the object will be fingerprinted using the word $\pi x^{(i)}$. Note that the same permutation π is applied to all users, and π will be kept secret. Keeping the permutation hidden from the users is equivalent to hiding the information of which mark in the object encodes which bit in the code.

To derive a tracing algorithm, let us define some notions. Let B_m be the set of all bit positions in which the users see columns of type c_m. That is, B_m is the set of all bit positions in which the first m users see a one and the rest see a zero. The number of elements in B_m is d. For $2 \leq s \leq n-1$, define $R_s = B_{s-1} \cup B_s$. For a binary string x, let $weight(x)$ denote the number of ones in x.

Suppose user s is not a member of coalition C which produced the word x. The hidden permutation π prevents the coalition from knowing which marks present which bits in the code $\Gamma_0(n, d)$. The only information the coalition has is the value of the marks it can detect. Observe that without user s a coalition sees exactly the same values for all bit positions $i \in R_s$.

For a bit position $i \in R_s$, the coalition C cannot tell if i lies in B_s or in B_{s-1}. This means that whichever strategy they use to set the bits of $x|_{R_s}$, the ones in $x|_{R_s}$ will be roughly evenly distributed between $x|_{B_s}$ and $x|_{B_{s-1}}$ with high probability. Hence if the ones in $x|_{R_s}$ are not evenly distributed then, with high probability, user s is a member of the coalition that generated x. With some computation, we can obtain a measure for d in $\Gamma_0(n, d)$ such that $d = 2n^2 \log(2n/\varepsilon)$ for $n \geq 3$, and the tracing algorithm can be formulated as follows:

Algorithm *Given $x \in \{0, 1\}^l$, find a subset of the coalition that produced x.*

1. *If $weight(x|_{B_1}) > 0$, then output "user 1 is guilty"*
2. *If $weight(x|_{B_{n-1}}) < d$, then output "user n is guilty"*
3. *For all $s = 2$ to $n - 1$ do; let $k = weight(x|_{R_s})$. If*

$$weight(x|_{B_{s-1}}) < \frac{k}{2} - \sqrt{\frac{k}{2} \log \frac{2n}{\varepsilon}} \tag{8.4}$$

then output "user s is guilty"

There is one thing needed to be clarified: if the word x found in the illegal copy contains some unreadable marks, these bits are set to zero before the word x is given to the algorithm. The algorithm then receives a word in $\{0, 1\}^l$.

8.6.3   Asymmetric fingerprinting

Usually, fingerprinting schemes are symmetric, that is, all users are able to recognize the fingerprinted copy. In electronic commerce, this property implies that it is not possible for the distributor to prove that a specific user and not the merchant distributed the object illegally. In order to handle this situation, Pfitzmann and Schunter [20] introduced asymmetric fingerprinting (see Figure 8.1). In this scheme only the buyer knows the data with the fingerprint. If the merchant later finds it somewhere, the merchant can identify its buyer and prove this fact to third parties.

This scheme consists of four protocols: key_gen, fing, identify, and dispute. In the key generation protocol key_gen, the buyer generates a public key pk_B and a private key sk_B and publishes the public key pk_B via a certification authority. Let

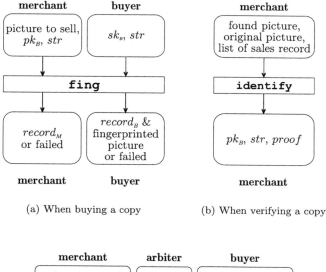

(a) When buying a copy   (b) When verifying a copy

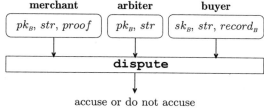

accuse or do not accuse

(c) In case of dispute

Figure 8.1   Asymmetric fingerprinting.

us consider a purchase of a picture in digital format. As inputs for the fingerprinting protocol `fing`, the merchant inputs the picture to sell, the buyer's identity pk_B and a string str to describe the purchase; str is used to match inputs from multiparties like a search key. Moreover the merchant may input a list of records from previous sales of the same picture. The buyer inputs str and his secret key sk_B. An output to the buyer is the picture to buy with a small error. The buyer may also obtain a record $record_B$ to be stored for future disputes. If the protocol fails, the buyer will get an output "failed." The output for the merchant is a record of the sale $record_M$ or "failed." When the merchant finds a copy and wants to identify the original buyer, he inputs the copy found to the algorithm `identify` with the picture the merchant sold and a list of sales records of the picture. The output of `identify` is either "failed" or the identity of a buyer pk_B and a signed string *proof* by the buyer. The dispute protocol `dispute` is a two- or three-party protocol between the merchant, an arbiter, and possibly the accused buyer. The merchant and arbiter input pk_B and *str*. The merchant additionally inputs the string *proof*. If the accused buyer takes part, he inputs *str*, his secret key sk_B, and $record_B$. The output of the protocol is a Boolean value for the arbiter whether he accuses or not. That is, the output shows whether the arbiter accepts that the merchant has found the picture bought by the accused buyer with *str*.

8.6.4 Traitor tracing

If only one person knows a secret and it appears on the evening news, then the guilty party is evident. When the set of people that have access to the secret is large, however, a more complex situation arises. If all of them share exactly the same data, the problem of determining guilt or innocent is unsolvable. One possibility to find a traitor from the secret sharers is to give a slightly different secret to the sharers. Chor et al. [1] applied this idea to reduce piracy. For this application, it is necessary to identify whether piracy is going on and to prevent information transfer to pirate users while harming no legitimate users. Furthermore, the legal evidence of the pirate identity should be provided. An application of their scheme to trace pirates who abuse a broadcast encryption scheme under the above requirements is presented.

The detailed operation of the Chor-Fiat-Naor scheme [1] is as follows: the distributor generates a base set R of r random keys and assigns m keys out of R to every user, which form the user's personal key. Note that different personal keys may have a nonempty intersection.

A traitor-tracing message consists of multiple pairs (*enablingblock, cipherblock*), see Figure 8.2. The cipher block is the symmetric encryption of the actual data, say a few seconds of a video clip, under some secret random key S. The enabling block allows authorized users to obtain S, and consists of encrypted video data under some or all of the r keys by the distributor. Each user can compute S by decrypting the encrypted video data using his keys, that is, the user's key set and enabling block become input to generate the decryption key for the corresponding cipher block.

Traitors may collude and give an unauthorized user a subset of their keys so that the unauthorized user can also decrypt the cipher blocks. The goal of the scheme is to assign keys to users in such a way that when a pirate decoder is captured and the keys it possesses are examined, it should be possible to detect at least one traitor.

It is expected that traitor-tracing schemes provide legal evidence for such

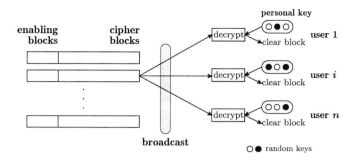

Figure 8.2   Chor-Fiat-Naor scheme.

treachery. Pfitzmann [20] focused on this point, and pointed out that the Chor-Fiat-Naor scheme cannot provide nonrepudiation because it is based on symmetric fingerprinting. Nonrepudiation is the property that prevents people from denying an action. By applying her asymmetric fingerprinting scheme, Pfitzmann provided an asymmetric traitor-tracing scheme with nonrepudiation [16].

8.6.5 Anonymous fingerprinting

Chaum [21] introduced a signature scheme that makes it possible to get the signature on a data from a signer without revealing the content of the data; this is called blind signature. Anonymous fingerprinting is an application of blind signatures. Pfitzmann and Waidner [18] introduced anonymous asymmetric fingerprinting based on a trusted third party and the asymmetric fingerprinting scheme [20]. Buyers can buy information anonymously, but can nevertheless be identified if they redistribute this information illegally, see Figure 8.3.

Electronic marketplaces are supposed to offer similar privacy as conventional marketplaces; that is, a certain level of anonymity in electronic purchase should be achieved. When people buy goods with cash, no one can trace the purchase in conventional marketplaces. It is undesirable for all this anonymity to be destroyed just to make buyers identify themselves for fingerprinting. With all previous symmetric and asymmetric fingerprinting schemes, buyers have to identify themselves during the purchase.

The basic idea of the anonymous fingerprinting is as follows: the buyer selects a pseudonym (i.e., a key pair (sk_B, pk_B) of a signature scheme), and signs under his true identity that he is responsible for this pseudonym. He obtains a certificate $cert_B$ from the registration center. With this certificate the registration center declares that it knows the identity of the buyer who chose this pseudonym (i.e., the

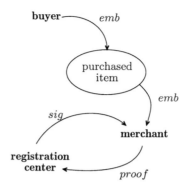

Figure 8.3   Anonymous fingerprinting.

registration center can identify a pseudonym with a real person). The buyer then computes a signature on the text identifying the purchase with no knowledge of the merchant, $sig := sign(sk_B, text)$ when he makes a purchase, and then embeds the information $emb := (text, sig, pk_B, cert_B)$ in the purchased data item. He hides this value in a bit commitment and sends the certificate and the commitment to the merchant in zero-knowledge. Bit commitment [22, 23] is a cryptographic technique to commit to data yet keep it secret for some period; detailed information can be found in [7, pp. 86–88]. When identification is needed, the merchant extracts emb and sends $proof := (text, sig, pk_B)$ to the registration center and asks for identification. In the response, the registration center sends back the buyer's signature to the merchant. With the signature, the merchant can then verify all values and has the evidence to accuse the buyer.

8.7 CONCLUSION

This chapter provided an overview and introduction to fingerprinting, including its examples, taxonomy, research history, and recent studies and developments. Essentially, fingerprinting is a technique to distinguish copies. With growing concern for digital copyright protection and copy control, this technique is used for copyright protection of intellectual properties in a digital format.

Fingerprinting is not designed to reveal the exact relationship between the copyrighted product and the product owner unless he or she violates its legal use. Compared with cryptography, this property may look incomplete and imprecise, but it may appeal to users and markets. High precision does not solve everything. It not only costs less than control by encryption but also may provide some anonymity to users. For copyright protection applications, fingerprinting is an easy, lightweight and efficient means; it may also complement copy-management techniques based on encryption and provide a fall-back defense when encryption keys are compromised.

REFERENCES

[1] Chor, B., A. Fiat, and M. Naor, "Tracing Traitors," in *Advances in Cryptology, Proceedings of CRYPTO '94*, vol. 839 of *Lecture Notes in Computer Science*, Springer-Verlag, 1994, pp. 257–270.

[2] Cambridge University Library, *Title Fingerprint Search: Cambridge Union List of Serials*, Cambridge, England, 1998.

[3] Kahn, D., *The Codebreakers – The Story of Secret Writing*, New York, USA: Scribner, 1996.

[4] Card International, *Iris-recognition ATMs Planned for Rollout in 1999*, Cambridge, England, Dec. 1998.

[5] Postel, J., "Out-of-Net Host Addresses for Mail," IETF RFC 754, The Internet Engineering Task Force, Apr. 1979.

[6] Zimmermann, P. R., *The Official PGP User's Guide*, Cambridge, Massachusetts, USA: MIT Press, 1995.

[7] Schneier, B., *Applied Cryptography*, New York, USA: John Wiley & Sons, 2nd ed., 1996.

[8] comp.security.pgp, *The comp.security.pgp FAQ*, Oct. 1998.

[9] Anderson, R. J., et al., *The Global Internet Trust Register 1999*, Cambridge, Massachusetts, USA: MIT Press, Apr. 1999.

[10] Brassil, J., et al., "Electronic Marking and Identification Techniques to Discourage Document Copying," in *Proceedings of Infocom '94*, Jun. 1994, pp. 1278–1287.

[11] Heintze, N., "Scalable Document Fingerprinting," in *Proceedings of the 2nd USENIX Electronic Commerce Conference*, Oakland, California, USA, 1996, pp. 191–200.

[12] Wagner, N. R., "Fingerprinting," in *Proceedings of the 1983 IEEE Symposium on Security and Privacy*, Oakland, California, USA, Apr. 1983, pp. 18–22.

[13] Blakley, G. R., C. Meadows, and G. B. Purdy, "Fingerprinting Long Forgiving Messages," in *Advances in Cryptology, Proceedings of CRYPTO '85*, vol. 218 of *Lecture Notes in Computer Science*, Springer-Verlag, 1986, pp. 180–189.

[14] Boneh, D., and J. Shaw, "Collusion-secure Fingerprinting for Digital Data," in *Advances in Cryptology, Proceedings of CRYPTO '95*, vol. 963 of *Lecture Notes in Computer Science*, Springer-Verlag, 1995, pp. 452–465.

[15] Low, S. H., and N. F. Maxemchuk, "Modeling Cryptographic Protocols and their Collusion Analysis," in *Information Hiding: First International Workshop, Proceedings*, vol. 1174 of *Lecture Notes in Computer Science*, Springer-Verlag, 1996, pp. 169–184.

[16] Pfitzmann, B., "Trials of Traced Traitors," in *Information Hiding: First International Workshop, Proceedings*, vol. 1174 of *Lecture Notes in Computer Science*, Springer-Verlag, 1996, pp. 49–64.

[17] Pfitzmann, B., and M. Waidner, "Asymmetric Fingerprinting for Larger Collusions," in *Proceedings of the 4th ACM Conference on Computer and Communications Security*, 1997, pp. 151–160.

[18] Pfitzmann, B., and M. Waidner, "Anonymous Fingerprinting," in *Advances in Cryptol-*

ogy, *Proceedings of EUROCRYPT '97*, vol. 1233 of *Lecture Notes in Computer Science*, Springer-Verlag, 1997, pp. 88–102.

[19] Boneh, D., and J. Shaw, "Collusion-secure Fingerprinting for Digital Data," *IEEE Transactions on Information Theory*, vol. IT-44, no. 5, Sep. 1998, pp. 1897–1905.

[20] Pfitzmann, B., and M. Schunter, "Asymmetric Fingerprinting," in *Advances in Cryptology, Proceedings of EUROCRYPT '96*, vol. 1070 of *Lecture Notes in Computer Science*, Springer-Verlag, 1996, pp. 84–95.

[21] Chaum, D. L., "Blind Signatures for Untraceable Payments," in *Advances in Cryptology, Proceedings of CRYPTO '82*, Plenum Press, 1983, pp. 199–203.

[22] Brassard, G., D. L. Chaum, and C. Crépeau, "Minimum Disclosure Proofs of Knowledge," *Journal of Computer and System Sciences*, vol. 37, no. 2, Oct. 1998, pp. 156–189.

[23] Naor, M., "Bit Commitment Using Pseudo-Randomness," in *Advances in Cryptology, Proceedings of CRYPTO '89*, vol. 435 of *Lecture Notes in Computer Science*, Springer-Verlag, 1990, pp. 128–136.

Chapter 9

Copyright on the Internet and watermarking

Stanley Lai and Fabrizio Marongiu Buonaiuti

9.1 DIGITAL COPYRIGHT AND WATERMARKING[1]

This section discusses some recent developments in copyright pertaining to digital technology, and addresses the copyright implications of tampering with, or reverse-engineering watermarking systems. Watermarking, the effusive method of tracking readership in the course of digital use, is often invoked as a cure-all solution to the copyright protection of multimedia data. Research on this technology has been formidable, as seen from other chapters of this work. However, standardization, effective investigation of interoperability issues, and the definition of a preliminary set of requirements for an effective watermarking system are still far from reached [2].[2]

Watermarks serve as tools for digital copyright protection. As the previous chapters discussed, there are various general scenarios to which watermarking may be applied. An example is image copyright protection by means of visible watermarks. Such a mark is visually apparent, but does not prevent the images from being used for other purposes. The visibility is intended to make apparent any commercial exploitation of the image, hence assisting enforcement of copyright. This watermarking system can also be used to indicate the ownership of original works.

---

1 Part of Section 9.1 has appeared as an opinion in the *European Intellectual Property Review*, no. 171, 1999, and part of Section 9.2 appeared in [1], published by CCH Editions Ltd, London.

2 The primary resource for this section, covering the technical intricacies of watermarking is [2].

Typically watermarks are used to prevent and detect unauthorized reproductions and distributions. If data or documents, which are disseminated on-line, are embedded with a watermark, a Web crawler can be subsequently used to search for unauthorized distributions (see Section 7.3.2). Digital watermarking is a relatively new discipline, and the search is still on for a truly robust blind public transparent-image watermarking algorithm, as suggest the attacks presented in Chapter 7. There are other limits to the present technology, for example, it is still not clear how many bits can be embedded into a piece of information of a given size.

This section proposes to study the treatment of generic watermarking systems as "technical protection systems" within the scheme of copyright as well as the larger context of reader privacy. By way of precursor, it may be helpful to discuss the latest copyright initiatives which affect the governance of digital disseminations in the on-line environment.

9.1.1   The WIPO treaties and WIPO's digital agenda

In 1996, the World Intellectual Property Organization (WIPO) convened a diplomatic conference [3], with the objective to revise the Berne Convention for the Protection of Literary and Artistic Works (the first international source in matters of copyright, establishing the so-called Berne Union for the protection of authors of literary and artistic works, concluded in 1886 and revised at a number of subsequent diplomatic conferences, most notably in Paris in 1971 (hereinafter the "Berne Convention") to cover digital use and dissemination. Two treaties emerged from the conference, the WIPO Copyright Treaty (WCT) and the WIPO Performances and Phonograms Treaty. It is the former which is directly relevant to the present discussion, and it is clear that its relationship with the Berne Convention is exclusive: Article 1 WCT.

Article 1(1) WCT provides that "this Treaty is a special agreement within the meaning of Article 20 of the Berne Convention for the Protection of Literary and Artistic Works, as regards Contracting Parties that are countries of the Union established by that Convention." Article 20 of the Berne Convention contains the following provision: "The Governments of the countries of the Union reserve the right to enter into special agreements among themselves, in so far as such agreements grant to authors more extensive rights than those granted by the Convention, or contain other provisions not contrary to this Convention." Article 1(1) of the WCT forbids any interpretation of the WCT which may result in a lower level of protection than that granted under the Berne Convention. The second sentence of Article 1(1) of the WCT deals with the relationship of the WCT with other treaties apart from the Berne Convention, and states that "this Treaty shall not have any connection with treaties other than the Berne Convention, nor shall it prejudice any rights and obligations under any other treaties." The WCT's relationship with Berne is clearly exclusive.

The provisions of the WCT relating to the "digital agenda" cover the following issues: the rights applicable for the storage and transmission [4, Art. 8] of works in digital systems, the limitations on and exceptions to rights in a digital environment [4, Art. 10], technological measures of protection [4, Art. 11], and rights management information [4, Art. 12]. Although the draft of the WCT contained certain provisions that were intended to clarify the application of the right of reproduction to storage of works in digital form in an electronic medium, they were not included in the final version. The Diplomatic Conference, however, adopted an Agreed Statement in the following terms:

> The reproduction right, as set out in Article 9 of the Berne Convention, and the exceptions permitted thereunder, fully apply in the digital environment, in particular to the use of works in digital form, It is understood that the storage of a protected work in digital form in an electronic medium constitutes a reproduction within the meaning of Article 9 of the Berne Convention.

As early as June 1982 a WIPO/UNESCO Committee of Governmental Experts clarified that storage of works in an electronic medium is reproduction, and WIPO officially states no doubt concerning that principle [5, p. 6], and [6, pp. 49–51].

9.1.2 Technical protection systems, rights management information, and their circumvention

In the preparatory work leading to the passing of the WCT, it was recognized that it is not sufficient to provide for appropriate rights in respect of digital uses of works, particularly on the Internet. In such an environment, no rights may be applied efficiently without the support of technological measures of protection and rights management. These issues are addressed by Articles 11 and 12 of the WCT.

Article 11

Under Article 11 of the WCT, Contracting Parties are required to provide "adequate legal protection and effective legal remedies against the circumvention of effective technological measures that are used by authors in connection with the exercise of their rights under this Treaty or the Berne Convention and that restrict acts, in respect of their works, which are not authorized by the authors concerned or permitted by law." On inspection, this "anticircumvention" clause is broad in its terms, its language betraying much of the controversy underlying its inception [7]. By way of summary, the controversy surrounding anticircumvention legislation has, in the past, centered around (i) its coverage of devices, particularly dual-use technology, and (ii) the prohibition of activities like software reverse-engineering, which are otherwise rendered lawful by the operation of a copyright exception, such as the fair use doctrine. In effect the concern, in relation to the latter, is that anticircumvention clauses would write the copyright exceptions out of copyright law.[3]

Article 11 of the WCT is an improvement on previous drafts. First it applies to the act of circumvention "for infringing purposes," rather than affixing liability on the manufacture or distribution of the device, in circumstances where there may be little or no anticipation that a device could be put to such a protection-defeating use. Secondly, there is no reference to "devices," as may be confronted in the proposed U.S. legislation implementing Article 11 WCT [9, S. 30], but to "measures" and "acts" of circumvention, which may potentially exclude dual-use technologies [7, p. 235], and [10, recital 30, Art. 6(1)]. Finally, the "circumvention" referred to in Article 11 only applies to acts "which are not authorized by the rights holders concerned or permitted by law." Within this formulation, copyright exceptions and exemptions remain intact, through ensuring that the sphere of application of Article 11 corresponds only to copyright infringement [6, p. 48]. Article 11 avoids any definition of "effective technological measures," probably in view of the resistance to its earlier drafts [11, Draft Art. 13 (3)], and [6, pp. 45–47].

Article 12

Article 12(1) WCT obliges Contracting Parties to "provide adequate and effective legal remedies against any person knowingly performing any of the following acts knowing, or with respect to civil remedies having reasonable grounds to know, that it will induce, enable, facilitate or conceal an infringement of any right covered by this Treaty or the Berne Convention: (i) to remove or alter any electronic rights management information without authority; (ii) to distribute, import for distribution, broadcast or communicate to the public, without authority, works or copies of works knowing that electronic rights management information has been removed or altered without authority." Article 12(2) defines "rights management information" as meaning "information which identifies the work, the author of the work, the owner of any right in the work, or information about the terms and conditions of use of the work, and any number or codes that represent such information, when any of these items of information is attached to a copy of a work or appears in connection with the communication of a work to the public."

---

3 For a discussion on the dilemma and controversy of traversing prohibitions between "acts" and "devices" of circumvention, see [8, pp. 197–207].

The Diplomatic Conference adopted the following Agreed Statement on Article 12 of the WCT:

> It is understood that the reference to 'infringement of any right covered by this Treaty or the Berne Convention' includes both exclusive rights and rights of remuneration. It is further understood that Contracting Parties will not rely on this Article to devise or implement rights management systems that would have the effect of imposing formalities which are not permitted under the Berne Convention or this Treaty, prohibiting the free movement of goods or impeding the enjoyment of rights under this Treaty.

The Agreed Statement evidently restricts the implementation of copyright-management systems to enforce any "Berne plus" rights and formalities.

In its final form Article 12 is a modification of its previous draft [11, Draft Art. 14 (1)], in requiring some connection to an infringing purpose [4, Art. 12 (1)]. It requires not only the knowing performance of a prohibited act, but also actual or constructive knowledge that such act will facilitate an act of copyright infringement. In addition, liability for distribution of altered works is imposed only if the distributor actually knows of the removal of rights management information. Particularly significant for the purposes of watermarking is the definition of "rights management information," especially covering watermarks which serve as signs of ownership and identification. The scope of Article 12(1) was broadened to include terms and conditions governing the use of the work, bearing upon the unlawful tampering of on-line licenses. Watermarking algorithms are similarly covered by Article 12(2)'s reference to "numbers or codes that represent such information."

9.1.3 Legal protection of watermarking systems

It is clear from the Articles 11 and 12 of the WCT that copyright-management systems are envisaged as playing a significant role for the copyright enforcement in the future. Insofar as watermarking forms part of rights management information (as defined by Article 12(2) WCT), it is protected against any unauthorized removal, alteration, distribution or importation in the course of digital dissemination. This bears upon "watermark invertibility."

A watermark is said to be invertible if authorized users are able to remove it from a document. In one context it may seen as desirable, since it would allow owners the flexibility to change the status of a document, according to its history. Conversely, invertibility is difficult to sustain if tampering resistance is sought [2, pp. 7–8]. Hence the greater the invertibility of a watermark, the greater the regulatory significance of Article 12 WCT.

The position of watermarks in relation to Article 11 WCT is less clear. It is uncertain whether watermarks constitute "effective technological measures," in the absence of any definition from the Treaty. Article 6(2) of the recent Proposal for a European Parliament and Council Directive on the Harmonization of certain aspects of copyright and related rights in the Information Society [7, p. 235], and [10, recital 30, Article 6(1)] offers the following definition:

> The expression 'technological measures' [...] means any device, product or component incorporated into a process, device or product designed to prevent or inhibit the infringement of any copyright or to prevent or inhibit the infringement of any copyright or any rights related to copyright [...] Technological measures shall only be deemed 'effective' *where the work or other subject matter is rendered accessible to the user only through application of an access code or process, including by decryption, descrambling or other transformation of the work or other subject matter, with the authority of the rightholders.* (emphasis added)

Insofar as a watermarking system performs functions of readership tracking and author/owner identification, it may not satisfy the above definition. Notwithstanding this, the rights available under Article 12 are sufficiently broad to address tampering with any watermarking system.

9.1.4   Watermarking interoperability

As with computer software, issues of interoperability transcend into the watermarking sphere, and the compatibility of different watermarking techniques is crucial when copyright protection is granted over various open environments. The Imprimatur Report on Watermarking [2] has stated that the compatibility of different watermarking systems may be addressed at two basic levels: intrinsic and format compatibility. According to this report, when speaking of intrinsic compatibility, two different watermarking algorithms can co-exist in the same environment only if the following conditions are satisfied: (i) they allow a predefined minimum number of bits to be inserted into the data, in such a way that the same information can be carried out by all the involved watermarks; (ii) watermarking algorithms must be homogeneous, in that private and public algorithms cannot be used together, nor blind/nonblind (readable/detectable) techniques can be mixed together. Format compatibility, simply put, refers to whether different watermarking formats bear the same kind of information.

This raises a question: whether it is permissible to reverse engineer (either through decompilation or disassembly) a watermarking algorithm for the purposes of securing interoperability with another format in a particular environment. In the European context the Directive, hereinafter the "Software Directive" [12], may come into play, provided the watermarking algorithm in question qualifies as "computer software" and satisfies the originality and minimal requirements necessary for copyright: if a micro-code is capable of copyright protection a fortiori a watermarking algorithm encompassing authorial information [13]. In practice there should be little doubt as to the software of a watermarking algorithm, since the algorithms consist of coding [2, p. 13] and could be seen as sets of instructions enabling a machine to perform a given function.

The regulatory regime of the Software Directive imposes stringent conditions on the decompilation of software [14–18]. Crucially, decompilation must be "indispensable to obtain the information necessary to achieve [...] interoperability," and fulfill the conditions in Article 6(1)(a)–(c). The interoperable developer must be a licensee or an authorized user [12, Art. 6(1)(a)], must not decompile interface information of which he has been previously made aware [12, Art. 6(1)(b)], and finally, must confine his decompilation only to those parts of the target program that contain the interface information he requires to create an independently created, interoperable program [12, Art. 6(1)(c)]. Beyond this, another three conditions [12, Art. 6(2)] are imposed on the use which may be made of the results of decompilation. Interface information may only be used for purposes relating to the interoperability of the newly created program [12, Art. 6(2)(a)], and the developer is restrained from divulging such information except for this purpose [12, Art. 6(2)(b)]. The final restriction prevents any interface information obtained through decompilation from being used to, inter alia, develop a copyright infringing program [12, Art. 6(2)(c)].

Interoperable developers in (re)search of watermarking interoperability should be mindful of the above restrictions on reverse engineering. The same is true for researchers of watermark invertibility who reverse engineer the watermarking process [2, p. 7].

9.1.5   Broader considerations of reader privacy

The copyright discussion on the use and development of watermarking should round off with a consideration of privacy concerns that bear upon the use of this technology. Writers [19, pp. 17–21, pp. 31–35], [20, pp. 228–238, p. 241], [21, pp. 140–141], and [22, p. 34, pp. 36–37] have described the capabilities of the ideal electronic copyright management system as follows:

- Detecting, preventing, and counting a wide range of operations, including open, print, export, copying, modifying, excerpting, etc.;

- Maintaining records indicating which permissions have actually been granted and to whom;
- Capturing a record of what the user actually looked at, copied or printed;
- Sending this usage record to a clearing house when the user seeks additional access, at the end of a billing period or whenever the user runs out of credit.

These attributes are manifested in regulating technologies which are invasive in character, especially where through the use of technologies such as watermarking, a systems operator may be able to generate predictive profiles of a particular consumer base: it has been argued that the freedom to read, listen, and view selected materials anonymously should be considered a right protected by the First Amendment in the United States [23, p. 184], and [24, pp. 985–6, 1003–30]. It is quite possible for management systems to preserve privacy by preventing the extraction of personal data, in order "to protect the privacy of individuals...the usage data can be aggregated or made anonymous before it reaches rights holders" [22, p. 36]. It has also been observed that the most effective way to protect individual privacy in the digital age is to design technological tools such that they prevent or limit the identification of individuals [25, pp. 181–83] or accepting anonymous digital cash [26, pp. 415–20, 459–70].

Developers of watermarking systems should be mindful of EC general purpose privacy laws [27] (contrast the approach taken in the United States, where legislative efforts in favor of privacy are more piecemeal; see for instace [28], concerning the privacy of video rental records), which may form a potential hindrance to copyright-management systems that are deemed too intrusive, for example, through revealing too much information about the user. The European IMPRIMATUR[4] project concluded that in developing a standardized model for copyright-management, reader privacy should be recognized as a fundamental right, and "privacy-enhancing" technology should be harnessed for all models [29, pp. 86–90]. In its latest Proposed Directive on "Copyright and Related Rights in an Information Society" COM(97) 628 final, the Commission in recital 33 acknowledges that technology incorporating rights management information may be used to process personal data about the use of the copyright work by individuals and to trace on-line behavior. Such technology must necessarily incorporate privacy safeguards in order to comply with the Data Protection Directive (95/46 EEC).

At the same time, the countervailing consideration is the use of watermarking to effectively enforce copyright; arguably one that should, in the public interest, override "not overly-intrusive" and hence unimpressive privacy arguments. Readership tracking should be deemed permissible insofar as such information that is

---

4 "Intellectual Multimedia Property Rights Model and Terminology for Universal Reference"

necessary for copyright enforcement is extracted and judiciously managed for enforcement purposes.

9.1.6   Conclusion

This section hopefully makes evident that watermarking as a technology is protected by copyright law, in the most recent WIPO initiatives. There is much scope for more research on the subject, and the dangers of missing the objective of reverse-engineering provisions in the Software Directive have been raised, and privacy concerns highlighted.

With the effluxion of time, we will be able to see whether, and to what extent, watermarking and the governance of digital copyright form an effective alliance.

9.2   CONFLICT OF COPYRIGHT LAWS ON THE INTERNET

The goal of this section is to examine the applicability of the new statutory rules on the conflict of laws in torts, as under the Private International Law (Miscellaneous Provisions) Act 1995—a statute making provision for the reform of parts of the rules on the conflict of laws within the United Kingdom, whose Part III is specifically dedicated to torts, hereinafter "the 1995 Act"—to a particular scenario of legal activities, bearing a relevance both from an information technology and an intellectual property perspective, that of activities implying infringement of copyright on materials made available on the Internet. It is acknowledged that, whereas the traditional solution to problems of coordination among different domestic legislative standards, originally brought about by the Berne Convention (see Section 9.1.1) with respect to conventional literary or artistic works, consisted in applying the national law of the author, or the law of the place of creation of the work *(lex originis)* on the basis of the national treatment principle, such a solution has in the long run proved less and less viable as allegedly discriminatory, in the light of growing suspicion and mistrust among different legal systems, with therefore inevitable reference to more articulated solutions. For example, while retaining as a general rule the lex originis to determine the subsistence and extent of copyright as a proprietary right, the law relating to the place where infringements are commited (lex loci commissi delicti), or any other law as applicable under the relevant rules of conflict of laws in torts. This in turn is applicable to infringements, as tortious invasions of property, the law relating to the place where they are committed *(lex loci commissi delicti)*, or any other law as applicable under the relevant rules of conflict of laws in torts.

Examination of this issue requires proceeding by subsequent stages, from an analysis of the new conflict of laws rules on tort as introduced by the 1995 Act, with particular regard to one of its most attractive features, the provision for a flexible clause of exception providing for the application of a law "substantially more appropriate" than the lex loci commissi delicti (the law of the place where the harmful event—or subject to specification, the resulting damage—occurred) as under the general rule. In this respect, a comparison is drawn between the latter option envisaged under the new law and a doctrinal elaboration due to the late English scholar, Dr Morris, and known as "the proper law of a tort" [30].

In the subsequent section the application of these principles to cases of copyright infringement will be evaluated. This implies addressing a number of questions of principle: may copyright infringement be considered a tort? Or, accordingly, may conflict of laws rules on tort suitably apply to such cases, in the particular perspective of deciding which copyright law will apply to the matters at hand? After attempting to answer these questions, consider whether the "proper law" approach may apply with regard to activities taking place on the Internet and whether this effectively helps solving problems, which would have been left unsolved by more rigid criteria such as the lex loci commissi delicti.

Finally, although the two-stages approach of the present essay is definitely cut between conflict of laws on one side and copyright protection on the other, a reference to some parallel and strictly related issues may not be omitted, with specific reference to the protection of personal data and the legal issues related to encryption technology.

9.2.1   The new rules on conflict of laws in torts in the U.K.

Part III of the 1995 Act introduced two changes of major significance to English conflict of laws in torts. The former consists in the codification of a subject so far left to the domain of the common law; the latter in the final abandonment of the leading common law rule, which had governed not merely choice of law but also jurisdiction of the English courts in tort actions.

The abolishment of the rule of double actionability; the lex loci commissi delicti

The rule of double actionability may be considered as a twofold mechanism, allowing an alleged tort committed abroad to be pursued in the English courts insofar as recognized as tort under both the law of the the place where it has been committed, the lex loci commissi delicti, and the *lex fori* (the domestic law of the courts where the issue arises). The rule as consolidated in dating case law and more recently specified in *Boys v. Chaplin* [31]—a case relating to the law applicable to liability in tort arising out of a road accident that occurred in Malta between English parties only, where, as explained later, English law was applied as more strictly connected to the elements of the case—clearly resulted in a restriction of the opportunities of the plaintiff who would have really been faced with an "uphill struggle" [32, p. 650] in order to satisfy so strict a requirement.

In the more recent case of *Red Sea Insurance v. Bouygues* [33–35]—a case of insurance of a building project in Saudi Arabia, where the insurer sought to rely on a direct cause of action which would have been allowed under the lex loci delicti commissi (Saudi Arabian) but not the lex fori (Hong Kong, presumed in accordance with English law), and the action was allowed as an exception to the rule of double actionability upon the specific facts of the case—a first step towards mitigation of the rule was actually taken, to the extent that the Judiridical Committee Privy Council ultimately granted recovery, which would have been allowed under the lex cause (the law applicable under conflict of laws rules, such as the lex loci commissi delicti) but not the lex fori, thus substantially setting aside the requirement of double actionability. Obviously, such an apparently revolutionary conclusion needs some specification: first of all, remember that decisions of the Privy Council—hearing as a final instance in point of law, substantially as the Judicial Committee of the House of Lords, cases from the supreme courts in dominions or Commonwealth countries, to the exception of those, such as recently Canada and Australia, which have waived its jurisdiction—are not as a matter of principle binding precedent on the English Courts and, conversely, the Privy Council itself in deciding of the issue was not bound by any recent authority. Secondly, in the merit of the decision, in the opinion of Lord Slynn, the double actionability rule was not actually overruled at all, simply an exception to it was applied on the basis of the facts of the case.

Actually, by the time the above case was decided, a proposal had already been considered by the Law Commissions for England and Scotland for a legislative reform of the subject, whereby the old rule of double actionability would have been definitively abolished. This project resulted in the Private International Law (Miscellaneous Provisions) Bill, which was made subject to extensive study by the House of Lords Special Public Bill Committee shortly thereafter [36].

The new regulation of the subject in the final text of Part III of the 1995 Act [37], begins with providing, under Section 9, a sort of preliminary *whereas*, whereunder a series of specifications is provided as to the meaning and scope of application of Part III. In fact, Section 9 of the 1995 Act addresses some of the crucial issues of private international law, such as the characterization of the issues in question as being in tort or delict, which is to be dealt with by the courts of the forum, an assumption by itself rather tautological, insofar as it does not provide for the law to be used to the purpose [38, pp. 893–894], [39, 40]. The latter question is then solved by a further paragraph in the sense that the applicable law shall apply also to the preliminary question of whether an actionable tort or delict has occurred, and, for the avoidance of doubt, that the provisions in Part III are to be deemed applicable equally to events occurring in the forum. That is, within the jurisdiction [37, Sec. 9, par. 7], as they are to events occurring abroad [37, Sec. 9, par. 4, 6], [41], [42, pp. 521–523], and [43].

It is then for Section 10 to provide that the consolidated rules of the common law bearing the requirement of double actionability, or providing as an exception for a single law to govern the issues of tort or delict arising in a given case, are to be intended as abolished, insofar as they do not apply to matters of defamation which are excluded from the operation of Part III of the 1995 Act [37, Sec. 10].

Coming finally to the solutions adopted by the 1995 Act, the general rule adopted in Section 11 consists of the applicability of the lex loci commissi delicti, as generally retained in foreign legislation on the basis of a strict principle of territoriality. Nonetheless, the weight of experience within the legal systems adopting this rule has suggested the addition of a series of specifications, to the extent that the lex loci commissi delicti is to be intended as the law of the place where the events constituting the tort or delict in question have occurred. A further provision in respect of actions on personal injuries or damage to property, in which case the law of the place where the victim or the property was at the time of the injury or damage will apply, whereas in respect of those cases still remaining in the gray area, a different solution has been devised, providing for a different law to be applicable. The law of the country where the most significant element or elements of the events in question occurred paves the way for the exception to the general rule, introduced by the subsequent Section 12 [37, Sec. 11], and [44].

The application of a substantially more appropriate law

Notably, Section 12 of the 1995 Act provides for a balance to be struck between the relevance of the factors connecting a tort or delict with the law applicable under the general rule and those connecting it with any other law as may be relevant in the specific case. With the effect that in case this balance tilts towards the latter law as substantially more appropriate to regulate the matters of the case, it shall then apply to the exclusion of the lex loci commissi delicti.

This solution, which may sound surprising in the context of a statute expressly aimed at providing that degree of certainty as to the applicable law which common law rules could not give, has actually not been brought about by the 1995 Act all of a sudden. In fact, a solution broadly conceived in such terms had already been retained in the common law, and notably in the cited case of *Boys v. Chaplin* [31], and earlier conceived in the doctrinal elaboration of one of the leading personalities in the English conflict of laws, under the meaningful banner of "the proper law of a tort" [30, 45], and [46, pp. 62–71].

To begin from the latter, the original and insightful inquiry traced in the very early 1950s as to the admissibility of a "proper law of a tort" represents a sort of confluence of both rules on conflict of laws in contract and in tort and, on the other side, of principles retained in either the English or the American legal systems. In fact, the formulation of this theory begins with the acknowledgement of the presence within English law of a notion of proper law with respect to contracts, whose lack was conversely resented in the American system, as shown by Paragraph 332 of the Restatement of Conflict of Laws of 1934 [47, Par. 332]—a nonlegislative consolidation of rules of U.S. law in specific areas.

On this premise, the perspective of introducing a "proper law" technique also in the field of torts is considered by Morris with regard to the advantages it would bring, if not in terms of stare decisis (authority of judicial precedent), in terms of flexibility and ultimate appropriateness of the law selected as applicable. In the absence so far of any authority within either English or Scottish law, reference was made to some breakthroughs by American case law, notwithstanding the general rule of choice of law in torts, as formulated in the Restatement of Conflict of Laws, was in the sense of applying the law of the place of wrong, intended as that where the last event giving rise to liability occurred [47, Par. 377].

In this respect, although the American rules on the conflict of laws in torts lacked the flexibility they enjoyed in the contractual field, a number of typical situations are clearly pointed out by Morris. A more flexible attitude appears to have been adopted by American courts with regard to the tort of conversion (i.e., undue appropriation), as well as in cases where the law of the place of the harmful conduct differs from that of damage. In one of these cases the doctrine of the proper law of a tort was introduced in the English conflict of laws by the House of Lords in *Boys v. Chaplin* [31], where the extent of tortious liability arising from a road accident that occurred in Malta involving exclusively English parties was held to be subject to the broader regime provided by English law, as more closely connected to the facts of the case.

Finally the 1995 Act gave the proper law of a tort an autonomous standing within English conflict of laws, thus emancipating it from the requirement of double actionability, where the House of Lords in *Boys v. Chaplin* had left it. We shall consider in the following subsection whether and to what extent, in the light of recent developments in the case law, this conflict of laws method may apply to copyright infringements on the Internet.

9.2.2   Information technology and intellectual property aspects

Our reference to the Internet requires some preliminary specifications. The Internet will be considered merely as a vehicle, and more precisely as a system of transmission, storage, and exchange of information. It is in this perspective that it becomes a virtual battlefield for intellectual property, not less than for other legal devices, notably the conflict of laws, specifically in torts. It follows that the interface between these two apparently separate developments of the present analysis is based on the indispensable coordination of the two: intellectual property law, mainly domestic in character, though part of a vital and irresistible process of harmonization, may not survive effectively without the support of a parallel system providing for the choice of the law to be applied, thus performing a role which is, and remains, indispensable, however further the process of harmonization and unification of domestic laws may proceed on the endless road to an ultimately unattainable absolute uniformity [48–51].

Internet as a means of exchange of information and the quest for legal protection

In this context, activities taking place on the Internet may be subject to a number of different sorts of protection: strictly under intellectual property law, both instrumentally, as under patent law covering the hardware, rather than software which is generally considered more suitably subject to copyright protection [6, 52], and under trademark law, with specific reference to domain names [53–56] and fundamentally, under copyright law, not less than general tort law, as in the specific case of passing off, or in the equivalent civil law cases of unfair competition, not to mention here cases arising from public policy or moral issues [57, 58].

Such a broad spectrum of legal issues has a direct reflection on the variety of cases arisen in the courts of different countries, and accordingly, only cases having a direct bearing on the treatment of the information provided on the Internet will be taken into account in this context. Specific reference to cases where tortious liability arises from dealing with copyrighted information, which giving rise to a civil liability for compensation which is not based on contract, may substantially be considered tortious, however of a special nature in comparison with the general figures of tort retained under the common law [59, p. 43], and [60].

Actually, the really controversial point is not related to the consideration of copyright infringement as tort for the application of the relevant rules, but rather to its strictly territorial character, so that an appropriate line of reasoning requires distinguishing between acts committed in the United Kingdom, subject to domestic intellectual property legislation, and those committed abroad, in which the fundamental role of international conventions has tended towards unifying the position between application of the lex originis (the law of the place of creation—or registration, if applicable—of the protected item) and of the lex loci commissi delicti mainly on the latter, substantially adopting a rule of territoriality alongside the national treatment principle. Ultimately, having the 1995 Act abolish the rule of double actionability in the U.K., which was the real obstacle in entertaining actions for infringement abroad of foreign intellectual property rights, a series of reasons seem to suggest an opening towards a more far-reaching perspective, which would allow the English courts to apply foreign intellectual property law when appropriate under the 1995 Act [37, S. 9, pp. 4–6], [61–64], and [65, pp. 504–513].

Copyright and conflict of laws on the Internet in recent case law

Having so far laid the essential framework of the difficult interaction between intellectual property and conflict of laws, an examination of its practical operation in the case law appears necessary. In this perspective, a coherent progression begins with those cases exploring the link between use of the Internet as a means of circulating information and copyright infringement, even within domestic boundaries. In this context, the first experiences are to be traced on the other side of the Atlantic, where since 1993 a number of significant cases have arisen, notably the various *Playboy* cases [66–68], those of *Sega Enterprises Ltd v. Maphia* [69], of *United States v. La Macchia* [70], as well as of *Religious Technology Centre v. Netcom On-line* [71] and of *Frank Music v. Compuserve* [72], and the Australian case of *Trumpet Software v. OzEmail* [73, 74].

All these cases may be considered jointly as they share common elements, the conduct being challenged as copyright infringement generally consisting in the reproduction on a "bulletin board" on the Web of materials—magazine photographs, computer games or software programs, or texts and songs—subject to the demander's copyright, in such a way as to render them publicly accessible and available for downloading by general users. In the whole of these cases the courts seized ultimately found for copyright infringement, although on the basis of a position, that of American copyright law, which does not thoroughly correspond to solutions retained under United Kingdom and generally European laws. In this sense American copyright law considers the mere uploading of information on a computer system a form of reproduction, therefore likely to constitute infringement, while other legal systems, notably those of Japan and Australia, relate infringement to the subsequent stage of distribution or transmission, therefore envisaging a particular perception of copyright as related to communication. Further differences arise with regard to the notion of right of display, recognized by the American courts in the case of *Playboy* [66] with respect to display on screen, which may be considered fairly beyond the more restrictive notion retained by the generality of European systems; further uncertainties relating instead to the legal qualification of actions like the mere "browsing" on copyright protected materials [75, pp. 286–288], and [76, pp. 552–556].

Similar cases have by now arisen also in European courts, such as the Court of

Session in Scotland in the case of *Shetland Times Ltd v. Dr Jonathan Wills* [77, 78], bearing on whether an interlocutory injunction was to be granted to the plaintiffs, owners and publishers of the newspaper *The Shetland Times*, to restrain the defendants, providers of a news reporting service named The Shetland News, from pursuing their activity of including among their news headlines a number of similar items appearing on *The Shetland Times*. Two essential questions are at issue: whether the headlines made available by the defendants on their Web site constituted a form of "cable program service" pursuant to Section 7 of the Copyright, Designs and Patents Act 1988—a statute making provision for the consolidation of relevant areas of intellectual property legislation in the U.K., to the exception, most notably, of registered trade marks, hereinafter "the 1988 Act"—and whether inclusion within that service of the items in question purported to infringement pursuant to Section 20 of the 1988 Act, provided incidentally that the headlines constituted literary works, as such subject to copyright protection under Section 3 of the 1988 Act. In the logical sequence of the questions, Lord Hamilton argued that whereas literary merit was not a necessary element of a literary work, the plaintiff had effectively made a prima facie case of infringement by inclusion in a cable program service as appropriate for the injunction to be granted, whereas the interactive character of the service pointed out by the defendants in resisting the application appeared merely incidental at that interlocutory stage. In the very end, although unfortunately an out of court settlement prevented the achievement of a final judgement [36; 44], the argument adopted by the court that interlocutory stage has paved the way in the direction considered more plausible by many writers, that is of guiding the Internet through the framework already laid down for previously developed means of communication [76, pp. 548–550], [65, pp. 495–496], and [75, pp. 288–293].

The case of *Shetland Times* has received some parallels in a few continental cases, notably those of *Association Générale des Journalistes Professionnels de Belgique v. SCRL Central Station* [79] in Belgium and *Re Copyright in Newspaper Articles Offered On-Line* [80] in Germany and the two subsequent *Queneau* cases in France [81–84], presenting similar issues of reproduction of literary works—parts of newspaper articles and pieces from a poem—on an Internet site: in different terms according to the circumstances of the cases the relevant courts ultimately upheld the plaintiffs' arguments as to the existence of copyright in the items affected and the suitability of reproduction of these on Web sites to purport to infringement under the relevant national laws, granting therefore prevalence to the instance of intellectual property protection on the opposite exceptions of lack of literary merit or noninfringing character of fragmentary reproduction and on the additional disclaimer of private use and accidental disclosure in the second *Queneau* case, where a security leakage had opened an Intranet site to public access [84].

Some further cases relating to different aspects are probably worth being considered, such as *Weber v. Jolly Hotels* [85, 86], where the central issue consisted in whether the mere fact of providing information on a passive Web site, on whose basis a contract was separately entered into, could attract the defendant to the forum of the plaintiff and, allegedly, to the application of its law in a situation where the latter court would not have personal jurisdiction under the general rule of *actor sequitur forum rei* (competence lies with the court(s) of the defendant's domicile), with the implied consequences also in point of applicable law. Faced with such a claim for exorbitant jurisdiction, which would render anyone providing information on the Internet virtually subject to the jurisdiction of whichever court in the world where a plaintiff may happen to sue him, the District Court of New Jersey more prudently held that a similar attribution of jurisdiction may derive only from an interactive use of the Internet, that is in case of business being actually conducted on it.

The alternative or complementary perspective, which we may pertinently address at this final stage, consists of having recourse to the various techniques of computer security, and more specifically to encryption technology, notably consisting in introducing information on the Web or on local computer systems in a particular technically elaborated format such as to render it accessible only to other users in possession of the appropriate decrypting key: a system which is already operative at a general and public level in the crucial field of electronic commerce and particularly of electronic funds transfer [87–90], similar to military networks, where the Internet as a phenomenon originated, but whose generalization and proliferation to the general or nongovernmental levels is likely to arise primary issues of public policy and general security, not less than of freedom of information [91–93].

This has been the scenario for the case of *Daniel Bernstein v. United States Department of State* [94, 95], where freedom of expression of scientific opinion by a researcher in the field of encryption programs, with particular regard to the possibility of circulating his own encryption model known as "Snuffle," has been faced with the restrictive limits imposed by the particularly sensitive American military security regulations, ultimately resulting in an order inhibiting the export of nonmilitary encryption products of the type produced by the plaintiff. Although the rigor of the American regulation in this respect may sound rather excessive, encryption technologies still undoubtedly remain a field for further legal and policy considerations, also with reference to the parallel broader issue concerning the protection of privacy, and in particular, of personal data [95–97].

9.2.3 Conclusions

Actual conclusions are probably beyond the reach of the present section, where we have attempted to address a particularly broad scope of issues, in the delicate perspective of casting a bridge between two areas of the law, the conflict of laws and intellectual property, the latter has traditionally been considered as mostly contained within the borders of domestic legal systems: a relationship which may no longer be considered as a mere subject of academic exercise. The reasons for this all undeniably will be with the development not only of the surrounding legal framework, but also, to an ever increasing extent, of the social, technological, and economic context.

It is in this sense that in the Internet there is a new, stimulating legal challenge in terms of adaptation of the existing legal devices, in a perspective of interaction and integration among domestic and international systems, aimed to address as coherently and homogeneously as possible the inescapable legal issues which it raises. It is by now evident that these issues are no more likely to be dealt with satisfactorily within the domestic legal systems on the basis of their not necessarily coherent rules on the conflict of laws and substantive regulations. There lies the ultimate ground for a quest for a proper law in the sense which we have tried to expose, whose need has to be perceived as an essential means towards achieving an ideal of efficient and harmonious coordination rather than conflict of the various domestic systems, up to a certain extent inevitably surviving in their own distinct identity.

Nonetheless, an acknowledgement cannot be omitted at this conclusive stage to the results so far achieved in the harmonization and potential unification of domestic intellectual property laws, carried out within different supranational and international organizations, at a regional and global level. Within the European Community and in the broader, though inevitably less integrated framework of the World Intellectual Property Organization, which have both reached in recent times particularly significant achievements, notably in the fields of protection of personal data [27, 98–102] and of harmonization of copyright laws, strengthened and consolidated by the reciprocal interaction, lastly consecrated by the E.C.'s commitment to introduce within its legal framework a new set of principles in accordance with those laid down in the WIPO Treaties [6, 10, 103, 104] (see Section 9.1).

REFERENCES

[1] Marongiu Buonaiuti, F., "The Proper Law of a Tort and the Internet," *Amicus Curiae,*

Journal of the Society for Advanced Legal Studies, London, England: CCH Editions Ltd, vol. 13, Jan. 1999, pp. 28 f.

[2] "General Requirements and Interoperability," Imprimatur Report on the Watermarking Technology for Copyright Protection, IMP/14062/A, 1998.

[3] "WIPO Diplomatic Conference on Certain Copyright and Neighbouring Rights Questions," 1996.

[4] "WIPO Copyright Treaty," 1996.

[5] "Document prepared by the International Bureau, WIPO/INT/SIN/98/9," 1998. Presented at the WIPO Seminar for Asia and the Pacific Region on Internet and the Protection of Intellectual Property Rights, Singapore.

[6] Lai, S., "The Impact of the Recent WIPO Copyright Treaty and Other Initiatives on Software Copyright in the United Kingdom," *Intellectual Property Quarterly*, 1998, pp. 35.

[7] Vinje, T. C., "The New WIPO Copyright Treaty: A Happy Result in Geneva," *European Intellectual Property Review*, 1997, pp. 230.

[8] Vinje, T., "Copyright Imperiled," *European Intellectual Property Review*, 1999, pp. 192.

[9] "U.S. Digital Millennium Copyright Act," 1998.

[10] "Proposal for a European Parliament and Council Directive on the harmonization of certain aspects of copyright and related rights in the Information Society OJ C108/6," 1998.

[11] "Partly Consolidated Text of the Copyright Treaty CRNR/DC/55," 1996.

[12] "Council Directive on the Legal Protection of Computer Programs 91/250/EEC of 14 May 1991 (Software directive)," 1991.

[13] "NEC v. Intel," *Federal Supplement*, vol. 643, 1986, pp. 590. Northern District of California.

[14] Lehmann, M., and C. Tapper, *A Handbook of European Software Law*, Oxford, England: Clarendon Press, 1993.

[15] Czarnota, B., and R. J. Hart, *The Legal Protection of Computer Programs in Europe—A Guide to the EC directive*, London: Butterworth, 1991.

[16] Band, J., and M. Katoh, *Interfaces on Trial*, Boulder: Westview Press, 1995.

[17] Dreier, T., "The Council Directive of 14 May 1991 on the Legal Protection of Computer Programs," *European Intellectual Property Review*, vol. 9, 1991, pp. 319.

[18] Huet, J., and J. C. Ginsburg, "Computer Programs in Europe: a Comparative Analysis of the 1991 EC Software Directive," *Columbia Journal of Transnational Law*, vol. 30, 1992, pp. 327.

[19] "Copyright Management and the NII: Report to the Enabling Technologies Committee of the Association of American Publishers," 1996.

[20] Stefik, M., *Internet Dreams: Archetypes, Myths and Metaphors*, Cambridge, Massachusetts, USA: MIT Press, 1996.

[21] Stefik, M., "Shifting the Possible: How Digital Property Rights Challenge Us to Rethink Digital Publishing," *Berkeley Technology Law Journal*, vol. 12, 1997, pp. 138.

[22] Smith, and Webber, "A New Set of Rules for Information Commerce-Rights-Protection Technologies and Personalized Information Commerce Will Affect All Knowledge Workers," *Commercial Week*, 6 Nov. 1995.

[23] Cohen, J., "Some Reflections on Copyright Management Systems and Laws Designed to Protect Them," *Berkeley Technology Law Journal*, vol. 12, 1997, pp. 161.

[24] Cohen, J., "A Right to Read Anonymously: A Closer Look at Copyright Management in Cyberspace," *Connecticut Law Review*, vol. 28, 1996, pp. 981.

[25] Glancy, D., "Privacy and Intelligent Transportation Technology," *Santa Clara Computer & High Technologies Law Journal*, 1995, pp. 151.

[26] Froomkin, M., "Flood Control on the Information Ocean: Living with Anonymity, Digital Cash and Distributed Databases," *Journal of Law and Commerce*, vol. 15, 1996, pp. 395.

[27] "EC Directive on the Protection of Individuals with Regard to the Processing of Personal Data and on the Free Movement of Such Data," 94/46/EC, 1995. Reported in OJ L.281/31.

[28] "The Bork Act 18 USCA," par. 2710.

[29] "First Imprimatur Consensus Forum," 1996. <http://www.imprimatur.alcs.co.uk/>.

[30] Morris, J. H. C., "The Proper Law of a Tort," *Harvard Law Review*, vol. 64, 1951, pp. 881.

[31] "Boys v. Chaplin," *Law Report, Appeal Cases*, 1971, pp. 356.

[32] Rogerson, P., "Choice of Law in Tort: a Missed Opportunity," *International and Comparative Law Quarterly*, 1995, pp. 650.

[33] "Red Sea Insurance v. Bouygues," *Law Report, Appeal Cases*, 1995, pp. 190. Privy Council.

[34] Dickinson, A., "Further Thoughts on Foreign Torts: Boys v. Chaplin Explained?" *Lloyd's Maritime and Commercial Law Quarterly*, 1994, pp. 463.

[35] Rodger, B. J., "Bouygues and Scottish Choice of Law Rules in Delict," *Scottish Legal Practice Quarterly*, vol. 1, 1995, pp. 58.

[36] "House of Lords, Session 1994-95, Private International Law (Miscellaneous Provisions) Bill [H.L.]," Proceedings of the Special Public Bill Committee, with Evidence and the Bill (as Amended), London (HMSO), HL Paper 36, 1995.

[37] "Private International Law (Miscellaneous Provisions) Act 1995, Chap. 42," 1995.

[38] Morse, C. G. J., "Torts in Private International Law: A New Statutory Framework," *International and Comparative Law Quarterly*, vol. 45, 1996, pp. 888.

[39] Collins, L., "Interaction Between Contract and Tort in the Conflict of Laws," *International and Comparative Law Quarterly*, vol. 16, 1967.

[40] Collins, L., *Interaction Between Contract and Tort in the Conflict of Laws*, Oxford, England: Clarendon Press, p. 352, International and Comparative Law Quarterly, 1994.

[41] Anton, A. E., "Loi du Royaume-Uni portant diverses dispositions en matiére de droit international privé," *Revue Critique de Droit International Privé*, vol. 85, 1996, pp. 267.

[42] Briggs, A., "Choice of Law in Tort and Delict," *Lloyd's Maritime and Commercial Law Quarterly*, 1995, pp. 519.

[43] Carter, P. B., "Choice of Law in Tort: the Role of the Lex Fori," *Cambridge Law Journal*, 1995, pp. 38.

[44] Rodger, B. J., "Ascertaining the Statutory Lex Loci Delicti: Certain Difficulties Under the Private International Law (Miscellaneous Provisions) Act 1995," *International and Comparative Law Quarterly*, vol. 47, 1998, pp. 205.

[45] Nygh, P. E., "Some Thoughts on the Proper Law of a Tort," *International and Comparative Law Quarterly*, vol. 26, 1977, pp. 932.

[46] Morse, C. G. J., *Torts in Private International Law*, Amsterdam, New York, Oxford: North Holland, 1978.

[47] "U.S. Restatement of Conflict of Laws," 1934.

[48] Cohen, B., "A Proposed Regime for Copyright Protection on the Internet," *Brooklin Journal of International Law*, vol. 22, 1996, pp. 401.

[49] Delacourt, J. T., "The International Impact of Internet Regulation," *Harvard Interna-*

tional Law Journal, vol. 38, 1997, pp. 207.

[50] Dixon, A. N., and L. C. Self, "Copyright Protection for the Information Superhighway," *European Intellectual Property Review*, 1994, pp. 465.

[51] Millé, A., "Copyright in the Cyberspace Era," *European Intellectual Property Review*, 1997, pp. 570.

[52] Longdin, L., "Technological Cross Dressing and Copyright," *New Zealand Law Journal*, 1998, pp. 149.

[53] "Pitman Training Ltd v. Nominet UK," p. 797, Fleet Street Reports, 1997, p. 797.

[54] "Avnet Inc. v. Isoact Ltd," p. 16, Fleet Street Reports, 1998, p. 16.

[55] "Prince Plc. v. Prince Sports Groups Inc." p. 21, Fleet Street Reports, 1998, p. 21.

[56] "Marks & Spencer Plc. v. One In A Million Ltd," p. 265, Fleet Street Reports, 1998, p. 265.

[57] "The Free Speech Coalition v. Janet Reno," *U.S. Law Week*, 1997, pp. 1125. Judgment C-97-0281, United States District Court for the Northern District of California.

[58] Taylor, P., "Note, *sub* Telecommunications-Internet-Free speech challenge to ban on child pornography," *Bulletin of Legal Developments*, 1997, pp. 221.

[59] Cornish, W. R., *Intellectual Property*, London, England: Sweet & Maxwell, 3rd ed., 1996.

[60] Trooboff, P. D., "Intellectual Property," in , *Transnational Tort Litigation*, Oxford, England: Clarendon Press, pp. 125–154, 1996.

[61] "Gareth Pearce v. Ove Arup," p. 641, Fleet Street Reports, 1997, p. 641.

[62] "Coin Controls v. Suzo," p. 660, Fleet Street Reports, 1997, p. 660.

[63] Cornish, W. R., "Note on Intellectual Property and the Conflict of Laws," in *Proceedings of the Special Public Bill Committee*, pp. 64–65, 1996.

[64] Beatson, J., "Note on Intellectual Property and Part III of the Private International Law (Miscellaneous Provisions) Bill," in *Proceedings of the Special Public Bill Committee*, pp. 61–63, 1995.

[65] Dutson, S., "The Internet, the Conflict of Laws, International Litigation and Intellectual Property: the Implications of the International Scope of the Internet in Intellectual Property Infringements," *Journal of Business Law*, 1997, pp. 495.

[66] "Playboy Enterprises Inc. v. George Frena et al." *Federal Supplement*, vol. 839, 1993, pp. 1552. District of Florida.

[67] "Playboy v. Chuckleberry Publ. Inc." *Federal Supplement*, vol. 939, 1996, pp. 1032. Southern District of New York.

[68] "Playboy v. Five Senses Production," *Intellectual Property Newsletter*, vol. 21, no. 6, 1998, pp. 4. U.S. Federal Court.

[69] "Sega Enterprises Ltd v. Maphia," *Federal Supplement*, vol. 857, 1994, pp. 679. Northern District of California.

[70] "United States v. La Macchia," *Federal Supplement*, vol. 871, 1994, pp. 535. District of Massachusetts.

[71] "Religious Technology Centre v. Netcom On-line," Judgment C-95-20091, 1995. United States District Court for the Northern District of California.

[72] "Frank Music v. Compuserve," Judgment C-93-8153, 1993. United States District Court for the Southern District of New York.

[73] "Trumpet Software v. OzEmail," Australian Federal Court judgement TG 21, 1996.

[74] Richardson, M., "Intellectual Property Protection and the Internet," *European Intellectual Property Review*, 1996, pp. 669.

[75] Dessemontet, F., "Internet, le droit d'auteur et le droit international privé," *Schweizerische Juristische Zeitung*, vol. 92, 1996, pp. 285.

[76] Bariatti, S., "Internet: aspects relatives au conflit de lois," *Rivista di Diritto Internazionale Privato e Processuale*, vol. 33, 1997, pp. 545.

[77] "Shetland Times Ltd v. Dr Jonathan Wills," p. 604, Fleet Street Reports, 1997, p. 604.

[78] Campbell, K. J., "Copyright on the Internet: The View from Shetland," *European Intellectual Property Review*, 1997, pp. 255.

[79] "Association Générale des Journalistes Professionnels de Belgique v. SCRL Central Station," p. 40, European Commercial Cases, 1998, p. 40. Tribunal de Première Instance, Brussels, 16 Oct. 1996.

[80] "Re Copyright in Newspaper Articles Offered On-Line," p. 20, European Commercial Cases, 1998, p. 20. U 127/95, Oberlandsgericht Düsseldorf, 14 May 1996.

[81] "J.-M. Queneau v. Ch. Leroy," p. 22, European Commercial Cases, 1998, p. 22. Tribunal de Grande Instance de Paris, 5 May 1997.

[82] "J.-M. Queneau c/ Boue et LAAS TGI Paris," La Semaine Juridique, vol. II, no. 52, 1997, pp. 569.

[83] Galizzi, P., "Internet—Publication on website of material protected by copyright," *Bulletin of Legal Developments*, 23 Feb. 1998, pp. 26.

[84] Olivier, F., "Queneau bis ou les faux-semblants de l'usage privé," *La Semaine Juridique*, vol. 52, 24 Dec. 1997, pp. 571.

[85] "Weber v. Jolly Hotels," Judgment 96-2582, 1996. United States District Court for the District of New Jersey. Full text at <http://lw.bna.com/lw/19971014/962582.htm>.

[86] Taylor, P., "Note, sub The Americas-United States, Civil Procedure-Jurisdiction-Internet," *Bulletin of Legal Developments*, 1997, pp. 249.

[87] "Commission Green Paper on Electronic Commerce," COM, p. 157, 1997.

[88] Caprioli, E. A., and R. Sorieul, "Le commerce international électronique: vers l'émergence de règles juridiques transnationales," *Journal du droit international*, 1997, pp. 323.

[89] Schneider, M. E., and C. Kuner, "Dispute Resolution in International Electronic Commerce," *Journal of International Arbitration*, vol. 14, 1997, pp. 5.

[90] Andersen, M. B., "Electronic Commerce: A Challenge to Private Law?" in *Saggi Conferenze e Seminari*, vol. 32, Centro di Studi e Ricerche di Diritto Comparato e Straniero, Rome, Italy, 1998.

[91] "WIPO Copyright Treaties Implementation Act," U.S. Federal Bill, H.R. 2281.

[92] "Collections of Information Antipiracy Act," U.S. Federal Bill, H.R. 2652. Available at <http://thomas.loc.gov/>, discussed in the House of Representatives; comments and reactions from either sides at <http://www.dfc.org/> and <http://www.cic.org/>.

[93] Marzano, P., "Sistemi anticopiaggio, tatuaggi elettronici e responsabilità on-line: il diritto d'autore risponde alle sfide di Internet," *Il Diritto di Autore*, 1998, pp. 149.

[94] "Daniel Bernstein v. United States Department of State," Judgment C-95-0582 of 25 Aug. 1997, 1995. United States District Court for the Northern District of California.

[95] Movius, D. T., "Bernstein v. United States Department of State: Encryption, Justiciability and the First Amendment," *Administrative Law Review (American Bar Association)*, vol. 49, 1997, pp. 1051.

[96] Kuner, C., "Rechtliche Aspekte der Datenverschlüsselung im Internet," *Neue Juristische Wochenschrift—ComputerRecht*, 1995, pp. 413.

[97] Bréban, Y., and I. Pottier, "Les décrets et arrêtés cryptologie: la mise en oeuvre effective

de l'assouplissement des dispositions antérieures," *Gazette du Palais*, vol. 118, no. 109–111, 1998.

[98] "Directive 97/66/EC concerning the processing of personal data and the protection of privacy in the telecommunications sector, O.J. L-24/1," 1998.

[99] Lai, S., "Database protection in the United Kingdom—The New Deal and its Effects on Software Protection," *European Intellectual Property Review*, 1998, pp. 32.

[100] Balz, S. D., and O. Hance, "Privacy and the Internet: Intrusion, Surveillance and Personal Data," *International Review of Law Computers & Technology*, vol. 10, 1996, pp. 219.

[101] Chalton, S., "The Effect of the E.C. Database Directive on United Kingdom Copyright Law in Relation to Databases: a Comparison of Features," *European Intellectual Property Review*, 1997, pp. 278.

[102] Smith, S., "Legal Protection of Factual Compilations and Databases in England—How Will the Database Directive Change the Law in this Area?" *Intellectual Property Quarterly*, 1997, pp. 450.

[103] Reinbothe, J., M. Martin-Prat, and S. von Lewinski, "The New WIPO Treaties: A First Résumé," *European Intellectual Property Review*, 1997, pp. 171.

[104] Khlestov, N., "W.T.O.-WIPO Co-operation: Does It Have a Future?" *European Intellectual Property Review*, 1997, pp. 560.

Index

Solving the Year 2000 Crisis, Patrick McDermott

User-Centered Information Design for Improved Software Usability,
　　Pradeep Henry

For further information on these and other Artech House titles,
including previously considered out-of-print books now available through our
In-Print-Forever® (IPF®) program, contact:

Artech House   Artech House
685 Canton Street   46 Gillingham Street
Norwood, MA 02062   London SW1V 1AH UK
Phone: 781-769-9750   Phone: +44 (0)20 7596-8750
Fax: 781-769-6334   Fax: +44 (0)20 7630-0166
e-mail: artech@artechhouse.com   e-mail: artech-uk@artechhouse.com

Find us on the World Wide Web at:
www.artechhouse.com